SO-AFE-208

Health, dignity, and development: what will it take?

Lead authors
Roberto Lenton, Coordinator
Albert M. Wright, Coordinator
Kristen Lewis

UN Millennium Project
Task Force on Water and Sanitation
2005

London • Sterling, Va.

First published by Earthscan in the UK and USA in 2005

Copyright © 2005
by the United Nations Development Program
All rights reserved

ISBN: 1-84407-219-3 paperback

For a full list of publications please contact:

Earthscan
8–12 Camden High Street
London, NW1 0JH, UK
Tel: +44 (0)20 7387 8558
Fax: +44 (0)20 7387 8998
Email: earthinfo@earthscan.co.uk
Web: www.earthscan.co.uk
22883 Quicksilver Drive, Sterling, VA 20166-2012, USA

Earthscan is an imprint of James and James (Science Publishers) Ltd and publishes in association with the International Institute for Environment and Development

A catalogue record for this book is available from the British Library

Library of Congress Cataloging-in-Publication Data

A catalog record has been requested

This publication should be cited as: UN Millennium Project 2005. *Health, Dignity, and Development: What Will it Take?* Task Force on Water and Sanitation.

Photos: Front cover Franck Charton/UNICEF; back cover, top to bottom, Christopher Dowswell, Pedro Cote/ UNDP, Giacomo Pirozzi/Panos Pictures, Liba Taylor/Panos Pictures, Jørgen Schytte/UNDP, UN Photo Library, Giacomo Pirozzi/UNICEF, Curt Carnemark/World Bank, Pedro Cote/UNDP, Franck Charton/UNICEF, Paul Chesley/Getty Images, Ray Witlin/World Bank, Pete Turner/Getty Images.

This book was edited, designed, and produced by Communications Development Inc., Washington, D.C., and its UK design partner, Grundy & Northedge.

The Millennium Project was commissioned by the UN Secretary-General and sponsored by the United Nations Development Programme on behalf of the UN Development Group. The report is an independent publication that reflects the views of the members of the Task Force on Water and Sanitation, who contributed in their personal capacity. This publication does not necessarily reflect the views of the United Nations, the United Nations Development Programme, or their Member States.

Printed on elemental chlorine-free paper

Foreword

The world has an unprecedented opportunity to improve the lives of billions of people by adopting practical approaches to meeting the Millennium Development Goals. At the request of UN Secretary-General Kofi Annan, the UN Millennium Project has identified practical strategies to eradicate poverty by scaling up investments in infrastructure and human capital while promoting gender equality and environmental sustainability. These strategies are described in the UN Millennium Project's report *Investing in Development: A Practical Plan to Achieve the Millennium Development Goals*, which was coauthored by the coordinators of the UN Millennium Project task forces.

The task forces have identified the interventions and policy measures needed to achieve each of the Goals. In *Health, Dignity, and Development: What Will It Take?* the UN Millennium Project Task Force on Water and Sanitation emphasizes that achieving the water and sanitation target and investing in water infrastructure and management are crucial to the achievement of all the Millennium Development Goals—a key point that is echoed in *Investing in Development*.

Consider, for example, the sanitation crisis. Four in ten of our fellow women, men, and children have no choice but to defecate in buckets, in plastic bags, in open fields, and alongside footpaths, streets, and railroad tracks, not occasionally but every single day. This persistent yet largely unrecognized humanitarian crisis must end if we are to reduce disease, hunger, and gender inequality; improve the lives of slum dwellers; and achieve environmental sustainability. Conversely, progress toward these and other Millennium Development Goals—particularly the reduction of poverty and gender inequality—is vital to achieving the water and sanitation target and to improving the use of Earth's water resources.

Health, Dignity, and Development has been prepared by a group of leading experts who contributed in their personal capacity and volunteered their time to this important task. I am very grateful for their thorough and skilled efforts, and I am sure that the practical options for action in this report will make an important contribution to achieving the Millennium Development Goals. I strongly recommend it to anyone who is interested in how countries can make the dream of safe drinking water and basic sanitation a reality for their poorest citizens.

Jeffrey D. Sachs
New York
January 17, 2005

Tables

Task force members

Task force coordinators

Roberto Lenton, The Earth Institute at Columbia University
Albert M. Wright, Independent consultant

Task force members

Ingvar Andersson, Senior Freshwater Advisor, United Nations Development Program (through June 2004)

Jamie Bartram, Coordinator, Water, Sanitation and Health Programme, World Health Organization (permanent observer as chair of UN-Water and on behalf of WHO)

Margaret Catley-Carlson, Chair, Global Water Partnership; Chair, International Center for Agricultural Research in Dry Areas

Ivan Cheret, Independent consultant, Paris

Kamla Chowdhry, Chair, Vikram Sarabhai Foundation, New Delhi

Bill Cosgrove, President, World Water Council (through December 2004)

Jennifer Davis, Professor of Development Planning, Massachusetts Institute of Technology, Cambridge, Mass.

Manuel Dengo, Chief, Water and Natural Resources, United Nations Department of Economic and Social Affairs

Halifa Drammeh, Deputy Director, Division of Policy Development and Law, United Nations Environment Programme

Gourisankar Ghosh, Executive Director, Water Supply and Sanitation Collaborative Council

Mi Hua, Sanitation Specialist, UN Millennium Project Technical Support Centre, Nairobi

Hans Olav Ibrekk, Adviser, Norwegian Agency for Development Cooperation, Oslo

Sir Richard Jolly, Fellow, Institute for Development Studies, University of Sussex, United Kingdom

Torkil Jonch-Clausen, Senior Advisor, Global Water Partnership, Copenhagen

Mike Muller, Director General, South Africa Department of Water Affairs, Pretoria

Dennis Mwanza, Managing Director, Water Utility Partnership, Dakar

Ravi Narayanan, Director, WaterAid, London

Noma Nyoni, Deputy Director, Institute of Water and Sanitation Development, Harare

Kalyan Ray, Chief, Building and Infrastructure Technology, United Nations Human Settlements Programme

Frank Rijsberman, Director General, International Water Management Institute, Colombo

Jamal Saghir, Director, Energy and Water, World Bank

David Seckler, Independent consultant, Greeley, Colo.

Vanessa Tobin, Chief, Water, Environment and Sanitation, United Nations Children's Fund

Gordon Young, Coordinator, World Water Assessment Programme

Task force secretariat

Kristen Lewis, Senior Policy Advisor and Task Force Manager

Christie Walkuski, Administrative Assistant

Other key contributors

Barbara Evans, Independent consultant, Macclesfield, U.K.

Guido Schmidt-Traub, Policy Advisor, UN Millennium Project

Susmita Shekhar, Senior Vice President, Sulabh International Social Service Organization, New Delhi

Preface

At the United Nations Millennium Summit in September 2000, the largest-ever gathering of world leaders adopted the Millennium Declaration. From the Declaration emerged the Millennium Development Goals, an integrated set of time-bound targets for extending the benefits of globalization to the world's poorest citizens and making real progress, by 2015, in tackling the most pressing issues facing developing countries.

Among those targets is Millennium Development target 10: to cut in half, by 2015, the proportion of people without sustainable access to safe drinking water and basic sanitation. In addition, sound water resources management and development is a key to achieving all of the Goals.

To help the international community as a whole reach the Millennium Development Goals, the UN Secretary-General and the administrator of the United Nations Development Programme (as chair of the United Nations Development Group) commissioned the UN Millennium Project, as an independent advisory body. The UN Millennium Project was a three-year effort to identify the best strategies for meeting the Goals. Ten task forces, each one focused on a specific substantive area and made up of independent experts from the relevant disciplines and sectors, performed the bulk of the UN Millennium Project's work; each task force was responsible for identifying what it would take to achieve one or more of the targets.

What's new about this report?

In the past 25 years, a number of commissions, expert groups, and high-level panels have produced reports and recommendations on water and sanitation. Indeed, many task force members have themselves been involved in these valuable exercises, and in our work we have deliberately sought not to "reinvent the wheel," but rather to build on past efforts and ongoing processes.

Millennium Development Goals

Goal 1	**Target 1.**
Eradicate extreme poverty and hunger	Halve, between 1990 and 2015, the proportion of people whose income is less than $1 a day
	Target 2.
	Halve, between 1990 and 2015, the proportion of people who suffer from hunger

Goal 2	**Target 3.**
Achieve universal primary education	Ensure that, by 2015, children everywhere, boys and girls alike, will be able to complete a full course of primary schooling

Goal 3	**Target 4.**
Promote gender equality and empower women	Eliminate gender disparity in primary and secondary education, preferably by 2005, and in all levels of education no later than 2015

Goal 4	**Target 5.**
Reduce child mortality	Reduce by two-thirds, between 1990 and 2015, the under-five mortality rate

Goal 5	**Target 6.**
Improve maternal health	Reduce by three-quarters, between 1990 and 2015, the maternal mortality ratio

Goal 6	**Target 7.**
Combat HIV/AIDS, malaria, and other diseases	Have halted by 2015 and begun to reverse the spread of HIV/AIDS
	Target 8.
	Have halted by 2015 and begun to reverse the incidence of malaria and other major diseases

The world is waking up to the water and sanitation crisis

International conferences and agreements on water and sanitation

Over the past 30 years numerous conferences and international agreements have provided the broad background for today's water resources policies and decisionmaking (UN WEHAB Working Group 2002).[3] In the past decade many international conferences have discussed and agreed on steps required to speed up the implementation of Agenda 21, a comprehensive plan of action for sustainable development adopted by more than 178 governments at the United Nations Conference on Environment and Development (UNCED) held in Rio de Janeiro in 1992. Water for sustainable development was discussed at the intergovernmental level in the sixth session of the Commission on Sustainable Development in 1998, and broad consensus was reached on key water issues; further international water meetings (such as the Second World Water Forum in the Hague in 2000 and the International Conference on Freshwater in Bonn in 2001) served as important forums for multistakeholder dialogues and generated new recommendations on how to address increasing water challenges. The United Nations Millennium Declaration and the preparatory process leading up to the World Summit on Sustainable Development further affirmed the role of water as a key to sustainable development and the urgency of immediate action.

The Millennium Declaration and the Goals and targets relating to water and sanitation

Water and sanitation are dealt with in several ways in the United Nations Millennium Declaration and in the final list of Millennium Development Goals and targets (UN General Assembly 2000).[4]

In chapter 4 ("Sustaining Our Future") of his report to the Millennium Summit the Secretary-General urged the Summit "to adopt the target of reducing by half, between now and 2015, the proportion of people who lack sustainable access to adequate sources of affordable and safe water" (UN 2000). In the Millennium Declaration the heads of state gathered at United Nations Headquarters in New York in September 2000 resolved, under the heading "protecting our common environment,"

> To stop the unsustainable exploitation of water resources by developing water management strategies at the regional, national, and local levels, which promote both equitable access and adequate supplies.

This resolution is explicitly highlighted as a goal in the Secretary-General's report to the UN General Assembly on the follow up to the outcome of the Millennium Summit (UN 2001, p. 34). In the statement of the United Nations Millennium Development Goals and targets, however, the overall goal relevant to this area (Goal 7) is stated more generally as "ensuring environmental sustainability," with three specific targets:

- Integrate the principles of sustainable development into country policies and programs; reverse loss of environmental resources.

Further international deliberations on water and sanitation have helped advance cooperation and action

- Halve by 2015 the proportion of people without sustainable access to safe drinking water and basic sanitation.
- Achieve significant improvement in the lives of at least 100 million slum dwellers by 2020.

Two conclusions can be drawn: first, the goal of "stopping the unsustainable exploitation of water resources by developing water management strategies at the regional, national, and local levels, which promote both equitable access and adequate supplies" appears to have been incorporated in that part of the first target that refers to reversing the "loss of environmental resources." Second, the target urged by the Secretary-General in his report to the Millennium Summit was incorporated (with some modifications) in the second target to reduce by half the proportion of people without sustainable access to safe drinking water.

The World Summit on Sustainable Development

One of the main outcomes of the World Summit on Sustainable Development (WSSD) in September 2002 was that water and sanitation were recognized as being inextricably linked to the eradication of poverty and to the achievement of sustainable development (UNDESA 2002b).[5] Water was identified by the Secretary-General as one of the five specific "WEHAB" areas (water, energy, health, agriculture, and biodiversity) in which concrete results are both essential and achievable. To provide focus and impetus to action on water issues, a document entitled "A Framework for Action on Water and Sanitation" was prepared for WSSD; it outlined the larger context in which the targets were established and provided a holistic view of the multiple impacts of increasing sustainable access to water supply and sanitation by the poor (UN WEHAB Working Group 2002).

WSSD reiterated the Millennium Development Goal to halve, by 2015, the proportion of people who are unable to reach or to afford safe drinking water and to set a new target on halving the proportion of people who do not have sustainable access to basic sanitation. This sanitation objective is now an integral part of target 10.

Several elements for a program of action on sanitation were clearly established in the WSSD Plan of Implementation (UNDESA 2002a), which particularly highlighted the need to incorporate sanitation within strategies for integrated water resources management. The water and sanitation targets are set out under the Plan of Implementation chapters on poverty eradication and protecting the natural resource base. Water resource management and protection were also recognized as fundamental to sustainable management of the natural resource base for economic and social development. It was also recommended that the participation of women be facilitated at all levels in support of policies and decisionmaking related to water resources management and project implementation. Water-related policies were included in virtually all of the natural resource objectives of the Plan of Implementation.

**There is a
very dynamic
process of
advancing
international
understanding
and
cooperation
on water for
sustainable
development**

Notably, the Plan of Implementation took a broad view of the actions required to achieve the Millennium Development Goal on water and sanitation, emphasizing the need, for example, to intensify water pollution prevention to reduce health hazards and protect ecosystems, and to adopt measures to promote sustainable water uses and address water shortages. The plan made a strong call for integrated water resources management by setting a new time-bound target to "develop integrated water resources management and efficiency plans by 2005, with support to developing countries, through actions at all levels."

Developments following the summit

Since Johannesburg, further international deliberations on water and sanitation have helped advance cooperation and action in this area. In late 2002, the United Nations affirmed the Right to Water, noting that such a right is "indispensable for leading a life in human dignity" and "a prerequisite for the realization of other human rights." In early 2003 water and sanitation (together with human settlements) were selected as the first themes to be discussed systematically by the Commission on Sustainable Development in the post-WSSD era, and became the focus of review and policy discussions of the UN Commission on Sustainable Development in 2004 and 2005. The Third World Water Forum in Kyoto, Japan, in March 2003 and the International Conference on Water for the Poorest in Stavanger, Norway, in November of that year also drew further attention to the subject.

In late 2003 the UN General Assembly adopted a resolution that proclaimed the period 2005–15 as the International Decade for Action—Water for Life (UN General Assembly 2004). The decade will officially start on World Water Day, March 22, 2005. Goals for the decade will be a greater focus on water-related issues and for actions to ensure the participation of women in water-related development efforts. Focus will also be on furthering cooperation at all levels, so that the water-related goals of the Millennium Declaration, the Johannesburg Plan of Implementation of the World Summit for Sustainable Development, and Agenda 21 can be achieved. The resolution emphasized "that water is critical for sustainable development, including environmental integrity and the eradication of poverty and hunger, and is indispensable for human health and well-being."

The institutional context

Although there is no global, comprehensive, intergovernmental structure for water, there is a very dynamic process of advancing international understanding and cooperation on water for sustainable development. These efforts are led by different governments; by the private sector and members of the civil society; by the work of various UN system entities and by other important regional and intergovernmental bodies; by such NGOs as WaterAid; and by several organized networks or partnerships, such as the Water Supply and

**Water
services are
often most
effectively
delivered
through
decentralized
organizations**

Sanitation Collaborative Council (WSSCC) and its WASH (Water Sanitation and Hygiene for All) partnership, the Global Water Partnership (GWP), the Gender and Water Alliance, and the World Water Council. Progress on water for sustainable development requires by its very nature a multistakeholder approach (UN WEHAB Working Group 2002).

Within the UN system, a number of different entities are involved in water and sanitation-related issues. Perspectives and approaches vary according to the mission and mandates that the governing bodies provide to the different UN entities. These entities have recently formed UN-Water, the United Nations Inter-Agency Committee on Water Resources, which was formally established as the interagency mechanism for follow-up of the WSSD water-related decisions and the Goals concerning freshwater in 2003. The way in which the international community as a whole currently supports water and sanitation issues is discussed in greater detail in chapter 12.

Global strategies, frameworks, and plans of action

The development of global plans or frameworks for action has been an inherent part of the process of advancing international cooperation on water and sanitation, starting with the International Drinking Water Supply and Sanitation Decade (box 1.2). Other important frameworks for action on water or sanitation since the decade ended include:

- The Dublin Statement and Report of the Conference on Water and Environment (1992).
- "Towards Water Security: A Framework for Action" prepared by the Global Water Partnership to achieve the Vision for Water in the Twenty-first Century (2000).
- Framework for Action outlined in the WSSCC's document, "Vision 21: A Shared Vision for Hygiene, Sanitation, and Water Supply and A Framework for Action" (2000).
- Numerous national and community level plans prepared under Vision 21's umbrella.
- Bonn Plan of Action (2001).
- "Framework for Action on Water and Sanitation" prepared by the WEHAB Working Group for the World Summit on Sustainable Development (2002).

Most of these plans and frameworks for action, however, have fallen short of a full strategy, in that they do not lay out the organizational means required for implementation, nor provide clarity on the amount, nature, and sources of financing required.

Local institutions

It is widely recognized that water services are often most effectively delivered through decentralized organizations and that voluntary community participation is critical to their success. Many institutions of local governance that now have a broader role were initially established to manage water. Aside from the ancient riverine civilizations of Asia and Africa, local governments in

Box 1.2

Lessons from the International Drinking Water Supply and Sanitation Decade

Source: Drawn from material contributed by task force member Gouri Ghosh.

The Mar del Plata United Nations Conference on Water held in 1977 was the first intergovernmental conference devoted exclusively to water, a milestone in the history of water development. As a result of the Mar del Plata action plan, the United Nations General Assembly in 1980 proclaimed the period 1981–90 as the International Drinking Water Supply and Sanitation Decade (IWSSD). The IWSSD was a period of accelerated and concerted effort to expand water supply and sanitation services to the unserved and underserved poor populations, spearheaded by a group of UN agencies (UNICEF, WHO, and UNDP) and the World Bank. The official reporting of progress was entrusted to WHO. The Interagency Steering Committee for Co-operative Action for the International Drinking Water Supply and Sanitation Decade succeeded in improving the coordination and cooperation among the multilateral and bilateral agencies participating.

Although the IWSSD did not reach its goal of total access in quantitative terms, much was learned from the experience of the IWSSD, including the further realization of the importance of partnerships, advocacy, knowledge dissemination, and comprehensive and balanced country-specific approaches to water and sanitation. Most important, perhaps, was the realization that the achievement of the goal would take far more time and cost far more money than was originally thought. Throughout the decade international organizations and bilateral donors developed a highly qualified group of dedicated water professionals, and water and sanitation were high on the development cooperation agenda.

As a result of the IWSSD new partnerships were developed, including the UNDP–World Bank Water Supply and Sanitation Programme (now the Water and Sanitation Programme), administered by the World Bank and funded by many bilateral donors, and the Water Supply and Sanitation Collaborative Council (WSSCC). The UN General Assembly resolution in December 1990 at the end of the decade emphasized the importance of intensifying the coordination of national activities undertaken with the assistance of all relevant agencies in the field of water supply and sanitation, in particular through the interagency group and the WSSCC. The WSSCC is a unique experiment of partnership within the UN system, providing an open platform to civil society, government, private sector, and research institutions to come together.

The Global Consultation for Safe Water 2000 held in New Delhi, September 1990, drew lessons from the decade, resulting in the New Delhi Statement: "Some for all rather than more for some." At the World Summit for Children in 1990, the goal of universal access to safe water and sanitation by the year 2000 was adopted to promote the survival, protection, and development of children. The 1992 International Conference on Water and the Environment, held in Dublin, developed four principles for water management and put integrated water resources management on the political agenda. The importance of universal access to drinking water supply and sanitation was further reiterated at the 1992 United Nations Conference on Environment and Development. There, world leaders endorsed Agenda 21's recommendations on the protection of freshwater resources. Thereafter, many other crucial international conferences recognized water and sanitation as the bedrock of public health and social progress and the key to improving people's survival, health, and development, including the World Summit on Sustainable Development in 2002.

It is necessary to recognize the plurality of institutions and to clarify their roles, relationships, and sequence of development

European countries, such as the Netherlands and Great Britain, were rooted in the need to cooperate to manage water on a collective basis in the public interest. This perspective is important not just for the design of water strategies, but also to provide an institutional framework for the achievement of other Goals (Muller 2004).

It is also necessary to recognize the plurality of institutions of local government and voluntary community participation and to clarify their roles, interrelationships, and sequence of development. Critical as well is understanding the different roles and responsibilities of men and women in water supply and sanitation provision, as well as recognizing that other factors, such as socioeconomic status, ethnicity, and age may place additional burdens on women in water resources management.

The focus of this report

In preparing this report, the Task Force on Water and Sanitation had a dual role. It focused on how to identify and communicate the strategies and actions needed to accomplish Millennium Development target 10 to cut in half, by 2015, the proportion of people without sustainable access to safe drinking water and basic sanitation; it also examined the requirements for water resources management and development posed by all of the Millennium Development Goals. For water supply and sanitation, it was responsible for identifying priority areas for action, developing strategies, proposing effective institutional arrangements for addressing these areas, and exploring both financial requirements and possible new sources of funding. For water resources management and development, its principal objective was to identify and communicate the water-related actions and strategies required to help achieve the Goals as a whole.

The report is organized as follows:
- Chapter 1 provides the context for the task force's work.
- Part 1 focuses on target 10. It explains why it is important to focus on domestic water supply and sanitation services, describes the Millennium Goals and targets related to water and sanitation, and provides a brief summary of international discussions on water and sanitation. It explores key issues that relate to the specific target for increasing sustainable access to water and sanitation, including current systems for monitoring and evaluation. It provides an overview of progress toward achieving the target on sustainable access to water and sanitation, including a brief review of existing information on costs. In addition, it examines constraints to meeting the target at the global, regional, national, subnational, and community levels, as well as the types of financial, institutional, and technical reforms that are needed.
- Part 2 explores issues related to water as a resource for achieving the entire set of Millennium Development Goals. It includes a discussion of the links between water resources management and specific Goals,

a review of the current institutional and monitoring apparatus at the global level, a diagnosis and typology of the problems faced in various parts of the world, and an examination of challenges to integrated water resources management in support of the goals.

- Part 3 outlines the task force's recommendations regarding the actions needed to move forward. It also translates these overall recommendations into an operational plan, with specific actions that need to be undertaken by key actors.

While the report focuses primarily on the water sector, the task force recognizes that reforms in other areas will have a strong impact on the ability of countries to reach target 10 and to optimize water use. These issues are addressed in *Investing in Development: A Practical Plan to Achieve the Millennium Development Goals* (2005), as well as in the reports of the other nine task forces.

**Households
with access
to safe,
reliable
domestic
water supply
and sanitation
services
are less
vulnerable**

Contribution to the Millennium Development Goals

Expanding access to domestic water supply and sanitation services, as called for in target 10, will bring the international community closer to meeting a number of other Millennium Development targets; in fact, for many of the targets, it is difficult to imagine how significant progress can be made without first ensuring that poor households have a safe, reliable water supply and adequate sanitation facilities.[1] Meeting target 10 is particularly vital in terms of the poverty, gender, and health Goals, and also has a significant impact on other Goals. For instance, as illustrated in table 2.1, in terms of the hunger Goal, healthy people are better able to absorb the nutrients in food than those suffering from excreta-related diseases, particularly intestinal worms; in terms of the education goal, reducing the incidence of water and excreta-borne disease among children improves school attendance.

Poverty

At both the national and international levels, it is difficult to find a definition of poverty that is not based at least in part on access to safe drinking water supply and basic sanitation services. For instance, the United Nations Development Programme's Human Poverty Index (UNDP 2003) is a composite of indicators of basic dimensions of deprivation: a short life (measured by the percentage of people expected to die before 40), lack of basic education (measured by literacy rates), and lack of access to, public and private resources (measured by access to health services, clean water, and sanitation, and percentage of malnourished children under five). Vulnerability is a critical dimension of poverty, and households with access to safe, reliable domestic water supply and sanitation services are less vulnerable than those who must figure out on a daily basis how to meet their needs.

Improved access to domestic water supply and sanitation brings with it considerable economic benefits at the household level (box 2.2). There is a strong link between health and household livelihood security; the inadequate water supply and sanitation services upon which the poor are forced to rely damage their health, causing relatively high health costs relative to income, an increase in morbidity, and a decreased ability to work. In addition, sufficient water supply is critical to the success of many household-based microenterprises. Other links include the following:

- Poor women and men spend a significantly greater proportion of their income on water than do the rich, and the absolute price they pay to water vendors is often ten times or more the tap price.
- Reducing the ill health and disease in children through improved water supply and sanitation services frees the time of the adults who care for them (particularly women) for more productive activities; it also keeps the children themselves from missing school, which has long-term economic consequences. Less illness (among both children and

Table 2.1	Millennium Goal	Contributions of domestic water supply and sanitation
Contribution of access to domestic water supply and sanitation to the Millennium Development Goals	**Poverty** To halve the proportion of the world's people whose income is less than $1 a day	• Household livelihood security rests on the health of its members; adults who are ill themselves or who must care for sick children are less productive. • Illnesses caused by unsafe drinking water and inadequate sanitation generate health costs that can claim a large share of poor households' income. • Time spent collecting water cannot be used for other livelihood activities.
	Hunger To halve the proportion of the world's people who suffer from hunger	• Healthy people are better able to absorb the nutrients in food than those suffering from water-related diseases, particularly worms, which rob their hosts of calories.
	Primary education To ensure that children everywhere complete a full course of primary schooling	• Improved water supply and sanitation services relieve girls from water-fetching duties, allowing them to attend school. • Reducing illness related to water and sanitation, including injuries from water-carrying, improves school attendance, especially for girls. • Having separate sanitation facilities for girls in schools increases their school attendance, especially after menarche.
	Gender equality To ensure that girls and boys have equal access to primary and secondary education	• Community-based organizations for water supply and sanitation can improve social capital of women. • Reduced time, health, and care-giving burdens from improved water services give women more time for productive endeavors, adult education, empowerment activities, and leisure. • Water sources and sanitation facilities closer to home put women and girls at less risk for sexual harassment and assault while gathering water and searching for privacy. • Higher rates of child survival are a precursor to the demographic transition to lower fertility rates; having fewer children reduces women's domestic responsibilities.
	Child mortality To reduce by two-thirds the death rate for children under five	• Improved sanitation, safe drinking water sources, and greater quantities of domestic water for washing reduce infant and child morbidity and mortality. • Sanitation and safe water in health-care facilities help ensure clean delivery and reduce neonatal deaths. • Mothers with improved water supply and sanitation services are better able to care for their children, both because they have fewer illnesses and because they devote less time to water-fetching and seeking privacy for defecation.
	Maternal mortality To reduce by three-fourths the rate of maternal mortality	• Accessible sources of water reduce labor burdens and health problems resulting from water portage, reducing maternal mortality risks. • Improved health and nutrition reduce susceptibility to anemia and other conditions that affect maternal mortality. • Safe drinking water and basic sanitation are needed in health-care facilities to ensure basic hygiene practices following delivery. • Higher rates of child survival are a precursor to the demographic transition toward lower fertility rates, and fewer pregnancies per woman reduce maternal mortality.
	Major disease To have halted and begun to reverse the spread of HIV, malaria, and other major diseases	• Safe drinking water and basic sanitation help prevent water-related diseases, including diarrheal diseases, schistosomiasis, filariasis, trachoma, and helminthes. 1.6 million deaths per year are attributed to unsafe water, poor sanitation, and lack of hygiene. • Improved water supply reduces diarrhea morbidity by 21 percent; improved sanitation reduces diarrhea morbidity by 37.5 percent; hand washing can reduce the number of diarrheal cases by up to 35 percent; additional improvements in drinking water quality, such as point-of-use disinfection, would reduce diarrheal episodes by 45 percent.
	Environmental sustainability To stop the unsustainable exploitation of natural resources; to halve the proportion of people without water and sanitation; to improve the lives of 100 million slum dwellers	• Adequate treatment and disposal of excreta and wastewater contributes to better ecosystem management and less pressure on freshwater resources. • Improved sanitation reduces flows of human excreta into waterways, helping to protect human and environmental health. • Inadequate access to safe water and inadequate access to sanitation and other infrastructure are two of the five defining characteristics of a slum.

Box 2.2

Economic benefits from improving water supply and sanitation services

Source: A summary of the WHO report is available at www.who.int/water_sanitation_health/en/execsummary.pdf.

A recent cost-benefit analysis by the World Health Organization found that achieving the global Millennium Development target on water and sanitation would bring substantial economic gains: each $1 invested would yield an economic return of between $3 and $34, depending on the region. The benefits would include an average global reduction of 10 percent in diarrheal episodes. If the global water and sanitation target is met, the health-related costs avoided would reach $7.3 billion per year, and the annual global value of adult working days gained because of less illness would rise to almost $750 million. Better services resulting from the relocation of a well or borehole to a site closer to user communities, the installation of piped water supply in houses, and latrines closer to home yield significant time savings. The annual value of these time savings would amount to $64 billion if the target is met.

The total benefits of such service improvements will vary across regions, as they depend on the existing levels of water supply and sanitation coverage and the region-specific levels of morbidity and mortality due to diarrheal diseases. Regions where the number of unserved is high and the diarrheal disease burden significant would realize the greatest benefits from improved services.

adults) means that adults miss fewer days of work, be it as employees, entrepreneurs, or farmers, with positive impacts on overall income and livelihood security. Each year in India, for example, 73 million working days are lost to water-borne diseases at a cost of $600 million in terms of medical treatment and lost production (UNDP 1981). Lower health costs mean more disposable income.[2]

- Access to water near the home can save significant amounts of time for women and girls—time that can be spent on productive activities and education, which lay the groundwork for economic growth. Forty billion working hours are lost each year in Africa to the need to carry water (Cosgrove and Rijsberman 1998), and improving domestic water supply services reduces female "time poverty."

- Having healthier children is, of course, a hoped-for end in itself, but higher rates of child survival are also a precursor to the demographic transition toward lower fertility rates, which in turn improves quality of life and spurs development.

Health

The importance of safe drinking water and basic sanitation to the preservation of human health, particularly among children, cannot be overstated. Water-related diseases are the most common cause of illness and death among the poor of developing countries. According to the World Health Organization, 1.6 million deaths per year can be attributed to unsafe water, poor sanitation, and lack of hygiene (WHO 2004a). Realizing the health-related Goals, particularly those targeting child mortality and major diseases, will require a dramatic increase in access to safe drinking water and basic sanitation services for poor women, men, and children in developing countries. It will also require changes in behavior and attitudes, particularly with regard to hygiene, a critical but often overlooked element in discussions usually dominated by questions of access and service provision (box 2.3).

The health impact of poor quality water supply and sanitation services and water-related diseases on developing countries is devastating (UN/WWAP 2003; WHO 2004a):

- At any given time, close to half the people in the developing world are suffering from one or more of the main diseases associated with inadequate provision of water supply and sanitation services: diarrhea, ascaris, dracunculiasis (guinea worm), hookworm, schistosomiasis (bilharzias, or snail fever), and trachoma.
- More than half the hospital beds in the world are filled with people suffering from water-related diseases.
- Billions of cases of diarrhea each year cause 1.6 million deaths, the vast majority among children under five, mostly in developing countries. 88 percent of diarrheal disease is attributed to unsafe water supply or

---

Box 2.3

Maximizing the health benefits from water supply, sanitation, and hygiene interventions

Source: Ghosh 2004.

Experience suggests that, to maximize the health benefits from water supply, sanitation, and hygiene interventions, it is critical to:

Think about health from the start
A common difficulty in multidisciplinary activities is that experts from one sector often develop most of the project, only involving experts from other sectors after fundamental decisions about the level of service and the types of intervention have already been made. If health benefits are a project aim, then public health specialists should be involved from the outset.

Focus on quantity as well as quality of water supply
Schemes that increase the number of public taps in either rural or urban settings, but do not significantly change the time required to fetch water will not increase household water consumption, regardless of how much water is available at the tap. Such interventions thus cannot be expected to reduce water-washed transmission of disease, and therefore can claim relatively few direct health benefits. By contrast, schemes that permit more household connections or reduce long travel times to less than half an hour can be expected to lead to increased water use and a resulting reduction in disease.

Focus on changes at the household level
Programs intended to improve environmental health must be driven by the impact they have at the household level. This is where most people (especially children) spend most of their time and are most vulnerable to contamination. Unless improvements can be shown to have an impact at the household level, they are unlikely to improve health.

Seek improved health indicators, rather than improved health statistics
Health impacts from water supply and sanitation interventions are notoriously difficult to assess. There are too many random variables to gain reliable information from statistics-based surveys. Better results come from observing practical outcomes, such as the use and maintenance status of facilities or improvements in hygiene practice, such as hand washing.

Billions of cases of diarrhea each year cause 1.6 million deaths, the vast majority among children under five

inadequate sanitation and hygiene. Improved water supply reduces diarrhea morbidity by 21 percent; improved sanitation reduces diarrhea morbidity by 37.5 percent; and the simple act of washing hands at critical times can reduce the number of diarrheal cases by as much as 35 percent. Additional improvement of drinking-water quality, such as point-of-use disinfection, would lead to a reduction of diarrhea episodes of 45 percent.

- Though not well documented, the trauma of watching a much loved young child die from a preventable, water-related disease, such as diarrhea, as do one in five in the poorest pockets of the world, no doubt has serious and lasting impacts on the psychological and emotional health of surviving parents and siblings.

- Some 6 million people worldwide are blind because of trachoma, and more than 150 million people are in need of treatment. It is the leading cause of preventable blindness. The disease is strongly related to overcrowding and the absence of nearby sources of safe water for washing the face and hands. Improving access to safe water sources and better hygiene practices can reduce trachoma morbidity by 27 percent.

- Intestinal helminths (ascariasis, trichuriasis, hookworm disease) affect hundreds of millions of people; 133 million suffer from high-intensity intestinal helminth infections, which often lead to severe consequences, such as cognitive impairment, massive dysentery, or anemia. These diseases cause around 9,400 deaths every year. Access to safe water supply and basic sanitation facilities combined with better hygiene practice can reduce morbidity from ascariasis by 29 percent. Overall, healthy people—as opposed to those sickened by worms—are better able to derive the maximum nutritional benefits from food; much of the caloric intake of people suffering from worms is captured by the parasites.

- Worldwide, an estimated 160 million people are infected with schistosomiasis. The disease causes tens of thousands of deaths every year, mainly in Sub-Saharan Africa. It is strongly related to unsanitary excreta disposal and absence of nearby sources of safe water. Basic sanitation reduces the disease by up to 77 percent.

- Arsenic in drinking water is a major public health threat. In Bangladesh, between 28 million and 35 million people consume drinking water with elevated levels of arsenic; the number of cases of skin lesions related to arsenic in drinking water is estimated at 1.5 million. Arsenic contamination of ground water has been found in many countries, including Argentina, Chile, China, India, Mexico, Thailand, and the United States.

- More than 26 million people in China suffer from dental fluorosis due to elevated fluoride in their drinking water, and more than 1 million cases of skeletal fluorosis are thought to be attributable to drinking water.

The vicious circle of poverty and ill-health is endemic among the poorest

- Cholera epidemics are a major risk where there are large concentrations of people and hygiene is poor (as in refugee camps and urban slums); an epidemic that began in Peru in 1990 spread to 16 other countries in Latin America, and ten years later cholera remains endemic following its absence from the continent for nearly a century.
- Water containers typically hold 20 liters of water and weigh 20 kilograms. Carrying such heavy loads, commonly on the head or back, for long distances each day, can result in headaches, fatigue, and pain or even serious injury to the head, neck, spine, and pelvis. Women are responsible for carrying water, and spinal and pelvic injuries can cause problems during pregnancy and childbirth; reducing water portage burdens can reduce maternal mortality risks. Children who carry water can also suffer serious and lasting injury.
- Improved health overall from clean water, sanitation, and better nutrition reduces susceptibility to anemia and other conditions that affect maternal mortality.

The vicious circle of poverty and ill-health is endemic among the poorest: poverty renders women and men ill-equipped to protect themselves and their children from biological pathogens and chemical hazards or to seek treatment for illness; and their poor health, impaired ability to work, and high health costs further mire them in poverty.

Adequate water supply and sanitation, coupled with hygienic behaviors (especially hand washing, safe water handling and storage, and the safe disposal of feces) are fundamental to health because the main culprit in the transmission of water-related disease is the "fecal-oral" cycle. Water and sanitation practitioners have a mnemonic device to describe the factors that fuel this destructive cycle—they refer to the "Five Fs" (UNDP 2004):

- *Fluid* (drinking contaminated water and having too little water to wash). Drinking contaminated water transmits waterborne fecal-oral diseases such as cholera, typhoid, diarrhea, viral hepatitis A, dysentery, and dracunculiasis (guinea worm disease). Insufficient quantities of water for washing and personal hygiene lead to water-washed disease; when people cannot keep their hands, bodies, and domestic environments clean, bacteria and parasites thrive, causing skin and eye infections, including trachoma, and fecal-oral diseases are more easily spread.
- *Feces* (the contamination of water, soil, and food with human fecal matter). Sanitation facilities interrupt the transmission of much fecal-oral disease by preventing human fecal contamination of water and soil. It is particularly important in controlling worm infections. Because children are the main victims of diarrheal diseases (which can be either waterborne or water-washed), they are also the mostly likely source of infection; the safe disposal of children's feces is thus critical. To balance

Traditional roles and tasks mean that poor women are hit hardest by inadequate services

human as well as environmental health, fecal matter should be treated as close to the point of defecation as possible.

- *Fingers* (unwashed hands preparing food or going into the mouth). Recent research shows that hand washing does more for reducing child mortality and the incidence of infectious intestinal diseases than the provision of safe water or even latrines. Yet hygiene gets surprisingly little focus.
- *Food* (eating contaminated food). Eating contaminated food presents the same health risks as drinking contaminated water, and careful food handling is key to combating gastrointestinal illnesses.
- *Flies* (spreading disease from feces to food and water or directly to people). Flies are particularly problematic where open-air defecation is the norm.

Breaking the oral-fecal cycle depends upon the adoption of healthful practices (such as hand washing) and use of technologies that contain and sanitize fecal matter. Addressing water and sanitation problems in developing countries is critical to reducing morbidity and mortality. Health is often viewed from a curative perspective; it is easy to forget how effective and affordable preventative approaches can be. Improving the quantity and quality of water that households receive, improving the management of human excreta, and promoting hygienic practices, such as hand washing and safe water storage in the home, are arguably the most effective health interventions that can be made in the world's poorest countries (boxes 2.4 and 2.5). For children in particular, improving access to water supply and sanitation is one of the most effective ways of improving health and quality of life.

Gender equality

The iconic image of a woman carrying water on her head is emblematic of a lifelong burden that keeps girls from attending school, prevents women from engaging in productive work, and fetters progress toward the Millennium Development Goals on universal primary education and gender equality.

Throughout the developing world, in urban as well as rural areas, the gender division of labor typically assigns to women a series of roles and responsibilities that, for the most part, men do not share. They include securing water for household needs such as drinking and washing; cooking and ensuring overall household food security; and caring for children, the elderly, and the ill.

These traditional roles and tasks mean that poor women are hit hardest by the inadequate services available in informal urban settlements. It is they who must spend much of the day waiting in line for water, thus forestalling their ability to engage in productive activities, adult education, or other domestic responsibilities, not to mention rest and recreation. They are in greatest physical contact with contaminated water and human waste, exposing them to a host of biological pathogens and chemical hazards, and are saddled with the unenviable task of finding a way to dispose of the family's wastewater and feces (no small challenge in areas where diarrheal diseases are endemic and

Box 2.4

Where does hygiene fit in?

Source: WHO 2004a; WSSCC website.

Hardware alone cannot improve health very much: What matters is the way in which it is used and the extent to which it is accompanied by efforts to promote changes in hygiene-related behavior. In some cases, this change is fairly automatic; people across the world need little encouragement to increase the amount of water they use for washing once it is readily available at the household level. In other cases, however, a significant amount of time and effort is required to alter hazardous practices that are wrongly considered "safe" or are simply not thought about.

Even after substantial investments have been made in water supply and sanitation hardware, hygiene behavior in these areas often remains a substantial risk to health. In many cultures, for example, the excreta of young children are considered safe and are thus not treated with the same hygienic concern as the excreta of adults. In fact, children are a significant reservoir of infection. This means that the feces of children can be just as infectious as those of adults. The practice of washing hands with soap after defecation is another example of a behavior that does not follow "automatically" from the provision of hardware, and yet has major health implications.

According to the World Health Organization, improved water supply reduces diarrhea morbidity by 21 percent; but the simple act of washing hands at critical times can reduce the number of diarrheal cases by up to 35 percent, and additional improvements of drinking-water quality, such as point-of-use disinfection and safe storage, would lead to a reduction of diarrhea episodes of 45 percent. According to the Water Supply and Sanitation Collaborative Council, safe disposal of children's feces leads to a reduction of diarrheal disease of nearly 40 percent.

Box 2.5

Household water treatment and safe storage

Source: WHO International Network to Promote Household Water Treatment and Safe Storage (www.who.int/household_water).

Helping households improve and maintain water quality at home has proven health benefits, is cost-effective, and contributes directly to meeting the Millenniuim Development Goals. Household water treatment and safe storage can serve as an immediate mechanism to reduce illness among the unserved. A recent study conducted among 400 households in a Malawian refugee camp indicated that point-of-use interventions resulted in 31 percent fewer cases of diarrheal disease in children under five. Moreover, other recent evidence demonstrates that household water treatment reduces diarrheal disease at levels comparable to sanitation and hygiene measures.

Promising treatment technologies include chlorination, combined chlorination and flocculation, solar disinfection, and filtration. Treatment needs to be accompanied by safe storage, which can be accomplished by using a container with a narrow opening and a dispensing device such as a tap or spigot to protect collected water. These measures are particularly important because the bacteriological quality of drinking water frequently declines after collection.

Although there are challenges, particularly with regard to achieving widespread adoption and sustainability of the interventions, household water treatment offers a rapid and affordable way of reducing the global burden of waterborne disease.

sanitation facilities nonexistent). Having no safe, private sanitation facilities in areas where people are living cheek-by-jowl means going the whole day without

Table 3.1

Improved and unimproved water and sanitation facilities

a. Not considered "improved" because of potential limits on the quantity of water available to a household through this source, not the quality of the water.

Source: WHO/UNICEF Joint Monitoring Programme.

	Improved	Unimproved
Water supply	Piped connection into dwelling, plot, or yard	Unprotected well
	Public tap or standpipe	Unprotected spring
	Borehole	Vendor-provided water
	Protected dug well	Bottled water[a]
	Protected spring	Tanker truck–provided water
	Rainwater	River, stream, pond, or lake
Sanitation	Connection to public sewer or septic tank	Service or bucket latrine
	Pour-flush latrine	Traditional latrine
	Pit latrine with slab	Public latrine or shared toilet
	VIP latrine	Open pit or pit latrine without a slab
	Ecological sanitation	Open defecation in bush or field

It appears, however, that the meaning of *improved* is still an issue. One interpretation has been proposed by a task force on monitoring established by the Water Supply and Sanitation Collaborative Council (WSSCC). According to the WSSCC task force, a person is said to have access to improved water supply if the person has access to sufficient drinking water of acceptable quality as well as sufficient quantity of water for hygienic purposes.[1]

As mentioned earlier, the target for sanitation was established at the 2002 World Summit on Sustainable Development (WSSD) and subsequently incorporated into the list of Millennium Development targets. The terminology chosen for this target is *basic sanitation.* In contrast, the terminology used in the JMP report is *improved sanitation,* which is defined in the JMP report as a sanitation system in which excreta are disposed of in such a way that they reduce the risk of fecal-oral transmission to its users and the environment. The WSSD definition of basic sanitation is broader; it links access to sanitation to improved human health and reduced infant and childhood mortality. The WSSD definition included:

- Development and implementation of efficient household sanitation systems.
- Improvement of sanitation in public institutions, especially in schools.
- Promotion of safe hygiene practices.
- Promotion of education and outreach focused on children, as agents of behavioral change.
- Promotion of affordable and socially and culturally acceptable technologies and practices.
- Development of innovative financing and partnership mechanisms.
- Integration of sanitation into water resources management strategies in a manner that does not negatively affect the environment (that is, it includes protection of water resources from biological or fecal contamination).

The WSSD definition is broader than what is envisaged in the JMP report and is more impact-oriented, particularly in communities that currently have

Issues of privacy and dignity are also important

very low levels of sanitation service. The WSSD is also not focused on the construction of a particular number of toilets as the target goal, but rather on the creation of an overarching process for improved health and hygiene through basic sanitation. The JMP is also concerned with this broader goal, but has been constrained by the need to ensure that its definition of and indicators for improved sanitation can be monitored using existing household survey instruments. The JMP also needs to ensure comparability of data across time and countries. Nonetheless, the JMP's emphasis on the use of particular household technologies ignores health risks associated with poor disposal of sullage[2] or wastewater from domestic sources (for example, risks such as filariasis and schistosomiasis). Moreover, issues of privacy and dignity are also important components of monitoring in sanitation, as they influence willingness to use sanitation facilities regularly (box 3.1).

With these considerations in mind, the task force defines *basic sanitation* as: the lowest-cost option for securing sustainable access to safe, hygienic, and convenient facilities and services for excreta and sullage disposal that provide privacy and dignity, while at the same time ensuring a clean and healthful living environment both at home and in the neighborhood of users.

This definition implies that technology for basic sanitation is not a context-free system, but rather a situation-determined, lowest-cost technology appropriate for the physical, environmental, and financial resources of both the supply side and the demand side of access. The specific technologies that meet these conditions may differ from place to place: in dispersed, low-income rural areas, the appropriate technology may be a simple pit latrine; in a congested urban slum area with reliable water service, it may be a low-cost sewerage system.

Box 3.1
What is sanitation?

Most professionals agree that sanitation as a whole is a "big idea" that covers, among other things:

- Safe collection, storage, treatment, and disposal, reuse, or recycling of human excreta (feces and urine).
- Drainage and disposal, re-use, or recycling of household wastewater (often referred to as sullage or grey water).
- Management, reuse, and recycling of solid wastes (trash or rubbish).
- Drainage of stormwater.
- Treatment and disposal, reuse, or recycling of sewage effluents.
- Collection and management of industrial waste products.
- Management of hazardous wastes (including hospital wastes and chemical, radioactive, and other dangerous substances).

Target 10 refers primarily to the first and second items on this list. It focuses on the collection, treatment, and disposal of human excreta and the drainage and disposal of household wastewater (sullage).

**There is a
need to strike
a workable
balance
between what
is desirable
to measure
and what is
possible**

With basic sanitation, access at the household level should be sufficient. Yet the goals of such access include broader impacts on public health and environmental pollution. Hence, at the very minimum, the definition of access should reflect a healthful environment at the neighborhood level. While household solutions may be sufficient in a rural environment or in a dispersed settlement, they would be woefully inadequate in an urban area, especially in urban slum areas or in congested urban areas and megacities. For such situations, we would need to go beyond access at the household level to provide proper collection systems, such as an appropriate form of sewerage, together with facilities for treatment and disposal of the collected sewage.

In defining indicators that will be used as the basis for monitoring, it is necessary to strike a balance between ideal but often impracticable indicators completely consistent with conceptual definitions and measurable indicators that can act as proxies for the definitions. It is such measurable indicators that should form the basis for developing the main monitoring instruments at the national and international levels. For instance, from a gender perspective, the definition of improved water supply would ideally include some measure of the distance between a household and its water source, as the distance women must travel for water has many impacts on their lives, from the amount of time they must spend on water gathering to questions of physical safety. Similarly, having separate sanitation facilities for men and women and, at schools, for girls and boys, as well as the physical location of such facilities, also affects regularity of use, women's physical safety, and girls' school attendance. Disaggregating service access data by gender would also yield important information, allowing for assessment of the degree to which both men and women are benefiting from interventions in this area.

However, if the information collected from, for instance, household surveys—among the most reliable methods—does not track access by gender, distance to water sources, or the presence of separate sanitation facilities for men and women, then creating monitoring indicators based on these considerations presents a host of operational difficulties. There is a need to strike a workable balance between what is desirable to measure and what is possible to measure, and cost is an important variable in this exercise.

Target 10 on water and sanitation

At the start, it is important to highlight four issues inherent in target 10:

First, the baseline date for these targets, which was not explicit in the original wording, needs to be clarified. Several other Millennium Development targets (1, 2, 5, 6, and 11) call for specific improvements with respect to some baseline year, but with the exception of target 11 on slum dwellers, they all specify this baseline year as 1990. Moreover, in the case of target 11, this ambiguity matters slightly less, since an absolute number of slum dwellers whose lives are to be improved is arguably an inappropriate way to measure

Sustainable access must be viewed from social, economic, and environmental perspectives

progress at the country level. This task force, therefore, needed to make its own determination of the baseline date. Taking into account that the UN Statistics Division and UNICEF use 1990 as their baseline year and that, as a result, the UN Secretary-General's report on progress toward achieving the Millennium Development Goals will use the same year, the task force adopted 1990 as the baseline date, to ensure maximum consistency with other UN publications and the work of the Secretary-General.

Second, sustainable access must be viewed from social, economic, and environmental perspectives. Access includes a physical dimension—for example, access to drinking water requires the existence of infrastructure in good working order—but also embraces a concept of use.[3] Access to sanitation, for example, cannot be measured simply by whether a toilet is installed, but must also determine whether that toilet is working and used for safe disposal of excreta with improved hygienic practices. Otherwise, the contribution of the toilet itself to human health will be negligible or even negative.

There are likewise two aspects of sustainability, a service aspect and an environmental aspect. In terms of service, sustainable access refers primarily to a type of service that is secure, reliable, and available for use on demand by users on a long-term basis. This is possible when there are credible arrangements to ensure a regular and reliable flow of adequate performance-determining resources—human, financial, institutional, and technical know-how, among others—needed to ensure proper functioning and satisfactory operation and maintenance of service infrastructure.

In terms of environmental impact, sustainable access refers to the effects on resources within or outside the service area of the technology and the processes required for adequate access. Thus, such technology and processes should not result in environmental damage or other negative consequences within or outside the service areas, such as exposing people to health risks or creating pollution or degradation of the local living environment or of downstream water resources. In a broader sense, the service should also be one that "meets the needs of the present [generation] without compromising the ability of future generations to meet their own needs" (World Commission on Environment and Development 1987); it should be one that does not compromise the goals of sustainable development, namely, economic development, social equity and justice, and environmental protection.

Third, the targets can and should be set (and monitored) at both global and national levels—and even subnational levels for large nations such as Brazil, China, India, and Nigeria. National targets must be owned by each country—some countries, for example, are well on track to achieving one or more of the above targets and can aspire to something much more ambitious than the Millennium Development targets, which are minimum targets for all countries. Likewise, intermediate milestones (for 2005 and 2010) should be set at both national and global levels (as well as subnational levels, where

National sector assessment reports and plans of action could serve as advocacy tools

JMP funding

Since its inception, the JMP has largely been funded from the regular resources of the two lead agencies, UNICEF and WHO. The role of managing the JMP, updating the country files with new survey data, producing regular reports on coverage, and maintaining the JMP's presence in the sector at global forums has on average received an input of between one and two person-years divided over a total of six people within the two executing agencies. In other words, the JMP has been operating on a shoestring. Costs for conducting the household surveys and tracking and collecting all of the data have not been borne by the JMP, but somehow should be taken into account to get an overall picture of the costs of monitoring progress toward the Millennium Development Goals. Although in the 1990s the JMP set out to fill an information gap, its scope has expanded considerably under the UN Secretary-General's mandate to monitor progress toward achieving the targets on water and sanitation.

To ensure proper representation at global forums, to support a yearly update of coverage estimates, and to promote the use of the JMP methodology and data at the national level, it is estimated that at least three fulltime professional staff are needed. If the mandate of the JMP were further expanded into national capacity building, including support to national sector assessments, much more program funding would be required. An estimated operating budget of little more than $1 million a year would allow the JMP to carry out its expanded role and to implement the recommendations of its advisory group. This would include capacity-building efforts in 25 priority countries, making use of the existing UNICEF and WHO infrastructure in each country. It also includes a pilot project to test a rapid water quality assessment protocol developed by WHO, to be introduced for regular water quality surveillance, with the potential to be run alongside a national-level household survey.

Chapter 4

Where are the needs greatest?

Any assessment of the chances of meeting the Millennium Development target for water and sanitation must begin with three caveats. First is the need to distinguish between the target for water supply and that for sanitation. Although both targets are mutually reinforcing and equally important, meeting the sanitation target is the far more daunting challenge for a variety of reasons, including lack of political will and commitment at the highest level, low effective demand for sanitation among the unserved, inadequate financing, the lack of institutions at the national level responsible for sanitation, the relatively low pay and status associated with work in the sanitation field as opposed to work in other sectors, and nearly universal cultural taboos surrounding discussion (much less the handling) of human excreta. In addition, the scale of the problem is far greater for sanitation than for domestic water supply; more than twice as many people (2.6 billion) lack access to sanitation than lack access to water supply (1.1 billion) (WHO/UNICEF JMP 2000).

Second is the need to tailor strategies for water and sanitation to specific circumstances at the regional, national, and subnational levels, and in rural and urban contexts. To be effective, interventions, approaches, costing, and financing mechanisms must be highly context-specific. Action plans rooted in generalities tend to be less effective than those that take advantage of local opportunities and address local constraints.

Third is the need to recognize the limitations of available data for monitoring progress. Although the data sources used in this report are the best, most reliable data sources available, they tend to understate the gaps in coverage. Measuring access to domestic water supply and sanitation services is a tremendously challenging task that requires striking a balance between what is conceptually desirable to measure and what is practical to measure.

Given these caveats, how should policymakers, advocates, donors, and others identify where the needs for intervention are greatest? The answer to this question is not as obvious as it might appear. It seems reasonable, for example, to simply identify areas where access to domestic water supply and sanitation services is lowest. The United Nations has used this criterion, along with information on progress toward the targets, to identify countries where existing coverage levels are low and where the rate at which access to services is expanding is low or even negative. Alternatively, areas where both access to services is poor and the incidence of water-related disease is high could be prioritized under the assumption that investments should be allocated where their impacts on health are expected to be the greatest. We consider each of these alternative approaches below.

Access to domestic water supply and sanitation services

The 2004 WHO/UNICEF Joint Monitoring Programme report (WHO/ UNICEF JMP 2004) describes regional coverage (map 4.1) for both improved drinking water and improved sanitation in the baseline year of 1990 and in 2002, which is the halfway point for the 2015 targets. The JMP report, which

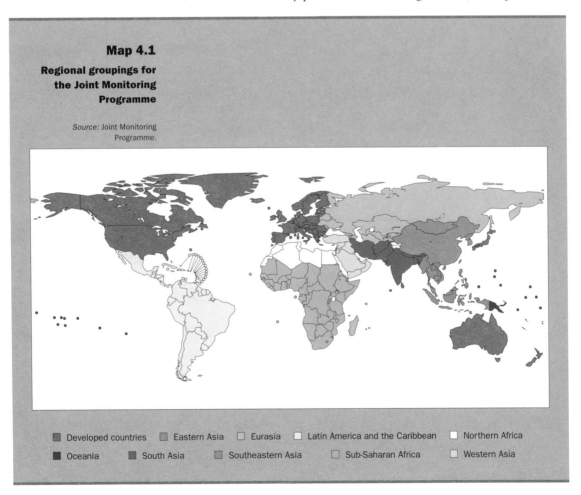

Map 4.1

Regional groupings for the Joint Monitoring Programme

Source: Joint Monitoring Programme.

Developed countries   Eastern Asia   Eurasia   Latin America and the Caribbean   Northern Africa

Oceania   South Asia   Southeastern Asia   Sub-Saharan Africa   Western Asia is the most reliable source of global water supply and sanitation information, indicates that Sub-Saharan Africa, Oceania, Eastern Asia, and Southeast Asia, are the regions where coverage is lowest for both water supply and sanitation.

In 2002, about 1.1 billion of the world's 6.2 billion people (18 percent) lacked access to improved water supply, and about 2.6 billion people (42 percent) had no access to even the most basic forms of improved sanitation (WHO/UNICEF JMP 2004). In the same year, drinking water coverage rates were lowest in Oceania (52 percent) and in Sub-Saharan Africa (58 percent). In absolute numbers, however, most of the 1.1 billion without access to improved drinking water sources lived in Asia (61 percent), and 26 percent lived in Sub-Saharan Africa (table 4.1).

In 2002, sanitation coverage was lowest in Sub-Saharan Africa (36 percent) and in South Asia (37 percent). As shown in table 4.2, most of those without

Table 4.1

Access to improved drinking water sources by region, 2002

Source: Adapted from WHO/UNICEF JMP 2004.

Region	Number of people in region lacking access (millions)	Share of regional population lacking access (percent)	Share of all unserved living in indicated region (percent)
Eastern Asia	303	22	28
Sub-Saharan Africa	288	42	27
South Asia	234	16	22
Southeast Asia	115	21	11
Latin America and Caribbean	60	11	6
Western Asia	23	12	2
Eurasia	20	7	2
Northern Africa	15	10	1
Developed economies	15	2	1
Oceania	3	48	<1
Total	1,076	na	100

Table 4.2

Access to improved sanitation by region, 2002

Source: Adapted from WHO/UNICEF JMP 2004.

Region	Number of people in region lacking access (millions)	Share of regional population lacking access (percent)	Share of all unserved living in indicated region (percent)
South Asia	938	63	36
Eastern Asia	749	55	29
Sub-Saharan Africa	437	64	17
Southeast Asia	208	39	8
Latin America and Caribbean	137	25	5
Eurasia	50	17	2
Northern Africa	40	27	2
Western Asia	38	21	1
Developed economies	20	2	1
Oceania	3	45	<1
Total	2,620		100

In 2002, about 1.1 billion of the world's 6.2 billion people lacked access to improved water supply

access to improved sanitation lived in Asia (73 percent), while 17 percent lived in sub-Saharan Africa. More than half of those without access to improved sanitation—nearly 1.5 billion people—live in just two countries, China and India.

Based on these 2002 coverage levels, along with projected population figures from the United Nation Population Division, UNICEF has estimated the number of people who must be reached with water supply and sanitation facilities by 2015 in order to meet target 10 (table 4.3). For water supply, meeting the target requires that services be extended to 359 million more persons in Sub-Saharan Africa, 444 million in South Asia, and 465 million in East Asia and the Pacific. With regard to sanitation, the challenge in Sub-Saharan Africa is of roughly the same scale as that for water supply; another 363 million persons must obtain access to sanitation by 2015 in order to meet the target. The sanitation challenge is much more daunting in both South Asia and East Asia, where services must reach more than 700 million in each region.

Current levels of access and the rate of progress toward the goal

The United Nations' *Human Development Reports* for 2002 and 2003 provide information on progress toward the Millennium Development target for safe drinking water and sanitation, using JMP data for 2000 and 1990 as the baseline year (UNDP 2002, 2003). The 2002 assessment was undertaken for all the United Nations member countries (except high-income OECD countries) and included Hong Kong and China. For 75 countries, representing 10.3 percent of the world's population, no assessment could be carried out because of data unavailability.

The results of the *Human Development Report* analyses indicate that 25 countries have already achieved the Millennium Development target for water. Of these, 4 (Singapore, Sri Lanka, Bangladesh,[1] and Maldives) are from Asia; only 1, Mauritius, is from Sub-Saharan Africa. Another 43 are considered to be "on track" toward achieving the goal, of which 8 are from Asia and 9 are from Africa. Finally, 25 countries are either lagging somewhat behind, consid-

---

Table 4.3

Number of people to whom access must be extended by 2015 to meet target 10

Source: WHO/UNICEF JMP 2004.

Region	Number of people to gain access to improved water supply (millions)			Number of people to gain access to improved sanitation (millions)		
	Urban	Rural	Total	Urban	Rural	Total
Sub-Saharan Africa	175	184	359	178	185	363
Middle East and North Africa	104	30	134	105	34	140
South Asia	243	201	444	263	451	714
East Asia and Pacific	290	174	465	330	376	705
Latin America and Caribbean	121	20	141	132	29	161
Former Soviet Union and Baltic states	27	0	27	24	0	24
Total	961	609	1,570	1,032	1,076	2,108

For several of the poorest countries insufficient data are available

erably behind, or are even slipping in their progress toward the targets. Among these, 13 are from Sub-Saharan Africa; only 4 (the Philippines, Viet Nam, Myanmar, and China) are from Asia.

The *Human Development Report 2003* assessment identifies two groups of countries that appear to need urgent changes of course in order to meet the goals. In the first group of countries, access to services is low and progress toward the goal is stalled or reversing. The report argues that these countries should receive the lion's share of the world's focus, resources, and assistance. In the second group of countries, the situation is somewhat less desperate, but the needs remain great. These countries either have medium coverage rates but exhibit stalled or reversing progress, or have very low levels of coverage and are progressing only very slowly. In addition, sufficient data are not available to classify another 32 countries; if the data were better, no doubt at least some of these would be included in these "urgent needs" categories.

In terms of access to water, the countries where access is poor and progress toward the goal is stalled or reversing include five in Africa (Ethiopia, Mauritania, Madagascar, Guinea, and Togo), one in East Asia and the Pacific (Papua New Guinea), two in the Arab States (Oman and Libyan Arab Jamahiriya), and one in Latin America and the Caribbean (Haiti). Countries with better prospects for meeting the goal but where challenges are still formidable include eight in Africa (Uganda, Malawi, Cameroon, Niger, Nigeria, Namibia, Côte d'Ivoire, and South Africa), two in East Asia and the Pacific (China and the Philippines), and one in Latin America and the Caribbean (Trinidad and Tobago). It is important to underscore that, for several of the poorest countries, such as Sierra Leone and Burkina Faso, insufficient data are available. It is likely that many such states would be included in this list.

In terms of access to sanitation, the countries where access to services is poor and progress toward the goal is stalled or reversing include ten in Africa (Ethiopia, Niger, Benin, Central African Republic, Mauritania, Madagascar, Guinea, Togo, Nigeria, and Mali), two in the Arab States (Yemen and Sudan), and two in Latin America and the Caribbean (Haiti and the Dominican Republic). Countries with better odds of meeting the goal but where challenges are still substantial include nine in Africa (Chad, Namibia, Côte d'Ivoire, Zimbabwe, Botswana, Malawi, Cameroon, South Africa, and Burundi), three in South Asia (India, Nepal, and Pakistan), three in East Asia and the Pacific (China, Indonesia, and Papua New Guinea), and two in Latin America and the Caribbean (Mexico and Brazil).

Low access to services and high incidence of water-related disease

A third perspective on identifying areas where the needs for accelerated action in domestic water supply and sanitation are greatest focuses on the links between water supply, sanitation, and health. It could be argued that resources expended in locations that have both low levels of access to improved services and high prevalence of water-related diseases will be most likely to generate substantial public health impacts.

Considering the intersection of access to water supply services and incidence of diarrhea, for example, leads to the identification of nine countries in which coverage is less than 50 percent and diarrhea prevalence is between 20 percent and 40 percent of households (map 4.2). Of these, eight are in Africa—Angola, Burkina Faso, Chad, Congo, Ethiopia, Eritrea, Guinea, and Mauritania—and one, Afghanistan, is in Asia. Indeed, with only one exception, those countries with the highest incidence of diarrhea are located in Africa and Asia. It is notable, however, that several Latin American countries with relatively high rates of coverage—countries that therefore do not emerge as high-need areas in the analyses above—have diarrhea prevalence rates of 10–20 percent.

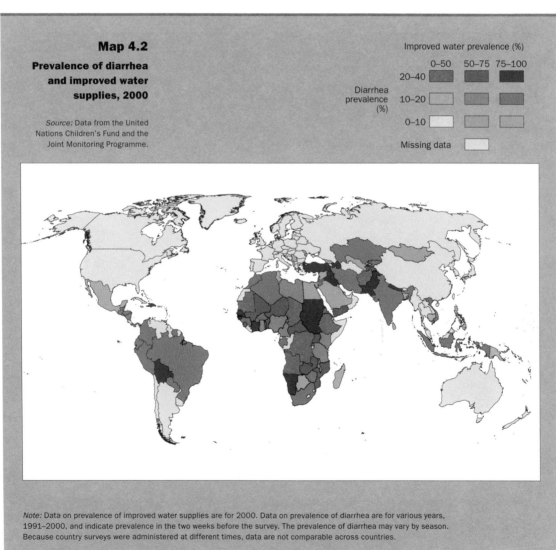

Map 4.2

Prevalence of diarrhea and improved water supplies, 2000

Source: Data from the United Nations Children's Fund and the Joint Monitoring Programme.

Note: Data on prevalence of improved water supplies are for 2000. Data on prevalence of diarrhea are for various years, 1991–2000, and indicate prevalence in the two weeks before the survey. The prevalence of diarrhea may vary by season. Because country surveys were administered at different times, data are not comparable across countries.

A similar analysis for sanitation services suggests that the number of countries in need of urgent action is greater; 15 nations have coverage rates below 50 percent and diarrhea prevalence between 20 percent and 40 percent (map 4.3). As with water supply, all "high-need" countries identified with this approach are in Africa and Asia. In Africa, these include Angola, Benin, Burkina Faso, Central African Republic, Chad, Congo, Ethiopia, Eritrea, Mauritania, Mozambique, Namibia, Niger, and Togo; in Asia, Afghanistan and Bangladesh.

Identifying greatest needs globally

Each of the three approaches to determining where water and sanitation needs are greatest is based on analyses that have important shortcomings. For example, data are typically aggregated and analyzed at the national level, which can mask large swaths of people, typically in rural areas and urban slums, who lack improved services or suffer from water- and sanitation-related disease

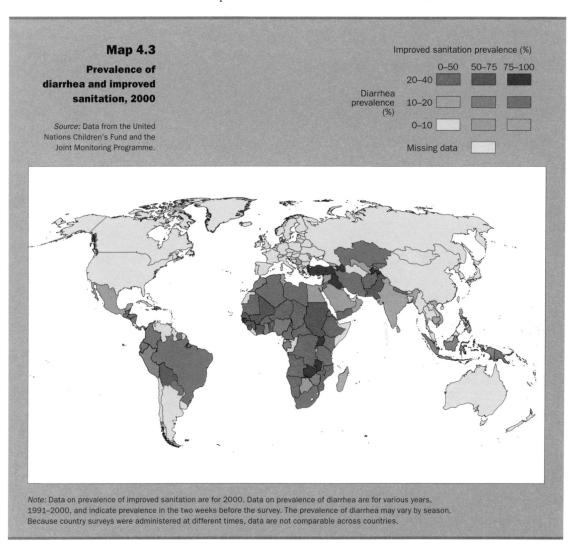

Map 4.3

Prevalence of diarrhea and improved sanitation, 2000

Source: Data from the United Nations Children's Fund and the Joint Monitoring Programme.

Note: Data on prevalence of improved sanitation are for 2000. Data on prevalence of diarrhea are for various years, 1991–2000, and indicate prevalence in the two weeks before the survey. The prevalence of diarrhea may vary by season. Because country surveys were administered at different times, data are not comparable across countries.

Governments know much less about those who lack water supply and sanitation services

in an otherwise fairly well-serviced, healthy country. Nonetheless, the general approach used here—defining criteria by which groups should be prioritized and using the best available data to identify where those groups are—is one that should underpin both international and national planning processes.

It is also important in such exercises to be clear about the choice of criteria, as well as the reasons for and effects of such choices. In this chapter, three alternative sets of criteria for identifying "high-need" countries are employed that, in broad strokes, produce a consistent conclusion that high-need countries are disproportionately found in Africa and Asia. Comparing the lists of specific high-need countries emerging under each of the three approaches, however, demonstrates that the choice of criteria—as well as the way in which particular criteria are operationalized—can have substantial impact on the way that priorities are shaped (table 4.4). Similar effects are almost certain to occur with subnational analyses as well.

Pinpointing greatest needs within countries

For water supply and sanitation professionals, it is already common knowledge that billions of people around the world do not have access to a minimum quantity of safe drinking water and adequate sanitation, and considerable empirical research has been undertaken to explain the reasons for low coverage rates in particular communities.[2] Governments, however, often know much less about those who lack water supply and sanitation services compared with those who do have access. Consequently, while a "one-size-fits-all" policy for the water and sanitation sector may appear attractively simple, such an approach may not reflect the supports and strategies needed to reach the unserved.

This section presents a simple typology of six kinds of communities in which a substantial proportion of households do not have access to improved water supply and sanitation services (figure 4.1). With respect first to water

Figure 4.1

A typology of communities with low water supply and sanitation coverage

		Density		
		Dispersed (rural)	Medium (village, small town)	Dense (urban/peri-urban)
Existing infrastructure	Little/no improved infrastructure	Type I: dispersed, little/no improved infrastructure	Type III: medium density, little/no improved infrastructure	Type V: high density, little/no improved infrastructure
	Low-functioning improved infrastructure	Type II: dispersed, dysfunctional improved infrastructure	Type IV: medium density, dysfunctional improved infrastructure	Type VI: high density, dysfunctional improved infrastructure

Table 4.4

High-need countries identified by various criteria

	Water supply			Sanitation		
	Low access, slow progress (UNDP 2003)	Moderate access and progress (UNDP 2003)	Low access, high diarrhea incidence (WHO/UNICEF JMP 2000)	Low access, slow progress (UNDP 2003)	Moderate access and progress (UNDP 2003)	Low access, high diarrhea incidence (WHO/UNICEF JMP 2000)
Africa						
	Ethiopia	Cameroon	Angola	Benin	Botswana	Angola
	Guinea	Côte d'Ivoire	Burkina Faso	Ethiopia	Burundi	Benin
	Madagascar	Malawi	Chad	Central African Republic	Cameroon	Burkina Faso
	Mauritania	Namibia	Congo	Guinea	Chad	Congo
	Togo	Niger	Eritrea	Madagascar	Côte d'Ivoire	Eritrea
		Nigeria	Ethiopia	Mali	Malawi	Ethiopia
		South Africa	Guinea	Mauritania	Namibia	Central African Republic
		Uganda	Mauritania	Niger	South Africa	Chad
				Nigeria	Zimbabwe	Mauritania
				Togo		Mozambique
						Namibia
						Niger
						Togo
Asia						
	Papua New Guinea	China			China	Bangladesh
		Philippines			India	
					Indonesia	
					Nepal	
					Pakistan	
					Papua New Guinea	
Arab states						
	Oman		Afghanistan	Sudan		Afghanistan
	Libyan Arab Jamahiriya			Yemen		
Latin America and Caribbean						
	Haiti	Trinidad and Tobago		Dominican Republic	Brazil	
				Haiti	Mexico	

supply and then sanitation, a brief description of each community type is provided, along with a summary of the principal explanations for low existing coverage levels, possible strategies for improving coverage, and illustrative examples. Acknowledging that access to water supply and sanitation is a function of many technical, financial, and institutional factors, a multifaceted analytical challenge has been distilled into one with a smaller number of dimensions. The horizontal axis represents the density of settlement, which carries with it a host of technical and cost implications for improving access to services. On

An urban bias in infrastructure investment policy often pushes Type I communities to the end of the queue

the vertical axis is the range of existing infrastructure. This variable serves as an indirect proxy for institutional considerations, such as the scope for collective action, based on the assumption that communities with existing but inadequately functioning water-supply infrastructure have a greater institutional foundation upon which to build than communities where collective water systems have never been installed. This is clearly a simplifying assumption that will not hold in all cases; however, it is a generalization that is consistent with experience in many of the case studies described in the following sections.

Efforts have been made to keep the number of categories small; many nuances in both the community characteristics and the service delivery considerations have thus been omitted. In addition, broader considerations, such as the status of governance and rule of law, have also been omitted from the typology. These issues are, however, discussed briefly in a separate section.

Across all six community types, unserved households tend to share two characteristics: they are poor, and they have limited voice in priority-setting and resource allocation decisions. While neither of these features is unique to the water and sanitation sector, each has important implications for the kinds of strategies needed to improve water supply and sanitation coverage to meet target 10.

Access to domestic water supply services

Water supply coverage is a function of both demand and supply considerations in each typology category.[3] For each community type, a summary of the principal demand considerations is presented, followed by a synopsis of the principal supply issues.

Type I: dispersed settlement, little or no improved infrastructure. Type I communities tend to be found in rural areas with agrarian economies. Household members—typically women and children—obtain water for domestic uses from surface water sources, and occasionally from water vendors. The time devoted to water fetching is often substantial, and both quantity and quality of water supply is lacking.

The reasons for lack of access to adequate supplies of water in Type I communities are found both in the economics of water supply and in development policy frameworks at the national level. Such settlements are generally unable to exploit economies of scale for community-level water supply solutions, so per capita costs of improvements are high, while the potential for cash contributions from households tends to be low. At the provincial and national level, an urban bias in infrastructure investment policy often pushes Type I communities to the end of the queue for government-financed water supply improvements.

Facilitating water supply improvements in Type I communities often requires substantial investment in institutional capacity building before sustainable improved water supply infrastructure can be installed. Frequently, the

Flexible strategies that allow in-kind contributions such as labor may be important in Type I communities

institutions needed to facilitate collective action for improving water supply are weak or completely absent. Partnerships with national or even international nongovernmental organizations (NGOs) may be necessary to develop community capacity for organization and planning of improved services.

If cost-sharing policies exist, flexible strategies that allow in-kind contributions such as labor may be important in Type I communities, where cash tends to be scarce. Another strategy for addressing the cost issues of water improvements in such communities is to consider the possibility of combining irrigation and domestic water supply initiatives. Millions of people throughout the developing world obtain their household water from irrigation facilities, yet planning and policy for irrigation is carried out largely without consideration of domestic users. Exploring the possibilities for incorporating both irrigation and domestic needs into water planning has the potential in many cases to lower costs, to replace environmentally damaging practices (such as tubewell irrigation, which can deplete water tables) with more sustainable ones (such as drawing seepage from irrigation canals through handpumps), and to ensure that the water people end up drinking is safe.[4]

Type II: dispersed settlement, existing infrastructure providing inadequate supply. Type II communities have some type of improved water supply infrastructure installed—typically shared facilities, such as borewells with handpumps—but are considered to be lacking access to services because the volume of water supplied per capita is insufficient or because the facilities have fallen into disrepair. Households either manage with these small quantities of water or supplement them with water from surface sources or vendors.

The water supply infrastructure in Type II communities has often failed because of inadequate maintenance. (Population growth in the community may also contribute to declining per capita supplies.) The public investment neglect and affordability issues that Type II communities suffer has been overcome, at least initially, but sustainability of the installed infrastructure is lacking as a result of inadequate financial resources for operation and maintenance, unavailability of spare parts or technical skills, a weak institutional arrangement for upkeep of the facilities, or some combination of those factors.

Understanding the reasons for the poor performance of a Type II community's water infrastructure is a critical first step in improving coverage. If the level of service installed is too expensive to be maintained by users, simply rehabilitating the existing infrastructure will result in another failure in the future. Even if the economic capacity for operation and maintenance does exist within the community, a different sort of mismatch between supply and demand may exist. In the village of Vellukara, India, for example, a piped water system with shared public taps fell into disuse because half of the village's households preferred to use private or shared wells (Davis and others 2001). These households were also unwilling to pay monthly fees toward the upkeep

The water supply infrastructure in Type II communities has often failed because of inadequate maintenance

of the system, which rendered it financially unviable and left the other half of the village reliant on distant surface water sources. This case illustrates how critical it is to understand the realities of demand for different types of facilities before embarking on projects.

Poor system performance may also arise if the communities lack the human capacity and training to maintain the supply systems in good working order. In the case of Ghana, for example, rural communities had historically not been a part of the planning process for water supply and thus had neither a stake in nor the capacity to ensure the longevity of the installed handpumps and piped systems. By one estimate, 60 percent of these facilities were nonfunctional at any given time before Ghana initiated major sector reforms in the 1990s (Klee-meier 2002). Accounts of this sort are very common, particularly in countries with weak local administrations. By extension, sustainable coverage expansion in Type II communities often requires considerable focus on training and building the capacity of local institutions.

In Ghana, for example, capacity building was undertaken gradually, with core planning functions transferred from central government to local government and communities. Ownership of water supply was transferred to the local governments and the communities. A number of public and private organizations brought their strengths to the new project, including four drilling companies, 32 local NGOs and community-based organizations, and several national and international NGOs. In Togo, a redesign of one of the country's largest rural water supply programs included strengthening of social intermediation programs and training of community technicians. In one village, Ayole—where a previous government-installed community handpump had broken down—a rehabilitation project was accompanied by technician training, the formation of a committee responsible for raising funds for operation and maintenance, and earmarked public funds at the district level for the provision of spare parts and extension services. The result was a well-functioning handpump and a community that, one year after its rehabilitation, successfully overcame a major failure of the pump (UNDP 1988).

It is important to note, however, that building capacity at the local level does not mean that central government has no role to play in sustainable service delivery. Indeed, the balance between the center and local service providers is critical to maintaining effective and reliable services. Whereas the prevailing wisdom in the development community advocates decentralization of water and sanitation services to the "lowest possible level," empirical evidence increasingly indicates that centralized institutions may be best suited to executing particular tasks within service planning, delivery, and monitoring.[5] For example, in one rural supply project in Azad and Jammu Kashmir, Pakistan, it was a set of centralized oversight mechanisms that ensured sustainable scheme designs and prevented disadvantaged groups from being excluded from project benefits (Davis 2003). In addition, realizing economies of scale in bulk

Type III communities are generally large enough to enjoy some economies of scale

water provision may require a lead agency at a higher level than the community. Furthermore, institutions not based in the community can be helpful in ensuring that the externalities of service provision do not simply get passed on to neighboring communities.

Centralized agencies may also need to provide ongoing support to local administrations and service providers undertaking responsibility for water supply for the first time. A growing literature also suggests that Type II communities need considerably more support after the construction phase of a project than was previously believed. Resources and capacity to provide training, technical assistance, and supply-chain support to communities must be available in the long term, whether through local government, NGOs, or external agencies. Because such "software" components of water supply planning receive much less emphasis (and funding) than do more visible construction projects, these elements so critical to sustaining installed infrastructure are often the most difficult to establish.

Type III: medium density, little or no improved infrastructure. Type III communities often represent the interface between rural and urban settlements—villages that have grown into small towns, but whose infrastructure systems have not yet evolved to a level comparable with larger cities. Some wealthier households may have installed private wells, while a substantial proportion of families obtain water from vendors or surface water sources.

Type III communities are generally large enough to enjoy some economies of scale—which means that piped networks will be feasible in at least part of the settlement—but are too small or dispersed for traditional urban utility management models to operate effectively. There often exists in Type III communities the economic capacity to make considerable improvements in water supply, but the absence of a supportive institutional framework often results in a variety of household-level solutions as opposed to a coordinated community-level effort. Type III communities are generally excluded both from national water supply programs targeting rural areas and from those focused on cities. Local government institutions are often weak and under-resourced. Few households have access to credit.

Extending coverage in Type III communities can happen quickly and sustainably, but planning mistakes are easy to make in this type of settlement. In particular, the question of whether such communities should be viewed more like large rural villages or small cities has considerable implication for the technologies and management structures that will be adopted. In the town of Lugazi, Uganda, for example, a piped network was installed, which provided private connections to a substantial proportion of households, as well as a limited number of public kiosks in the central business district. Households that once used spring water now obtain water supply from their own or their neighbors' private connections, from public kiosks, or from vendors who also

Extending coverage in Type III communities can happen quickly and sustainably

patronize the kiosks. In all cases, users pay the full cost of the level of service they receive. In the neighboring town of Wobulenzi, the water-planning paradigm was more like that of a rural village. Water user groups were established and were given responsibility for managing neighborhood kiosks throughout the town, and most established prices that were lower than the cost of supply. Private connections were also made available to households and businesses that wished to pay the full cost of this improved level of service. These two very different models stemmed from fundamentally different views of the character and the future of the communities and gave rise to two unique sets of financial and institutional challenges (Wandera 1999; Whittington and others 1999).

Much less is known about effective strategies for extending sustained coverage in small towns, as compared with either rural or dense urban settlements. It appears that allowing for a variety of service options and expecting the composition of technologies to change rapidly are important planning principles in these dynamic communities. Considerable empirical research has also demonstrated that provision of financing—even at market rates—can unleash latent demand for improved services and allow households in small towns to move more quickly toward community-level piped networks. In towns where such economic capacity does not exist, policies that promote small-scale independent providers can also increase the range of options available to households and lower service costs through competition and innovation (Collignon and Vezina 2000). Growing recognition of the policy vacuum regarding water supply and sanitation services for Type III (and IV) communities has spurred several important research and policy-experiment activities. In Peru, for example, the Water and Sanitation Program is currently undertaking comparative analysis of several different management models in a number of small towns (Water and Sanitation Program website).

Type IV: medium density, existing infrastructure providing inadequate supply. Small towns in the Type IV category have installed water supply facilities that provide an insufficient volume of water per capita per day. Households typically supplement their water supply with water purchased from vendors or perhaps drawn from surface sources. If the level of community-level service continues to slide, wealthier households will tend to exit the public system in favor of self-provision (for example, through private wells). Over time, the situation deteriorates as revenues decline, and households with the greatest ability to withstand tariff increases (and provide cross-subsidies to poorer households) invest in private solutions instead.

As with Type II communities in rural areas, it is important to understand the reasons that existing infrastructure in Type IV towns is not providing adequate supply. Simply rehabilitating a poorly designed system will not provide sustained access to improved services in the long run. In many cases, small town systems are overbuilt as a result of designs based on perceived demand and peak estimates,

A variety of institutional models are being employed to improve water services in Type IV communities

rather than on dialogue with users themselves. Although technically sound, such systems cannot be supported given the economic base of the community. In Mali, for example, the "overscaled" design of facilities was identified as one of the key explanations for the high rates of failure in small-town water systems.

The unsustainability of overbuilt systems can be further exacerbated by the institutional arrangements for water supply services that are typically found in small towns. Services managed by local government may suffer from underfinancing, particularly for operation and maintenance, when funds for water are intermingled with the community's general accounts. Water user associations or other civic groups dedicated to water supply service delivery may perform better with respect to financial and accountability matters, but they often lack technical capacity and have limited access to state or national sources of support in the event of major problems.

A variety of institutional models are being employed to improve water services in Type IV communities, from regional utilities in South Asia to local *juntas* in Latin America. There is also increasing private-sector involvement in the management of small-town water systems. In Uganda, the national government financed the rehabilitation of several dozen Type IV towns as a prelude to establishing management contracts with six private operators (Kayaga 2003). The World Bank is also supporting pilot projects in franchising for small town water systems (Roche and others 2001).

Type V: high density, little or no improved infrastructure. Urban areas lacking water supply infrastructure typically fall into two categories: newly constructed neighborhoods to which trunk lines have not yet been extended or unregularized areas where the installation of trunk infrastructure is costly or prohibited by law. Households in Type V communities typically obtain water from vendors (ranging from pole vendors to tankers); from privately or communally managed stationary tanks; or from friends, family, or employers located in networked areas.

In areas of new construction, urban development policy and regulation is typically the cause of lack of access. Development permits, for example, may be granted without the requirement of providing basic services. Indeed, at times, urban development authorities actually work at cross purposes with water and sanitation agencies. In Lima, Peru, for example, a decision of the Vice Ministry for Construction and Sanitation that inadequate water supply was available to develop an outlying area of the city was overturned by the Ministry of Housing, which was under strong political pressure to develop new areas for a national low-cost housing program (Davis 2004).

In urban slums—defined as unplanned areas in which the majority of residents have title neither to their land nor their homes—both the high cost of water supply improvements and an unsupportive policy environment constrain access to service. Such settlements are often located on marginal lands at considerable

Awareness campaigns need to make better use of modern marketing strategies

as a prerequisite for receiving improved water supply. Although this bundling strategy has been successful in some communities, in others it has led to the construction of "white elephants" that households have little interest in using or maintaining.

In some cases, communities' understanding of the links among sanitation, hygiene, and health is limited, and awareness-raising efforts can help generate demand for improved sanitation services. In many other instances, however, households have simply pursued other investments in a rational priority-setting process. Awareness campaigns may need to take greater advantage of modern marketing strategies, focusing on basic human emotions, such as pride, shame, and competition to make real progress in rural sanitation. Such programs could also, where feasible, provide information about the potential for human waste to be used as a resource in agriculture. Some sanitation technologies—such as the twin-pit latrine—are well suited to the collection and safe removal of excreta, which can be applied as fertilizer to crops.

Subsidies for improved sanitation services have been declining in recent years. For Type I and II communities, the costs of simple technologies may be low, but so too is effective demand for them. Improving affordability with well-designed subsidies—paired with social marketing efforts—may be more cost-effective than implementing large-scale education and marketing campaigns in an effort to influence household investment decisions. Recent experience with a particularly promising approach called community-led total sanitation suggests that, in some instances, subsidies can inhibit community action. In community-led total sanitation, communities themselves analyze the effects of open defecation and address the problem by building latrines cheaply from local materials and establishing community mechanisms for ensuring that everyone uses them. When community members think that a subsidy may be in the offing, they do not participate in the community effort. It is important to stress that this approach has been successful in rural areas, with basic latrines made from often freely available local materials and volunteer community labor; this "no subsidies" approach may not be applicable in areas where latrines cannot be constructed so inexpensively, such as urban slums.

Type III and IV communities: medium density, little or poorly functioning infrastructure. As is the case with water supply, sanitation planning at the rural-urban interface can be particularly challenging. Households in these communities have often been exposed to sewerage systems and would appreciate the convenience and status that toilets with sewers would convey. However, these are costly technologies, and on-site facilities may be a more appropriate choice given the economic base of the community. In some small towns in Peru, for example, fewer than 10 percent of households have connected to piped sewerage networks, although the results of community assessments indicated this level of service was preferred by a majority of residents (Davis

Communities at the urban-rural boundary are also often good candidates for recycling sewage water in agriculture

2004). Once households were confronted with the substantial connection fees and monthly service bills, however, a majority decided to retain their existing (on-site) service.

It may be possible to respond to the demand for sewerage service in Type III and IV communities by adopting lower-cost technical options. In Brazil, for example, a system of "condominial" sewerage was developed in the 1980s with the aim of extending sanitation services to low-income communities. This technology has now become a standard sanitation solution for entire urban areas in Brazil, irrespective of income levels. Condominial sewers reduce per capita costs of service by replacing the traditional model of individual household connections to a public sewer with a model in which household waste is discharged into branch sewers, and eventually into a public sewer through a group (or "block") connection (Watson 1999).

For households that cannot afford a sewer network connection, public facilities may be a good alternative, if they are carefully designed. Countless anecdotes exist in the water and sanitation sector regarding public facilities that, once constructed, quickly fell into disrepair because communities lacked the interest or skills to maintain them. Examples do exist, however, of public facilities that function reliably and are well maintained. They all have the common feature of having in place attendants who take care of them, as well as being operated on a pay-per-use basis. In India, the NGO Sulabh International has installed 5,500 pour flush toilets that are operated on a fee basis and are maintained by attendants who live at the facilities. Through gradual technology development, careful attention to sustainability, and strong efforts in marketing and promotion, Sulabh's facilities are considered to be a model for sustainable public sanitation services (Sulabh International website).[7]

Communities at the urban-rural boundary are also often good candidates for recycling sewage water in agriculture (Ensink and others 2002). This practice can save enormous costs of treating sewage water, while creating substantial benefits in the form of usable water and fertilizer for agriculture. Care must be taken to ensure that the concentration of fertilizer nutrients in the water is not too high, and agricultural workers using recycled sewage water should also be equipped with protective gear, such as gloves and boots. In sum, although recycling sewage water in agriculture is not without its problems, these problems can be managed. The savings in water treatment and the benefits in food production make this practice highly desirable.

Type V and VI communities: high density, little or poorly functioning infrastructure. Improving sanitation in urban areas is perhaps one of the most formidable challenges facing target 10 and the water and sanitation sector more generally. Given the high densities of these communities, on-site technologies are often unworkable because of limited land availability and the potential for contamination of drinking water supplies. Sewerage systems, on the other hand, are

The high per capita cost of sanitation services is often the result of overly stringent technical standards

expensive to construct and can generally not be operated and maintained with revenues obtained from low-income households. As with water supply services, challenges related to insecure tenure and landlord-tenant arrangements often undermine efforts to improve sanitation services in these communities.

In many instances, the high per capita cost of sanitation services is the result of overly stringent technical standards adopted without modification from industrial countries.[8] In the past decade many innovative technical solutions have helped resolve this bottleneck to expanding sanitation coverage. Condominial sewerage (discussed above) is one example of a lower-cost technology that has been successful in some areas. Another technical innovation involves "unbundling" of sewer networks into several smaller systems serving different zones within a city. In Bangkok, Thailand, for example, the Metropolitan Administration prepared a wastewater master plan for the entire metropolitan area in 1968. Though technically sound, the plan was found to be prohibitively expensive and was shelved for 16 years. In 1984, the master plan was revised under a Japanese technical assistance program such that the inner part of Bangkok was divided into 10 sewerage zones, each with an independent collection and treatment system. The total sanitation investment among the 10 zones is lower than the amount that would be required for a single project that covered the entire city. Moreover, each zone-level project is technically simpler than a citywide project would be. As a result, the Bangkok Metropolitan Administration has been able to implement various sanitation projects in different zones of the city, using a more affordable phased investment program. (For more details, see the case study in the appendix to this volume).

In much of the literature on urban sanitation, institutional constraints are considered to be as important as technical and financial challenges in explaining low rates of coverage. Whereas low-income urban communities tend to have more influence than, say, dispersed rural villages, they still often lack the capacity for organizing, planning, and levying demands on government and service providers. For their part, municipal water and sanitation agencies often find it difficult to initiate a dialogue with low-income communities—and often have little incentive to do so. Partnerships between government, service agencies, communities, and civic organizations can thus be useful in facilitating dialogue and collective action in pursuit of improved sanitation services for the urban poor.

In West Bengal, India, for example, the Medinipur District Rural Sanitation Project was launched in 1990 and involves UNICEF, state- and district-level governments, a religious NGO (the Ramakrishna Mission), and voluntary grassroots community-level organizations. The project was designed as a "people's movement" and strives to discourage open defecation through education and social marketing. Community mobilization and education is carried out by trained motivators from the communities, using home visits, motivational camps, exhibitions, and the use of visual aids, such as flash cards and calendars.

Over the course of just 10 years, the project has increased coverage of improved sanitation services from almost zero to 80 percent. Development and production of the latrines was undertaken locally, which improved cultural appropriateness and affordability of the designs while also providing an economic opportunity for local women trained in latrine component manufacturing. To date, approximately 1.2 million latrines have been delivered through the program throughout West Bengal. The impact of widespread latrine development has been accompanied by a remarkable reduction in cases and deaths associated with diarrheal diseases (Chowdhry 2002; Sengupta 2001; UNICEF 1994, 2002).

For countries with very low access to basic sanitation, increasing the effectiveness of management of excreta at the household level may have the biggest health implications, and it may be the biggest challenge. For this reason some countries may legitimately decide to focus their efforts at this level in the short

Table 4.6

Typology of unserved and underserved communities for sanitation

	Density	Existing service	Proximate explanations		Possible policy and planning responses
			Supply side	Demand side	
I	Dispersed (rural)	Little or no improved infrastructure: open defecation	• No institutional home for sanitation. • Low priority and limited public investment in rural sanitation.	• Poverty. • Limited access to credit. • Low demand for sanitation improvements.	• Social marketing and education. • Partnerships with civic organizations. • Targeted subsidies and credit programs.
II	Dispersed (rural)	Service from dysfunctional private facilities, such as latrines	• No institutional home for sanitation. • Limited post-construction support for sanitation. • Limited private-sector skills for operation and maintenance. • Mismatch between levels of service supplied and demanded.	• Poverty. • Limited access to credit. • Low demand for sanitation improvements.	• Social marketing and education. • Partnerships with civic organizations. • Targeted subsidies and credit programs.
III	Medium density (small town)	Service from dysfunctional private and public facilities, open defecation	• No institutional home for sanitation. • Limited resources available for operation and maintenance. • Constraining standards for service improvements.	• Limited access to credit. • Limited demand for sanitation improvements. • Demand captured by private household investment.	• Social marketing and education. • Partnerships with civic organizations. • Regulatory reform (standards, new construction). • Innovative technologies.

term. In other cases specific linkages between elements of sanitation mean that a more complete solution may be better. For example, in a particularly congested urban community some form of off-site (sewered) sanitation may be the only viable technical choice, in which case there will probably need to be some interventions to improve management of solid wastes and stormwater drainage; otherwise the sewers won't work.

The key issue is that each community, region, or country needs to work out the most sensible and cost-effective way of thinking about sanitation in the short and long term and then act accordingly. Flexibility and pragmatism should be the key words—and both professionals and politicians need to try to see past "experience" and ideas that are developed elsewhere. A pragmatic local approach with an eye to wider environmental and health issues is likely to result in more progress than blind adherence to a rigid global definition. The key elements of the preceding discussion on sanitation are summarized in table 4.6.

Table 4.6

Typology of unserved and underserved communities for sanitation

(continued)

	Density	Existing service	Proximate explanations		Possible policy and planning responses
			Supply side	Demand side	
IV	Medium density (small town)	Service from dysfunctional private facilities	• No institutional home for sanitation. • Limited post-construction support for sanitation.	• Limited access to credit. • Limited demand for sanitation improvements. • Demand captured by private household investment.	• Social marketing and education. • Partnerships with civic organizations. • Regulatory reform (standards, new construction). • Innovative technologies.
V	High density (urban or periurban)	Little or no improved infrastructure: open defecation or use of facilities in other neighborhoods	• No institutional home for sanitation. • Growth (newly incorporated areas). • Investment restrictions in unregularized areas. • High per capita cost of service. • Perceptions of poverty. • Constraining standards.	• High proportion of rented dwellings. • Insecure tenure. • Limited access to credit. • Poverty. • Low demand for sanitation improvements.	• Land tenure reform. • Social marketing and education. • Partnerships with civic organizations. • Regulatory reform (standards, new construction). • Innovative technologies.
VI	High density (urban or periurban)	Service from shared public facilities	• No institutional home for sanitation. • High per capita cost of household level supply. • Perception of poverty. • Constraining standards. • Limited funding and incentives for operation and maintenance.	• High proportion of rented dwellings. • Limited access to credit. • Poverty. • Low demand for sanitation improvements.	• Land tenure reform. • Social marketing and education. • Partnerships with civic organizations. • Regulatory reform (standards, new construction). • Innovative technologies.

Chapter 5

What's holding us back?

To understand how to move forward to meet the Millennium Development Goals, it is first necessary to analyze what's holding us back. Understanding why 2 in every 10 people in the developing world lack access to water supply, and 5 in 10 lack access to sanitation services, is fundamental to identifying effective strategies for meeting target 10. Clearly, the explanations vary across communities, countries, and regions, but a common set of political, financial, institutional, and technical challenges confronts most developing countries in their quest to expand water supply and sanitation services.

Political constraints

One of the chief constraints to expanding water supply and sanitation coverage is the lack of political will, by which we mean an absence of political leadership and government commitment to allocating sufficient national resources to the sector, and to undertaking the reforms necessary to improve performance and attract investment (box 5.1).[1]

There are many underlying reasons for a lack of political will. For decisionmakers in finance ministries, for example, investments in water supply and sanitation are perceived as having lower returns than funds spent in other sectors (for example, on roads or energy). Another reason is the failure of technical specialists, civil society actors, and others to make a compelling case to decisionmakers concerning the social and economic benefits of access to water supply and sanitation services. It is easier to make the case where political leaders, as well as policy and decisionmakers, are themselves aware or convinced of the social, economic, environmental, and spiritual benefits from access to water supply and sanitation. Politicians, in particular, tend to respond to public pressures and demands from their constituencies; hence, they tend to give higher priority to water supply in response to higher demand for water. Experience

Information can be one of the most effective tools for overcoming political resistance

shows that where political leadership and commitment have been accompanied by social marketing, significant progress has been made not only in access to water supply, but also to sanitation.

The capture of water and sanitation planning and institutional processes by powerful political interests also acts as a barrier to service expansion. The kinds of changes needed to prioritize improved water supply and sanitation services to poor households often threaten status quo arrangements that confer substantial benefits on politically influential groups. The resistance that often emerges can be difficult to overcome, particularly when vested interests exploit the plight of the unserved to argue against policy or institutional reforms. Building broad-based, informed coalitions, ideally led by an influential political champion, is critical for mounting initiatives that prioritize the poor and redirect resources toward low-income households.

Indeed, information can be one of the most effective tools for overcoming political resistance. Decisionmakers often need education about the social and economic benefits of improving water supply and sanitation to make a case for prioritizing the sector in policy and planning processes. Public education campaigns, such as the "report card" and public meeting approaches employed in parts of South Asia, can help mobilize broad support and exert pressure for change on elected officials. Equally important, civic organizations and the public need information regarding the ways in which existing subsidies are captured by middle- and upper-income households and prevent expansion of service to the poorest.

Broad policy and institutional reform is also essential for reducing political interference in the day-to-day operations of water and sanitation agencies in many countries. So long as water supply and sanitation service providers are reliant upon the state for budgetary transfers, and so long as agency staff are vulnerable to interference by officials in decisions related their careers, priority setting, pricing, and investment will continue to favor those with political connections—which almost never includes the poor. "Ring fencing"[2] of agencies to help make financial and personnel management processes more transparent

---

Box 5.1

Water is a political issue

Source: UN-HABITAT 2004.

"Local elections took place two months back. Our only demand was water—whoever gave us water would get our votes."

—Sagira, a pavement dweller in Mumbai, India.

"For a few weeks before the municipal elections, one of the candidates who lives just on the other side of this hill used to supply water to us in long hosepipes from taps in his house. After the elections, the hosepipes disappeared and our water supply stopped. Now if we go to him to ask for water he drives us away as if we are beggars. It is so humiliating!"

—A woman from Laxminagar, a slum settlement of about 700 families in Pune, India.

"Confidence-building" measures can help pave the way for deeper, subsequent reforms

and less vulnerable to corruption, as well as the enactment of civil service legislation to improve incentives for good performance, are two examples of the kinds of reforms that can help reorient planning and decisionmaking toward communities with relatively weak political voice.

It is also worth noting that, in the water and sanitation sector, change is often triggered by a crisis, such as a drought, a precipitous drop in service levels, an outbreak of disease, or a financial failure. Political shifts, such as decentralization or elections, can also be opportunities for reform, as can external shocks, threats, and opportunities, such as the possibility of privatization or donor pressure. Indeed, timing is one of the basic challenges of the sector—how to make progress within one political cycle after decades of neglect or how to interest politicians in measures that are not likely to yield visible results during their terms of office. It is thus important to look for historic opportunities to make large strides and also to pursue buy-in around a few simple first steps that can yield short-term benefits to the politicians and policymakers. Such "confidence-building" measures that build capacity, trust, and social capital can help pave the way for deeper, subsequent reforms (Kingdom and Van Ginneken 2004).

Institutional constraints

Two types of institutional constraints[3] stand in the way of expanding access to water supply and sanitation services: the lack of appropriate institutions at all levels, and chronic dysfunction of existing institutional arrangements. At the community level, potential users of services are often constrained by the absence or underutilization of institutions to facilitate collective or individual action. At the national and subnational level, sanitation often has no institutional home at all, creating a policy vacuum and a corresponding lack of prioritization in budgetary decisionmaking.

Among existing institutions involved in the extension, operation, and maintenance of water supply and sanitation services—including formal organizations such as utilities and local governments, less formal associations such as village committees, and principles or practices such as laws, regulations, and customs—persistent problems at the heart of constraints to expanding access to service include inadequate capacity, inappropriate incentives, lack of accountability, and absence of a sound regulatory system. are. For women, legal barriers to owning and inheriting land can also serve to limit their access to water.

Capacity building

Institutions responsible for service provision—whether village water and sanitation committees or large urban utilities—need technical, financial, managerial, and social intermediation capacity that is lacking in many parts of the developing world. Technical capacity is particularly critical for extending services to

Capacity building is also essential in the area of gender-sensitive programming and policymaking

low-income communities, where innovative technologies and service-delivery systems can be tailored to meet the needs of poor households. Similarly, considerable research suggests that reaching the poorest of households with water supply and sanitation services can be facilitated by the participation of social intermediation professionals.[4]

Capacity building is also essential in the area of gender-sensitive programming and policymaking. Because of differences in production, labor, responsibilities, and resources, women and men have different interests in, and derive different benefits from, the availability, use, and management of water. Women, for instance, generally prioritize water for domestic uses such as drinking and washing, whereas men may focus on irrigation. As a result, they often have different criteria to evaluate the adequacy, equity, timeliness, convenience, and quality of various interventions. Without a thorough gender analysis, planners have a distorted picture of communities, natural resource uses, households, and water users. Understanding the differences between women's and men's roles (who does what work, who makes which decisions, who uses water for what, who controls which resources, who is responsible for the different family obligations) is part of a good analysis and can contribute to more effective initiatives.

Capacity is enhanced through adherence to the principle of management at the lowest appropriate level, expressed through mechanisms such as devolution of responsibility to local governments and communities, backed by technical assistance for appropriate capacity building and funding. However, lack of financial and managerial authority and capacity can be particularly problematic when responsibility for water supply and sanitation service delivery is decentralized to local administrations. From planning and conflict resolution to revenue management and accounting, local governments often need considerable strengthening before they are able to administer services in an effective and sustainable manner. Devolution of responsibility to local levels that are not accompanied by devolution of financial authority often leads to paralysis of sector performance. Decentralization programs also inherently prejudice households living in areas of weakest administration, which are typically the rural poor. Moreover, the financial difficulties of the water and sanitation sector often make it difficult to attract and retain good engineers, managers, and social intermediation professionals—particularly in locations outside large urban areas. Lastly, when responsibility is decentralized to communities without a sound system of regulation and oversight, communities can sometimes compete among themselves for scarce water supplies in ways that can lead to economic inefficiencies; thus decentralization also needs to be accompanied by effective regulatory and oversight mechanisms, as well as be embedded in an overall system for management of water resources.

With respect to households, capacity building often requires little more than tapping into the skills and endowments that already exist among community members. In some cases, improving access to information can go a

It is also important to strengthen capacity for monitoring

long way toward making households aware of their rights and their options for obtaining improved water supply and sanitation services. Alternatively, forming or supporting civic organizations can be a way of developing community capabilities for organizing, planning, and even implementing local water and sanitation projects.[5] In other cases, partnership with local and international nongovernmental organizations (NGOs) would be the feasible option.

Capacity building is often thought to pertain only to emergent institutions, such as local governments receiving authority for water and sanitation planning in a decentralizing country. In such a situation, however, the role of central government is also changing, and national institutions often need strengthening in new and unfamiliar capacities. National and provincial agencies, for example, may need assistance in shifting from design and construction to contracting, procurement, and oversight. It is also important to strengthen capacity for monitoring of sustainable access to water supply and sanitation services at the national level.

Incentives

Capacity building can provide individuals and institutions with the tools and skills to improve water supply and sanitation services, but not necessarily with the motivation to do so. From the household to the international level, current incentive structures often work against extension of water supply and sanitation services to the poorest, as well as against the long-term sustainability of installed infrastructure.

In urban areas, for example, service providers may either be prohibited from installing trunk infrastructure, or may be reluctant to do so, in communities with insecure land tenure. Not only are households without a title denied access to network services, but they often cannot obtain titles without evidence of long-term residency—such as bill payment receipts from the water supply and sanitation agency. Families without titles are also reluctant to invest in private, individual water supply and sanitation facilities such as wells and latrines, given that they feel vulnerable to clearance actions by government.

From the perspective of service providers, assignments to projects benefiting low-income communities are viewed with disappointment by many agency staff. Not only do they place employees in less attractive work environments (urban slums or rural areas), but they also tend to emphasize simple technologies that are viewed as posing few interesting technical challenges. Even where improved services are installed, service providers often view low-income communities as having limited revenue potential, which in turn can engender inadequate maintenance and high rates of failure of systems serving poor households.

The "ribbon-cutting" culture of water and sanitation agencies the world over—in which rapid progress toward construction objectives is prioritized over virtually all other activities—has also been well documented. This attitude is the

Accountability is needed to impel individuals and institutions in the right direction

consequence of demands placed on agency staff by elected and unelected leaders, who themselves are under pressure to deliver new construction projects to constituents. As a result, human and financial resources are allocated disproportionately to construction rather than operation and maintenance, thus placing the sustainability of installed infrastructure at great risk. In addition, professional status becomes increasingly associated with large-scale design, the latest technologies, and construction activities. Promotions (and elections) may easily be decided on the basis of extending a new water or sewer line; they are rarely influenced by the fact that an existing water supply and sanitation system continues to function well, or by a reduction in unaccounted-for water. This description of professional incentives favoring new, large construction projects is also relevant to donor agencies and multilateral development banks. In most organizations, incentives are largely structured around the number and value of new projects, rather than around the performance or sustainability of existing initiatives.

Accountability

Accountability is a special form of incentive. It is needed to impel individuals and institutions in the right direction. Accountability mechanisms are essential to hold government, service providers, and international institutions responsible for their action (or inaction) in improving sustainable access to water supply and sanitation services. Accountability implies both a measurable standard of performance and a consequence for the failure to meet that standard. In a competitive market, for example, a service provider who does not meet his or her obligations to customers will suffer the consequence of losing business to a competitor.

Given the limited scope for competition in water supply and sanitation service delivery, this market approach to accountability has limited applicability for reaching target 10. One promising alternative strategy for improving accountability in water supply and sanitation service delivery is the decentralization of planning and budgeting to local institutions. Decentralization offers the potential of increasing the influence of communities and households over decision-making, through elections, social norms, and expressions of public opinion. Decentralization can also improve accountability by separating policymaking for example, for tariff setting) from service delivery activities. It is important to note, however, that decentralization will have limited (or even negative) effects if it is implemented in areas with inadequate capacity or if central government does not maintain an active role in oversight by retaining control over certain key functions, such as setting standards or redistributing resources to subsidize service for the poor. One method of capturing the gain from decentralization is through benchmarking of performance of service providers.

At the international level, the global institutional structure for supporting water and sanitation issues is still not fully aligned with the Millennium Development Goal initiative. In particular, the accountability of the international

The regulator should have a clearly defined mandate and authority, with independent funding

community could be substantially enhanced by the development of an effective system to assess and report regularly on what actions have been taken to meet the goals and on the extent to which those actions have advanced progress toward achieving the goals.

Regulatory system

Absence of a sound regulatory system and a strong regulator are generally held to be constraints to good performance by public as well as private sector operators. The overall aim of regulation is to ensure that such sector goals as target 10 are reached, confidence is established in the sector to attract private investor participation in financing and service delivery, and that the interests of both users and service providers are protected. A key complement, especially where private sector participation is involved, is establishment of instruments for arbitration. Good regulation is critical in public sector systems and particularly so in decentralized administrations.

The regulator should have a clearly defined mandate and authority, with an independent source of funding. The primary responsibility of the regulator should be to supervise operators, both public and private. Two types of regulation are necessary: quality regulation and economic regulation.

Quality regulation is used to track the quality and efficiency of service providers. It entails monitoring service operators to determine whether they are meeting their contractual obligations to provide access to service coverage and quality of service within the authorized tariffs, rather than merely providing access to dysfunctional infrastructure. To do so effectively, the regulator should define goals and performance standards so that actual service delivery can be compared with them. In addition, he or she should define the tariff policy, provide information on required investment to meet stated goals, and advise on funding sources to meet investment goals.

The minimum standards to be followed should be defined by central government, leaving regional governments to define local standards, provided that they are not lower than the national standards. Best practice suggests that both public and private service providers should operate under the specified targets, with rewards for exceeding such targets and sanctions for failure to meet them in terms of costs and timeliness. Quality regulation is also needed to monitor the implementation of reform measures and the flow of resources into the sector.

Economic regulation is required for tariff-setting on the basis of agreed upon objective criteria. It seeks to ensure that the interests of both operators and users are protected. A key principle is to ensure that consumers are not made to pay for the inefficiencies of service providers. Competition between operators and benchmarking are considered to be powerful instruments in economic regulation. Competition helps to improve performance and reduce costs, hence reducing charges and improving affordability. Benchmarking

Central government should provide incentives for good reporting

yields information that can be used for performance comparison and tariff setting. Its outputs can give signals that can help to determine whether programs are on track to achieve targets. The information it provides can give signals that can be used for making mid-course adjustments to technical strategies in order to improve sector performance. In view of the importance of such information, central government should provide incentives to local governments and operators for good reporting.

Financial constraints

Poverty is a principal impediment to increasing access to services, from the household to the national level. Within communities, some households simply cannot afford the costs of improved services without assistance from other families or from the state. Compared with the rich, many poor households pay a much higher proportion of their incomes toward their daily needs for water supply and sanitation services from informal private providers. Such households do not have access to credit markets; yet without such access, they cannot finance expansion of service to their communities or the costs of a piped connection, neither can they afford the cost of installation of private wells or latrines.

At the national level, too, it is common wisdom that wealth is positively associated with access to water supply and sanitation services at virtually every level of analysis (figure 5.1). Middle- and upper-income countries enjoy higher service coverage rates than lower-income countries, just as wealthier households within a given community are more likely to have improved services as compared with their poorer neighbors. (It is interesting to note, however, the large variation around the general trend; some low-income countries have given political priority to expanding services to their populations and thus have higher rates of coverage than income alone would predict.) Expanding access to water supply and sanitation requires money—whether from national

Figure 5.1

Access to water supply rises as national income rises

Per capita national income and access to water supply in selected countries, 2000

Note: R^2 = 0.77.

Source: WHO/UNICEF JMP 2000; World Bank 2004.

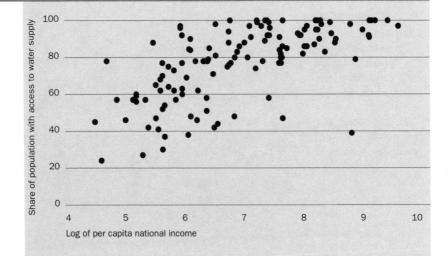

and subnational government tax revenues, user charges, cross-subsidies from users who can afford to pay, private-sector investment, or official development assistance.

In terms of water supply, about 5 of 10 people have household connections (tapped water into their house or yard); 3 of 10 used another improved water source, such as a public standpipe; and 2 of 10 used unimproved sources. As can be seen in figure 5.2, having these household connections, the highest level of service, is correlated closely with income. Similarly, as can be seen in figure 5.3, the level of sanitation service also rises in tandem with income.

Funds must be available not simply to construct new water supply and sanitation facilities, but also to support their operation and maintenance over the long term. The many defunct piped networks, handpumps, and latrines throughout the developing world are due in part to inadequate resources for

Figure 5.2

The richest are twice as likely to use drinking water from an improved source as the poorest

Average share of population using improved drinking water in 20 developing countries, by wealth quintile

Source: Data from selected surveys for 20 developing countries. Adapted from WHO/UNICEF JMP 2004.

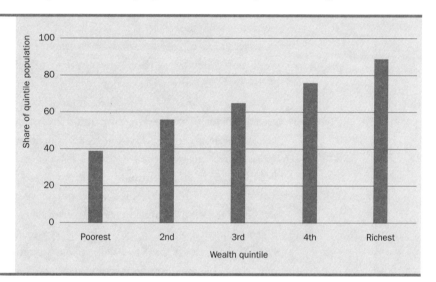

Figure 5.3

The richest are four times more likely to use improved sanitation than the poorest

Average share of population using improved sanitation in 20 developing countries, by wealth quintile

Source: Data from selected surveys for 20 developing countries. Adapted from WHO/UNICEF JMP 2004.

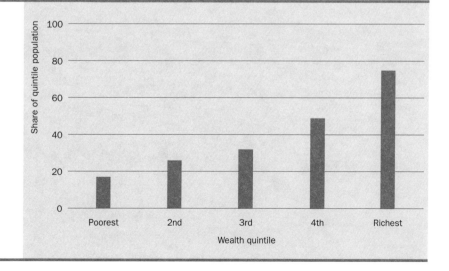

Realizing these benefits requires the willingness to plan, manage, and implement effective maintenance

proper maintenance. They are powerful reminders that, without this concern for financial sustainability, investments made in pursuit of target 10 will likely yield only temporary benefits. Indeed, experience suggests that the payoffs to effective preventive maintenance and savings in terms of lower operating costs, reduced adverse external impacts, and extended infrastructure life are very substantial, and are generally underestimated by cuts in budgets intended to meet specific fiscal targets. Realizing these benefits, however, requires the capacity and willingness to plan, manage, and implement effective maintenance. It also obliges a commitment to ensuring the reliable flow of funds for financing maintenance in a timely manner.

In discussing financial constraints, a distinction should be made between the absolute lack of resources for expanding water supply and sanitation coverage, and the need to redistribute potentially sufficient existing resources, so that target 10 can be met. In some countries, sufficient financial resources exist to provide universal coverage, but their concentration among wealthier households leaves a substantial proportion unserved.

Sizable gains in coverage can result from policy and institutional arrangements that encourage the redistribution of resources; they can also result from loan financing facilities that can also help households and communities to express latent demand for services. In other countries, however, pervasive poverty creates binding financial constraints to coverage expansion. Here the challenges are to mobilize the necessary resources from the international community, while also working to ensure that budgetary processes, policies, and institutional arrangements within countries give priority to investment in basic water supply and sanitation services for the poor. A second challenge is the recognition that the poor cannot be expected to bear the full cost of improved access to water and sanitation. Yet governments as well as donors often direct their resources not to poor communities and countries where the needs for access are the greatest, but rather to areas where there is political capture by politicians or where the criteria for donor success, such as reforms, are in place.

Many towns and municipalities in developing countries are constrained by a lack of access to loan-financing facilities. Because of their limited revenues from user fees and taxes, these communities often rely on transfers from central government to finance construction of improved water supply and sanitation networks. Transfers, however, are subject to fluctuations in the national economic and political climate, thus undermining cities' ability to undertake long-term water and sanitation planning.

Many water and sanitation utilities are characterized by weak managerial and financial capacities. In many cases, political pressures prevent them from charging service prices that would cover recurrent costs, even in communities with the collective financial capacity to cross-subsidize service for the poorest. This, together with poor demand management and high levels of unaccounted-for water, often make it impossible for utilities to generate sufficient cash flows

Overly
optimistic
expectations
from private
sector
investments
are another
constraint

for recurrent expenditures. As a result, their creditworthiness is weak, and they are unable to attract investment for expansion. Indeed, many water and sanitation agencies have difficulty funding proper operation and maintenance of the systems they currently manage, much less expanding services to keep pace with the rapid growth in their communities. Reliance on recurrent funding from state or national government for operation and maintenance is even more tenuous than that for construction. Thus, instead of moving toward financial self-sufficiency and universal coverage, agencies deliver subsidized service largely to their communities' wealthiest households that have more political or social influence. In other cases, financial regulations require that revenues from water supply are sent to national coffers and are prevented from being used for water supply operations and maintenance. Where such revenues have been ring-fenced for the exclusive use of the water supply agencies that collected them, significant improvements have resulted in performance.

Overly optimistic expectations from private sector investments are another constraint. Some developing-country governments are reducing national expenditures for water supply and sanitation with the expectation that the investment gap will be filled by the private sector. Recent evidence suggests that this attitude appears to be overly optimistic (figure 5.4). After peaking in 1997, external private financial flows have decreased steadily during the past several years.[6] The features of investment in water and sanitation facilities—including its "lumpiness," payback periods of 20 years or more, and political difficulty of charging cost-recovering tariffs—make it difficult to attract private investment. The frequency with which water and sanitation concessions in both developing and industrialized countries have been postponed or cancelled over the past several years is evidence of how difficult it is to design and implement successful private-sector involvement in water supply and sanitation services. And private sector investment does not go to the areas of greatest need (where coverage is lowest); it has been estimated that between 1990–97, less

Figure 5.4

**Private investment
in infrastructure
has fallen off in
recent years**

*Annual private investment
in infrastructure,
1990–2000*

Source: World Bank data
on private participation in
infrastructure projects.

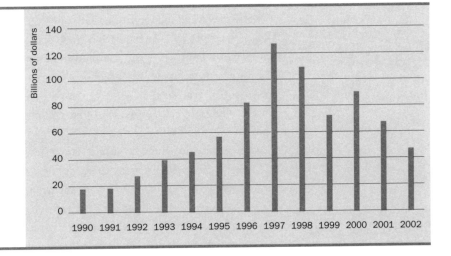

Achieving environ-mentally acceptable sanitation solutions is a major technical challenge

amounts required for agricultural uses, there are often situations in which the physical availability of water resources on a sustainable basis (and access to technologies suited to that environment) limits efforts to increase sustainable access to water and sanitation. It is important to note, however, that in other cases what is termed "water scarcity"—at least as regards water for domestic purposes—is often the result of decisions at various levels to prioritize water allocation to other uses and to expend limited budgetary resources on activities other than accessing, treating, and transporting water for household use. It is also important to recognize that, although water and sanitation are often seen principally as a challenge of capital investment, the provision of water and sanitation services is an ongoing business that has to be understood and managed as such if it is to achieve and sustain its goals. Where a water supply system is poorly planned or poorly managed, the consequences often include excessive loss of water through leakages and waste, as well as loss of the revenue needed to run it effectively through unmanaged consumer connections. Finally, achieving environmentally acceptable sanitation solutions is a major technical challenge, particularly in urban and periurban areas—indeed, some approaches may lead to a period of transitional environmental pollution, since increasing access to sanitation under conditions of water stress means that there will be more and more pollutants being disposed into less and less water.

In some instances, sustainable access to water may be limited by the physical availability of water itself—where countries or communities have an inadequate water supply at a reasonable distance either in terms of quantity or quality (whether because of low rainfall, topography, hydrology, or geography) or might face such constraints in the future, because of such factors as population increases or climate change. Sometimes, one or more particular challenges—such as arsenic contamination, salinity, guinea worm infestation, or groundwater depletion—need to be overcome to ensure a safe drinking water supply.

At a global level, the withdrawal of water supplies for domestic, industrial and livestock use is projected to increase by at least 50 percent by 2025. According to the International Food Policy Research Institute and the International Water Management Institute (Rosegrant and others 2002), "current trends show a water crisis could occur, leading to a breakdown in domestic water service for hundreds of millions of people—most significantly in the developing world—as well as devastating loss of wetlands, serious reductions in food production, and skyrocketing food prices. If current trends worsen even moderately, farmers will drive down water tables by extracting increasing amounts of water to get sufficient supply for their crops, the institutes predict. The accelerated pumping could cause key aquifers to fail after 2010 in northern China, northern and northwestern India, West Asia, and North Africa."

Although the greatest impact of such a worsening of water trends would be in the area of food production and rural livelihoods (the IWMI/IFPRI report

**Any strategy
to achieve
the water and
sanitation
Goals must
take into
account
the costs**

estimates a loss of food production equivalent to India's entire annual cereal crop or the combined annual harvest of Sub-Saharan Africa, North Africa, and West Asia), the availability of water for drinking and sanitation purposes could also be threatened in the most water-stressed areas. Such availability could also be affected by climate change and increased climate variability, especially since poor countries are the most vulnerable and have the least storage capacity to be able to overcome the effects of climate variability and change and natural disasters (UN/ISDR 2004).

Strategies to prevent this crisis scenario—principally investment in infrastructure to increase the supply of water for irrigation, domestic, and industrial purposes; conservation of water and improved efficiency of water use in existing systems through water management and policy reform; and improvement of crop productivity per unit of water and land—extend beyond the narrow water and sanitation sector and relate to the proper management of water resources as a whole, as discussed in part 2. Nevertheless, they will be a necessary component of any strategy to increase sustainable access to water supply and sanitation in areas in which the physical availability of water is a limiting factor.

The relative availability of water will of course have a strong impact on the costs of increasing sustainable access to water and sanitation. Some estimates of the costs involved in meeting the water and sanitation target appear to assume that the water resource itself is free, and need to be adjusted to include not only the costs of capture but the opportunity costs of the water itself. Many poor women and men without access to water supply and sanitation live in places where the shadow value of water is high, and the costs involved in increasing access to water supply and sanitation will be greater in water-stressed environments, reflecting water's scarcity value.

Thus, any strategy to achieve the water and sanitation Goals must take into account the costs of meeting the Goals as differentiated by ecological settings. To this end, a sound analysis of water resource availability and technological options to address the particular challenges of water-stressed environments is needed. Since conditions are enormously context specific, it would be necessary to segment the overall problem by distinguishing among different ecological conditions—for example, coastal areas, alluvial river basins, drought-prone regions, and small island states—and assessing the technological options for increasing access to drinking water supplies required in each case.

Strategies to achieve the water and sanitation Goals must also take into account that additional water supplies can be generated through demand management and reductions of water wastage, primarily in cities, through such mechanisms as tariff structures and leak detection. But the potential value of demand management approaches should take into account at least two potential caveats. First, since water wasted through leakage may be reused, in calculating the benefits of reducing wastage, the additional cost of providing access to people whose water supply currently depends on such leakages must

Many constraints lie outside the sector

be factored in. Second, higher levels of efficiency can sometimes lead to higher levels of risk. Experience in South Africa, for example, has led to some concern that very high levels of water efficiency lead to vulnerability to drought and climate variability more generally.

Two final points should be considered. The first is that poorer countries and communities, especially those located in water-stressed areas, must learn how to live with perennial water scarcity and design their development around it. Most cities in arid zones do not, for example, have limits on multistoried houses or on water-consuming flushes. The second point is that groundwater protection is a high priority in many water-stressed areas. Overexploitation of groundwater for agricultural purposes increases the cost of water supply for drinking purposes, which is further increased by the need for additional treatment.

Conclusion

One of the most striking implications of the previous sections is that many of the constraints to improved access to water supply and sanitation services lie outside the sector itself. The inadequate financial allocations to water supply and sanitation services in most developing countries are the result of budget-setting processes in which water and sanitation are pitted against any number

---

Box 5.2

Overcoming constraints and increasing access: the South African experience

Source: World Bank 2002.

Although not reflected as such in the *Human Development Report*'s figures in 1994, 15.2 million (38 percent) of South Africa's population of 40 million lacked access to basic water supply (defined in South Africa as 25 liters of water per person per day within 200 meters from home). In addition, just over 50 percent (20.5 million) lacked access to basic sanitation (defined as a ventilated improved pit latrine or its equivalent).

South Africa has used a combination of policy instruments and investments to expand coverage quickly and dramatically in just eight years. Devolution of responsibility for water supply and sanitation from the national level to the local government level using community-based approaches has been accompanied by policy reforms and an accompanying legislative framework. A capital works program was launched, which has provided infrastructure to meet the needs of nearly 10 million rural people, and municipal programs have extended services to their growing populations as well. Finally, the "free basic water supply" program has provided water to some 27 million people as of July 1, 2002. South Africa now expects that, within seven more years, all citizens will have access to basic water supply.

Clearly, the experience of South Africa is not a model that can simply be transferred to other settings, but it does provide insight into the challenges of attaining the Millennium Development Goals. At a recent international conference, Ronnie Kasrils, minister of water affairs of South Africa, identified the three key factors that led to success in South Africa as strong political leadership, a willingness to take action without having planned every last detail, and adequate financial resources. Jan Pronk emphasized the third point ("money, money, money") and added four additional "how-to" principles: setting clear goals, organizing your tax base, focusing on water and sanitation, and involving local governments. These "how-to" principles are universally applicable.

of competing claims for limited resources. Lack of responsiveness and account-ability in water and sanitation service provision often stems from broader civil-service legislation and the balance of power between central and local government, both of which are established at the national level. Governments that are committed to improving long-term access to water supply and sanita-tion services must, by extension, be prepared to make hard choices regarding budget priorities, the devolution of powers to local administrations, and the restructuring of incentives and accountability networks among the public, pri-vate, and civic sectors.

It is also important, however, to recognize that all of the constraints described here are surmountable. Consider, for example, the case of South Africa (box 5.2) where access to water supply increased from 62 percent to 86 percent in 1994–2000. A systematic assessment of the impediments to extending water supply and sanitation service coverage, however, enables the systematic develop-ment of strategies to address them—a topic to which we turn in part 3.

Chapter 6

The special challenge of meeting the sanitation target

Whereas the financial, institutional, and technical constraints discussed in chapter 5 pertain to expanding both water supply and sanitation services, in practice, sanitation and hygiene receive substantially less attention, funding, and priority than water supply in virtually every country the world over. It should thus not be surprising that the WHO/UNICEF Joint Monitoring Programme (JMP) has recently warned that, "[w]ithout a sharp acceleration in the rate of progress, the world will miss the sanitation target by half a billion people" (WHO/UNICEF JMP 2004, p. 14). The international community is dangerously off track from its goal of halving the proportion of people lacking even basic sanitation services by 2015.

Perhaps the most daunting aspect of the sanitation target is simply the scale of the problem. Today more than twice as many people lack access to basic sanitation services as lack access to improved water supply. Meeting the Millennium Development target for sanitation requires bringing improved sanitation to 1.4 billion people over the next 10 years, or more than 383,000 people every day. The cost of meeting this challenge is much higher than the cost of meeting the challenge for water supply, not only because so many more people must be served, but also because of the higher unit cost of sanitation infrastructure, especially for urban areas. Moreover, the socioeconomic and public health costs of failure to meet the target are much higher and more widespread for sanitation.

Recognizing the magnitude of the sanitation crisis in turn raises questions about how the global community allowed the problem to grow to such immense proportions. That at least 2.6 billion people around the world are forced to defecate in plastic bags, buckets, open pits, agricultural fields, and public areas in their communities should generate a collective outcry for immediate, concerted efforts to expand access to improved sanitation facilities. Yet,

**Some govern-
ments and
development
organizations
view sanita-
tion as simply
a household
amenity**

coverage rates in the developing world are barely keeping pace with population growth; indeed, in some parts of Africa the percentage of households with access to sanitation is actually declining. Why does sanitation command so little attention from local and national governments and from the international community?

A collective or an individual service?

The absence of sanitation from planning and policy dialogues can be traced in part to the lack of a national-level institution with responsibility for sanitation in the majority of countries in the developing world, as discussed more fully in chapter 7. This institutional vacuum, however, is itself symptomatic of a broader tension that exists regarding the allocation of responsibilities for improving and managing sanitation services. Many of the public health benefits stemming from improved sanitation are shared by the community at large, rather than accruing principally to individual households (which, it could be argued, is the case for improved water supply).[1] As such, some have argued that community institutions, such as local, regional, and national governments, have an interest in—and an obligation toward—allocating resources for sanitation improvements. At the same time, households do benefit from the increased convenience, safety, privacy, and dignity of improved sanitation facilities in their homes or neighborhoods. Some governments and development organizations, viewing sanitation in a restricted sense as simply a household amenity, have thus argued that it should be considered a household responsibility, thereby discounting the public components and public benefits of sanitation. These different perspectives on the nature of responsibility for sanitation have quite different implications for an "appropriate" institutional arrangement to support service improvements.

Perceptions about the locus of responsibility for sanitation services have also been shaped by the nature of the public and private components of water versus sewer networks. In the case of urban water supply, for example, service provision typically begins with installation of public infrastructure such as water intake and treatment facilities, transmission lines, and main distribution lines. Only once these assets are in place can households install connections to the distribution network and make use of private internal plumbing systems. Because all public components of the water system have been installed prior to these individual private connections, the costs of the entire system are known and can be allocated among consumers when setting service prices.

Historically, urban sewerage systems have been installed in a fashion similar to that of urban water supply. Infrastructure development starts with the trunk sewerage system and sewage treatment facilities, followed by the sewer network in each community. Once these public components have been installed, residents can connect their homes to the sewer network. In many developing countries, this approach has been markedly less successful for sanitation than

Gender inequality is one explanation for low effective demand for sanitation

for water supply. Sewer systems installed using this approach have often been highly underutilized (as in Accra, Ghana) or have not been used at all (as in Bombay, India). In other cases, plans to install citywide sewer systems are simply never implemented because of their prohibitive cost. An alternative approach for expanding sanitation services in developing countries is clearly required.

The nature of demand for improved sanitation

Underlying these very different experiences with improved water supply versus sanitation are differences in the nature of demand for the two services. Considerable research has documented, even among very poor households, higher-than-expected effective demand for improved water supply (defined as willingness and ability to pay for a service at a particular price). Effective demand for improved sanitation, by contrast, is regularly found to be less than the cost of its provision. This is so both for private demand and for public demand for the public component of sanitation.

Many observers have suggested that low demand for sanitation is simply the result of communities' poor understanding of the links between sanitation, hygiene, and health. In some cases this is true; often, however, households with limited resources have simply pursued other investments in a rational priority-setting process. In situations where both water supply and sanitation services are scarce or of poor quality, demand for improved access to water almost always outstrips demand for sanitation. The benefits of the former are immediate and perceptible, and they accrue to a household irrespective of whether other households also invest in improved services. By contrast, the benefits of sanitation are generally less immediate and obvious to the household, have significant public-goods characteristics (improved health for the community as a whole), and may not materialize unless other households also act—a factor over which a given household may have little influence.

Another explanation for the low effective demand for sanitation is gender inequality. As discussed in chapter 2, women tend to place a higher value on household toilets than do men for a number of reasons, among them privacy, cultural norms, care-giving responsibilities, and the risk of sexual harassment and assault (box 6.1). Yet the limited political and personal power of women in many developing countries means that some of sanitation's strongest advocates are virtually absent from decisionmaking and priority-setting processes. When women have little control over household expenditures, for instance, demand as gauged by willingness to pay will not capture the true extent of household or community demand for sanitation. In addition, the unique sanitation needs of women and girls (for example, during menstruation and during and after pregnancy) receive little recognition when discussions about sanitation and hygiene occur.

A mismatch between demand for improved sanitation and the type of services provided is often implicated in cases of unused or underused sanitation infrastructure, such as in Accra and Bombay. At the heart of strategies to

Box 6.1

**Unheard voices
of women**

Source: UN-HABITAT 2004.

"I gave birth to my children while I was living in the same *jhuggi* (slum). After giving birth to the child I do not eat food for two days and so there is no need to go to a latrine. But after two days I go to the same place in open to defecate. When I go out to defecate my elder children do baby sitting for the younger ones but there are times when the babies are left alone in the *jhuggi* with no one to take care of them."

—Miradevi, age 35, Sanjay Amar Colony, an urban slum in Delhi, India.

"I go out in the open to defecate. Due to the continuous stare of men, I have to get up again and again in between the process of defecation."

—Babita, age 27, Sanjay Amar Colony.

achieve the Millennium Development target for sanitation, then, is the recognition that institutional, financial, and technical supports must be focused principally on understanding and responding to the felt needs, preferences, beliefs, priorities, and constraints of households and communities regarding improved services—as well as being sensitive to the gender dimension of expressed demand. It is increasingly evident that people are willing to pay for things that matter to them, including sanitation.

Unfortunately, little is known about the best means of promoting demand for improved sanitation facilities. One important insight from research into sanitation preferences is that, among the reasons that people invest in improved services, health does not figure particularly prominently. More frequently, households cite the convenience, privacy, dignity, safety, community status, or reduction of odors and insects that improved facilities afford them. It is thus critical to understand and exploit the right "levers" to motivate individuals and communities to act. Treating access to basic sanitation as both a right and a shared responsibility of all households in a given community may have greater impact on attitudes and behaviors than traditional appeals only to individual-level concerns about health.[2]

It is also instructive to consider how industrial countries have approached this challenge of low effective demand for improved sanitation among households that they, too, once faced. In general, public infrastructure components have been highly subsidized by governments of industrialized countries, reflecting an understanding that the public health benefits of sanitation generate substantial positive externalities that merit public investment. In Britain, for example, urban authorities borrowed more than £7.7 million for sewerage works during the period 1880–91. Eventually the public provision of sanitation became an uncontroversial and indeed, expected, part of life (Chaplin 1999).

Similarly, for many municipalities in the United States, public financing of sanitation infrastructure was seen as the only option for ensuring investment adequate to protect public health. In nineteenth-century Boston, for example, lower-than-expected connection rates among households to the city's new

Progress in sanitation requires that public agencies broaden their traditional role

water and sewer network prompted the city to cover the cost of service pipes for all unconnected households. In 1850, an influential state sanitary survey concluded that government must accept responsibility for financing public sanitation infrastructure because, left to their own devices, "a large proportion" of Massachusetts residents would be "unable or unwilling to take on personal responsibility to conduct their lives in accord with recommended sanitary principles" (Rosenkrantz 1972 as quoted in Bartlett 2003). Until recently, grants of up to 70 percent or more were provided for innovative sanitation technologies in the United States.

Today, of course, scientific evidence and public awareness of the links between improved sanitation, hygiene, and health is much stronger than in nineteenth-century Britain and America. Nevertheless, households lacking access to improved services often still need support to appreciate fully the health and economic benefits of sanitation and hygiene. Governments can sponsor public education campaigns that identify the central role that sanitation and hygiene play in controlling cholera and other diarrheal diseases, thereby encouraging such safer personal habits as hand washing, and increased household investment in sanitation. At the same time, governments must accept responsibility for ensuring the provision of the public components of sanitation infrastructure and services, investments that underpin public health and environmental objectives and for which effective demand among households will invariably be low.

Reorienting public institutions for sanitation service delivery

As the emphasis on strategies to expand access to sanitation shifts toward influencing household and collective action at the neighborhood level, governments at all levels are confronted with new challenges. Progress in sanitation requires that public agencies broaden their traditional service-provision role to include encouraging and supporting desired household and community actions. Most public agencies are unfamiliar with or ill-suited for this role. Water and sanitation service agencies are typically modeled after utilities in industrial countries, and as such are organized around the goals of maximizing operational efficiency for public sanitation components (trunk sewers and treatment plants). Indeed, most water supply and sanitation agencies in industrial nations have very little direct interaction with hygienic behavior of households at all. Hygienic household behaviors are entrenched or are promoted through other channels, and the infrastructure that underpins them (reliable, abundant piped water and household toilet facilities) is universally available. In many developing countries, of course, these conditions do not apply. Institutional arrangements are thus needed, over and above those needed for normal utility functions, to target household behaviors and collective decisionmaking in communities, promoting solidarity, social capital, and the kind of hygienic culture that affords value to improved sanitation facilities.

Engaging community-level institutions should be at the center of efforts

World Development Report 2004: Making Services Work for Poor People notes that in "conventional" service delivery arrangements, the same agency is often responsible for both service delivery and oversight, while the "citizen/consumer" is a passive recipient rather than an active participant (World Bank 2003). As discussed above, *World Development Report 2004* notes that the prevailing "supply-driven" approach to sanitation has led to the installation of infrastructure that communities did not want or could not afford. Over time, households that were never reached with services or that obtained services that failed or did not meet their needs have been forced to turn to self-provision or to unregulated third-party providers. Recent research in India indicates that as many as 8 percent of rural households across the country invested their own money and used small private providers to construct latrines (Kolsky and others 2000). Self-provision accounts for about 1 million privately installed septic tanks in Manila and in Jakarta. Research in Africa confirms that the role of the small-scale private sector in sanitation provision is significant (Collignon and Vezina 2000). These findings are further supported by data from the JMP: between 1990 and 2000, the increased number of people served with sanitation reported by the JMP was much larger than the expected impacts of the public investment that occurred during this period

Reorienting public institutions to broaden their focus toward an emphasis on influencing citizen/consumer behavior, as well as toward engaging community-level institutions in planning appropriate interventions, should be at the center of efforts to expand household access to private sanitation. For many countries, such a shift in strategy has major implications for institutions both within and outside the sector. For example, the prevailing custom of linking sanitation exclusively with water supply in policy and planning should be reconsidered. Greater progress in expanding access to basic sanitation may result from also forging strong linkages with other services that engage households in a more direct and continuous manner, such as health, education, agricultural extension, and rural development. The role of local government, community organizations, and small-scale private providers should grow for household- and community-level services in parallel with the growth of centralized service delivery agencies to provide public sanitation services to complement private services.[3]

Where all three aspects of sanitation (the household level, community/neighborhood level, and the public level) remain confined within a traditional "utility" organization, partnerships with other services that engage households in a more direct and continuous manner can help infuse the agency with the new skills needed to target household and community decision-making more effectively. A study soon to be published by the Water Supply and Sanitation Coordinating Council (WSSCC and others forthcoming) notes that the needed human resources can be found in a wide variety of locations, including:

The ultimate goal should be having the right skills and mix of staff

- *Government agencies:* health, education, environmental, rural development, and urban planning departments, as well as local government.
- *Civil society:* nongovernmental organizations, community-based groups, self-help groups, microfinance organizations, households themselves.
- *Private sector:* small-scale private providers, personal hygiene product companies, building contractors, advertising agencies, and the media.

Where the number of unserved in a given area is considerable, agencies might consider employing a "franchising" approach to partnership arrangements in sanitation. In such arrangements, agencies contract with one or more large civic or private organizations that, in turn, subcontract other smaller organizations that operate at the community level. The principal organizations are responsible for training their subcontractors, as well as for ensuring that performance is uniform and of high quality. For the public agency, the need for only a small number of contracts in the franchising model reduces administration and monitoring costs. For unserved communities, this arrangement offers a dramatic increase in locally based, accountable organizations providing improved sanitation services.

Clearly the types of efforts needed to effect change in the prevailing sanitation paradigm require considerable resources and energy. Equally important is the recognition that powerful stakeholders have vested interests in seeing that the status quo for sanitation service provision is maintained. This observation is certainly not unique to developing countries. More than 140 years ago, middle-class Victorians in Britain failed to grasp the urgent need to increase access to basic sanitation for everyone; they felt that public expenditure on such services would be wasted and, worse, would divert scarce public resources from more important needs.

The same concerns exist today in countries seeking to meet the Millennium Development Goals and are compounded by the institutional barriers of dismantling organizations that are structured to deliver the wrong sorts of services. The costs of such radical institutional change may simply be too high for some politicians. As a result, some countries may prefer to take a gradual approach to changing the way services are offered, perhaps by experimenting in geographically defined pilot areas or by shifting staff on temporary reassignments. The ultimate goal should be having the right skills and mix of staff working at the right locations.

Changing roles for government

Public water supply and sanitation agencies are thus being asked to pull back from many of the service-provision activities they are comfortable with, as well as to develop new capacities or partnerships for activities that promote and respond to demand for improved sanitation at the household and community levels. For their part, national governments should assume responsibility for the broad overall strategic planning for sanitation services and must also strengthen

Shifts in the way public resources are used for sanitation are also in order

and recommit to their role as a regulator of services, promoting innovation and expansion of access while also protecting both citizens and the environment.

Shifts in the way public resources are used for sanitation are also in order. The case can clearly be made for public investment in collective assets, such as trunk sewers and wastewater treatment plants, as well as sanitary facilities in schools; as noted earlier, however, at the household and community levels, evidence suggests that the most effective use of public funds may be in powerful marketing and promotion of sanitation and hygiene. Supporting ancillary services such as microfinance may also help households and communities to express latent demand for service improvements, as well as to support an emerging market of small-scale service providers who can respond to varied and changing demand at the community and household levels.[4]

This is not to say that there is no role for targeted subsidies to increase access to sanitation by poor households. As noted previously, sanitation and hygienic behaviors have significant positive public health impacts, which justify public investment. (Not to mention the strong human rights and human values arguments described in chapter 2.) At the same time, the implementation of subsidy programs for sanitation—particularly latrine construction programs in rural areas—have focused largely on funding of hardware with little or no attention paid to the critical issues of community members' felt needs, priorities, and beliefs. As a result, many of these programs fail because they do not address a principal constraint for sanitation improvement; low expressed demand, not affordability, was at the heart of the problem. In other programs, households (particularly the poorest) are unable to make up the funding gap between the subsidy provided and the cost of the standard facility offered. In addition, problems with technology choices, including too few options, inappropriate designs, or poor construction, undermine households' confidence in the program and their willingness to risk investing scarce family resources.

It is not surprising that a discussion of government's role in improving access comes back to the same themes that underpin the discussion of traditional sanitation providers. Without an emphasis on policies and planning strategies that embrace and respond to local knowledge and priorities, progress in expanding improved sanitation services in the developing world will continue to be slow. Governments can encourage these shifts in the sanitation sector by:

- Commissioning (and funding) research into communities' priorities, needs, preferences, and practices, as well as into factors that motivate behavior change.
- Funding an effective national hygiene promotion program.
- Funding an effective national sanitation marketing program.
- Supporting policies that spur expansion of services, such as the provision of microcredit and support for small-scale, independent service providers.

A full complement of technologies is now available

- Promoting and financing innovations in low-cost sanitation technologies, especially those appropriate for congested settlements.
- Requiring and financing hygiene curricula and separate sanitary facilities for girls and boys in schools.
- Targeting public funds toward elements of sanitation systems for which public benefit is greater than the private benefit (for example, trunk infrastructure, shared facilities, environmental infrastructure, and household facilities for the small proportion of households whose effective demand is not high enough to obtain hygienic sanitary facilities).[5]
- Supporting the development of community-based "franchising" approaches that are flexible, sustainable, and replicable on a large scale.

New technologies or better use of existing technologies?

Clearly innovation is needed in the institutional, policy, and financial arenas to meet the Millennium Development Goal for sanitation. With respect to technical innovation, most experts agree that a full complement of technologies is now available for the provision of safe and reliable sanitation services in almost any setting.[6] For many countries, however, sanitation planners are unable to take advantage of many of these technical options. They are constrained by policies, planning regulations, technical norms and standards, and conventions that limit the range of sanitation options.

Technical conventions and standards are usually developed for good reasons, and often when they are promulgated, they embody the technological "state of the art." Often, however, standards constrain innovation and eventually hinder progress toward access targets. This is particularly true for sanitation norms that have been adopted from other countries or regions without sufficient adaptation for local conditions. Furthermore, written norms tend to reflect an idealized solution in which a uniformly high level of service is provided. While desirable in the longer term, such standards may be prohibitively costly for immediate use, may no longer be necessary as a result of technological advances, or may be irrelevant for local circumstances (as in the case of norms that do not apply to highly congested urban areas or dispersed rural districts).

Innovation and flexibility with technical standards will allow developing countries to expand sustainable access to sanitation more rapidly and cost effectively. Technical designs should also reflect the new emphasis on local decisionmaking that is increasingly infusing planning and policy work in the sector. For example, allowing households, neighborhoods, and communities to choose from among a range of technological options based on their preferences and willingness to pay—rather than requiring a uniform standard across an entire city or region—would result in a self-selected technological mix, accelerate progress, and bring improved services to more households in the short term. Decentralizing urban sanitation planning allows phased implementation of affordable investments within different zones of a city, thereby overcoming the constraint of the lumpiness of investments, especially in large urban areas. Connecting public sanitation infrastructure to neighborhood-level infrastructure—rather than to household-level infrastructure, as is done in the developed countries—allows for more rapid and cost-effective progress, and also helps create pressure for households to join in collective action to improve sanitation within their communities.

Changing technical norms and standards for sanitation services can, however, be very challenging. Entrenched resistance may arise from technocrats who have a stake in preserving the status quo and whose training is rooted in accepted practices. Organizations whose culture does not encourage or value innovation may also resist such changes. Elected officials may be reluctant to champion the relaxing of norms, lest they be perceived as advocating "substandard" sanitation services to the public. It is clear, however, that many governments cannot afford waterborne, sewered sanitation for all, and that "top-shelf" technologies are not a cost-effective option for many of the communities and households that currently lack access. This is an area in which the international community clearly has an important role to play. Not only can international organizations support (preferably indigenous) research, development, and piloting of appropriate sanitation technologies, they should also undertake parallel policy advice and efforts to encourage the adoption of appropriate standards in countries seeking to expand sanitation coverage to the unserved.

Alternative planning approaches for urban sanitation

Considering the difficulty that planners have had with traditional, supply-oriented approaches to the installation of sanitation infrastructure, a number of innovative alternatives have emerged that deserve attention in the Millennium Development context. As one example, experiments with reversing the service provision chain for urban sewerage have occurred in several developing countries. Instead of investing first in wastewater treatment facilities and trunk sewers, priority was given to providing an initial minimal level of sanitation services to households, as well as some mechanism for removing wastes from the community. For network systems, initial investments thus include some form of hygienic private or shared toilet facility for households, along with a feeder sewerage system that carries wastes safely away from the neighborhood. For on-site systems such as those using septic tanks, emphasis should be put on the installation of two parallel systems of soil absorption that should be used one at a time and interchanged on an annual basis. They should also be supported by a fleet of septic-tank-emptying trucks, together with public facilities for septage treatment. Similarly, facilities should be provided for pit-emptying services for on-site facilities, such as ventilated improved pit latrines and pour-flush latrines.

Because these household- and community-level sanitation services are those whose benefits are most readily perceived by households, they are also the services for which households tend to be most willing to pay. Hence, it

Experiments with reversing the service provision chain for urban sewerage have occurred in several developing countries

should be possible to treat household and neighborhood sanitation infrastructure and services as private facilities exclusive to the communities concerned. Many cities in the developing world, such as Manila and Jakarta, have achieved this minimal level of sanitation service at the household level for millions of people. In most cases, however, such investments have not been followed by the development of community- or public-level sanitation infrastructure, such as feeder and trunk sewerage systems, to convey the household-level wastes away from the community for treatment and safe disposal. As a result, septic tank and feeder network effluents regularly flow into open streams and drainage channels, creating public health risks, environmental damage, and unpleasant living conditions. Even in the many cities of Latin America where relatively complete feeder and trunk sewerage systems have been constructed, only about one third of them have sewage treatment plants. Public health concerns are thus generally addressed in the immediate neighborhoods, but environmental damage from untreated waste continues unabated, often affecting the poor who live downstream.

The term "sanitation ladder" is often used to describe these types of planning approaches that seek to make progress in a gradual way (figure 6.1). Starting with immediate, household-level access to sanitation facilities, then moving gradually toward collective infrastructure components, such as feeder sewerage at the community or neighborhood levels, and eventually to trunk sewers and treatment plants. This approach has clearly helped to make progress in cities that would otherwise have taken much longer to move toward the top of the sanitation ladder. At the same time, achieving localized sanitation improvements can actually generate environmental pollution and, at times, health risks for downstream neighboring communities. How should such

Figure 6.1

Urban water and sanitation services are much more expensive than simpler rural services

Note: Estimated costs include overhead charges of 15 percent, as well as operation and maintenance costs. Costs in dollars per person are not to scale.

Source: van de Guchte, and Vandeweerd 2004.

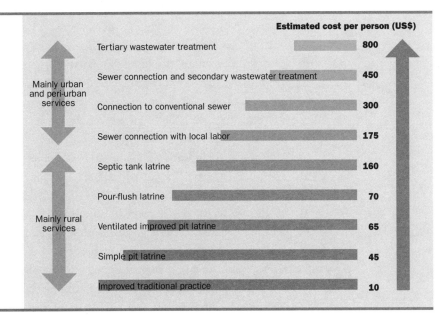

Estimated cost per person (US$)

Tertiary wastewater treatment	800
Sewer connection and secondary wastewater treatment	450
Connection to conventional sewer	300
Sewer connection with local labor	175
Septic tank latrine	160
Pour-flush latrine	70
Ventilated improved pit latrine	65
Simple pit latrine	45
Improved traditional practice	10

Mainly urban and peri-urban services

Mainly rural services

An important first step is to clearly define responsibilities for household, community, and public provision

tradeoffs—between the short and long term and between access to basic sanitation services (on one hand) and health- and environment-related benefits (on the other)—be managed? How long a transitional period should be tolerated between the attainment of basic sanitation for households and concomitant production of negative environmental externalities? These are difficult policy questions with which countries and their international development partners will continue to grapple.

Breaking the full set of sanitation objectives into manageable steps—from the safe collection, storage, and disposal or reuse of human excreta to the treatment and disposal, reuse, or recycling of sewage effluents and hazardous waste—can help create opportunities for progress where the entire challenge seems overwhelming. In many cases, more progress can be made by first focusing on a few solvable problems rather than by waiting until adequate resources and support are available for a full-scale intervention. Indeed, this phased approach was pursued in many of the countries that now enjoy universal access to sanitation services. This is not to say that the approaches of 100 years ago should be followed blindly. Much more is known today about, for example, environmental protection, which should generate more effective and sustainable solutions. Yet, while it may be desirable to develop a holistic strategic plan for improving sanitation, practicality and resources may dictate that a phased or stepped approach must be taken for implementation of such strategic plans. An important first step to addressing this problem is to clearly define responsibilities for household, community, and public level sanitation service provision.

Alternative planning approaches for rural sanitation

The scale problems in sanitation are even greater in rural areas, where the absolute poor in low-income countries most off-track in reaching the sanitation targets tend to be concentrated. The majority of the rural population lives in sometimes remote, dispersed settlements; others, in countries such as Egypt, live in very high density settlements. The number of such communities and the wide areas over which they tend to be distributed makes reaching them a formidable task. What is required is a significantly scaled-up approach that can be applied simultaneously over a wide area—an approach that centers on community mobilization and actions that support and encourage such mobilization. That kind of approach supports community members in their efforts to discuss sanitation practices with households that are within their boundaries and to devise locally appropriate and affordable strategies for improving services. Where necessary, government, civic, and external organizations may support these community-planning processes by providing information, technical support, or even financial support or loans for facility construction.

One such approach is the franchise approach described earlier. It is being tried in community-based sanitation programs in Indonesia, where parent

Required is a significantly scaled-up approach that centers on community mobilization

NGOs are establishing "daughter" NGOs at the local level to mobilize communities to plan and provide themselves with sustainable access to basic sanitation. Depending upon local circumstances and preferences, services may be provided at the household, neighborhood, and community-wide levels. Key to this approach is the principle of "rights and responsibilities," which provides that all people in a village community have both the right to a clean and healthful living environment and a shared responsibility to avoid disposing of their waste in ways that adversely affect the cleanliness and healthfulness of their living environment. This principle of rights and responsibilities is central to efforts that focus on total sanitation coverage or "no open defecation" within project communities. Examples of total sanitation coverage include the Orangi Pilot Project in Pakistan, the condominial and simplified sewerage system in Brazil, and community-led total sanitation, all of which are discussed in the case studies (appendix 1).

Community-led total sanitation has been implemented in a number of countries, such as Bangladesh, India, Cambodia, Indonesia, Mongolia, and Zambia. It has also been implemented for more than 20 years in rural sanitation programs in Tanzania (in the Wanging'ombe Rural Sanitation Project financed by UNICEF) and in Zimbabwe. As practiced in Bangladesh, it starts with strict proscriptions against capital subsidies.[7] It begins with a community-organized appraisal of current sanitation practices (typically, open defecation). Residents undertake a mapping exercise in which their households and places where defecation occurs are identified. Facilitators accompany residents on a tour of the community. The group visits defecation areas; calculates the amounts of feces produced; analyzes routes of contamination (through dirt, flies, and animals, for example); and estimates how much excreta each person in the community ingests each day. The resulting combination of disgust, shame, religious precepts for cleanliness, and self-respect typically trigger a collective decision to end open defecation in the community.

Alternatives to open defecation are pursued by households per their preferences and ability to finance the improvements; simple pits and various types of latrines are typically installed. Emphasis is placed on local designs and affordable materials. Communities that have undergone the community-led total sanitation process often erect signs at the entrances to their villages proclaiming that they are totally sanitized. The resulting social solidarity can provide a base for further collective action.

Galvanizing support for sanitation and hygiene

The absence of sanitation and hygiene from much of the discussion about water, health, and development has found various explanations over the years. What is clear is that excreta and its disposal have been, and continue to be, unpopular subjects from the local to the international levels. Without strong champions to raise public awareness and generate concern, the sanitation cri-

Simply studying what people are doing can prompt discussion and debate

sis has not been met with anything resembling the kind of response necessary to make substantial and sustainable gains. It is instructive to consider how another "difficult" topic—HIV/AIDS—was freed from its own cultural taboos and transformed into a leading global health concern.

It is true, of course, that HIV/AIDS has affected both wealthy and low-income families in both rich and poor countries around the world, providing a foundation for solidarity that is broader than that in the case of sanitation. Nonetheless, the way in which that solidarity was cultivated—through simple, consistent messages and a single, coherent call for action—has much to do with the successful marshalling of support and resources to combat HIV/AIDS. For sanitation, the impact of a similar coordinated awareness campaign has already been felt, as evidenced by the addition of the sanitation target to the original Millennium Development Goals in Johannesburg.

The Water Supply and Sanitation Collaborative Council deserves much of the credit for leading this international call to action for sanitation. The Council's advocacy campaign Water, Sanitation and Hygiene for All (WASH) has had considerable impact at the international level. The Council's effectiveness arises from its structure as a coalition of key-sector players, whose efforts and messages have been effectively coordinated to reinforce one another. The WASH campaign has also highlighted the importance of simple and accurate information for shaping opinion and raising awareness. Several key information gaps still remain which, if pursued, could help identify the most effective and appropriate ways to increase access to sanitation.

At the national level there is also a need for information and coherence of action. Focused efforts to document the ground reality of sanitation practices can help initiate dialogue among decisionmakers, professionals, communities, and households about ways to address deficits in service. Simply studying what people are doing and exploring how they have changed their hygiene habits over time can also prompt discussion and debate.[8] Eventually, however, decisions regarding public funds and institutional restructuring to advance the sanitation agenda will require the cooperation of elected officials. Again taking a lesson from global experience with HIV/AIDS, it must be recognized that politicians have a stake in significant development issues; they should be drawn into, rather than be excluded from the debate.

Finally, the strengths of the WASH campaign can and should be replicated at local level. By drawing more people into the process of promoting sanitation, both the strength and the coherence of the message will grow until it is undeniable. Developing a critical mass of concerned, vocal advocates for improved sanitation within communities is not only helpful for propelling change at all levels, it is essential for sustaining the service improvements effected far beyond the Millennium Development Goals process.

Chapter 7

Technology and infrastructure

To expand services to the millions of people who need to be reached in order to meet target 10, technology and infrastructure are indispensable. They are needed to produce savings in time, labor, and cost; they are needed to deliver convenience, efficiency, and reliability of service. Fortunately, a wide range of technological options is available for possible use in the expansion of service; however, not all of them are appropriate or available for use in every situation. Hence, there is a need for guidance on technology selection, strategies for cost reduction, and the need for innovation in technology and infrastructure. A starting point should be a quick review of available technological options.

Available technological options

Available technological options differ in many ways. They differ in scale and cost. There are options for different community sizes and densities. There are options for community types, such as rural areas, small urban towns, large towns, and megacities. For water supply, for instance, there are different types designed to match the occurrence and sources of water, treatment needs, the socioeconomic status of intended users, and the location and size of the consumption area in relation to the source (tables 7.1 and 7.2). While each of the various options has its time and place, the question that arises is how best to choose among them.

The choice among technological options should be driven in part by the approach to be followed in providing coverage and, in part, by factors specific to the technologies. In choosing technology for a particular approach, the recommended criteria are the same five that should be satisfied in a financing strategy for target 10, plus a sixth criterion. They are:

- Maximum scalability.
- Minimum transactions costs.
- Full financial accountability.

Table 7.1 Water source	Abstraction structure	Abstraction equipment	Required treatment	Applicable situations
Surface water (rivers, streams, lakes)	Dams Direct pumping (lakes, perennial rivers, ponds) for storage in adjacent surface reservoirs (Metropolitan Water Board, London)	Electric pumps	Clarification involving removal of solids and turbidity; disinfection; corrosion prevention treatment (water conditioning)	Large-scale; for large cities or a number of cities and communities
Ground water	Small-diameter wells • Boreholes • Tube wells	• Electric/hand pumps	• Mostly disinfection to combat distribution system contamination • Mostly no treatment for household use	• Large-scale systems • Institutions • Domestic and small-scale agricultural uses
Wells	Large-diameter wells • Dug wells • Mechanically dug	Hand pumps, mostly; also electric	Mostly no treatment necessary other than disinfection	• Village community use • Household uses
Ground water Spring water	Protected spring box	Springs provided with protective box with open bottom and outlet pipes overflowing continuously, leading directly to distribution or to storage tanks	No treatment normally provided because such spring water is normally potable	Rural sites
Rainwater	• Roof catchment into domestic tanks • Ground surface catchment into storage ponds (as in Bermuda)	• None • Simple mechanical pumps	None or simple disinfection	• Islands with no surface or groundwater sources • Small rural communities • Households
Saline water	Pumping from ground or surface, such as seas	Electric pumps	Desalination, including reverse osmosis	Water-scarce areas with access to sea or saline water sources

Table 7.1

Water supply technologies

- Closed revenue cycle.
- Technical feasibility.
- Operational and environmental sustainability.

These are discussed at length in chapter 9 under "financing strategy for the poorest." In addition, the choice between alternative technologies for expansion of service should also take into account a number of other factors:

- Supply and demand.
- Sustainability of service.
- Type of service provision.

Table 7.2	Type of system	Purpose	Technological options	Conditions suited for use
Selected technological options for sustainable access to sanitation	On-site sanitation	Excreta disposal	Simple, unventilated, double-pit toilet: used one pit at a time while the other rests until fully decomposed contents are safe to use on land	Low water usage; poor soil permeability; low water table; low to medium housing density
			Pour-flush toilet with twin soakaway pits, reused and rested alternately; intended for emptying	Medium water use; ablution water; good soil permeability; low water table; low to medium housing density
			Pour-flush toilet plus septic tank with twin-pit soakaway pits, reused and rested alternately	High water usage; poor soil permeability; high housing density; high water table
			Compost toilets (Ecosan toilet)	Low water usage
		Wastewater disposal	Separate twin-pit soakaway system for sullage disposal	Medium-high water usage; on-site sanitation to dispose of excreta
	Off-site sanitation	Wastewater conveyance	Low-volume flush water closets with simplified sewerage or with small diameter, shallow-depth, and flat-gradient sewers	High water usage; poor soil permeability; high housing density; high water table; on-site sanitation to dispose of excreta
		Primary treatment	Pour-flush toilets or low-volume flush water closets with Imhoff Tank and sludge-drying beds	Small communities and medium towns with high water usage
			Low-volume flush toilets with conventional primary treatment, screening, grit removal and sedimentation	For medium to large towns and megacities
		Secondary treatment	Trickling filters with sludge digesters of co-composting of sludge with garbage	Long-term solution to wastewater disposal in medium to large cities
		Alternative treatment options	Constructed wetlands	Areas where odor risk is low
			In-stream wetlands and waste-stabilization ponds	

- Type of access.
- Desired level of service.
- Community preference.
- Institutional and technical capacity considerations.

Matching supply and demand

A fundamental problem in the past has been a mismatch between supply and demand, rooted in a failure both to appreciate the importance of responding to user preferences and to understand the real ability of people to pay for services. Traditionally, sector planners have developed demand projections from population growth projections translated into hypothetical demand (such as presumed willingness to forgo something important to pay for new service). This supply-driven approach leads to a waste of scarce resources because the intended consumers often ignore the installed facilities altogether, making them very expensive in per capita beneficiary cost (Wright 1997). For example, in Accra, Ghana, after 20 years, only 130 connections had been made to a

It is imperative to respond to user demand

sewerage system intended for 2,000 connections. In Howrah, India, no one connected to a sewerage system built for workers; and in Addis Ababa, Ethiopia, after 10 years, only 10 percent of the expected connections had been made to the new sewerage system (Wright 1997). Tempting as it can be for professionals to push their favorite technologies, it is imperative to respond to user demand as expressed in their preferences and their willingness to contribute to acquisition, operation, and maintenance expenses. Even the poorest community should have to incur a cost in the form of cash (however small) or in-kind contributions toward the capital cost of the types of desired technologies.

Sustainability of service

It has been noted in chapter 3 that the concept of sustainability has an operational or service aspect and an environmental aspect. To be sustainable in operational and service terms, access should be secure, reliable, and available on demand by users on a long-term basis. For this, the following are required:

- A choice of technology that is responsive to demand.
- Proper design of the chosen technology.
- Installation of the infrastructure in accordance with the design.
- Use of the installed facility as intended in the design.
- Maintenance of the facility to ensure proper functioning.
- Availability of competent technical staff or technical support for all of these requirements.
- A reliable flow of revenue to pay for all of these requirements.

Sustainability suffers when any one of these factors is absent. Each of them involves the performance of actors, which is driven by the incentives they face. Thus, sources of perverse incentives, like free-rider problems and principal-agent difficulties, should be identified and corrected.

Types of provision, access, and service level

Expansion of service can be achieved through public or private provision, through self-provision, or by informal sector provision. Service can be delivered through private access, such as house connection to a public water-distribution system or to a public sewerage system; it can also be delivered through on-site facilities, through vendors, or through private contractors. Each of these means of service delivery has a corresponding type of technology that is appropriate (table 7.3). For example, the use of self-provision, informal provision, public provision, or private-sector provision determines, in part, the scale of service. This, in turn, determines what type of infrastructure or technological option would be appropriate. Thus, sewerage is not a technology of choice for private provision, nor is roof catchment technology appropriate for public provision. If the scale is large, economies of scale become important in technology choice. Factors of the type illustrated in table 7.2 should be taken into account in technology choice, irrespective of financing constraints.

Table 7.3

Water and sanitation service levels

Access to water supply service				Access to sanitation service			
Type of provision	Type of access	Type of service	Technology needed	Type of provision	Type of access	Type of service	Technology needed
Public or private sector provision	Private access	House connection	Public intake structures; treatment; public distribution systems	Public or private sector provision		Sewerage plus treatment plants	Low-volume flush water closets; house connections; simplified sewerage; oxidation ponds or ditches; trickling filters; Imhoff tanks
		Yard tap at household level	As for house connection, plus home storage tanks		Private access	Septic tank systems	Septic tanks; soakaway pits or absorption trenches; water closets or pour-flush toilets
	Public access	Public standpost		Self-provision		Pour-flush toilets	
Informal-sector provision		Vendor service	Water tanker trucks; home storage tanks			VIP latrines	Squat slabs over pits or connected to offset pits
Self-provision	Private access	Private wells	Hand or electric pumps; home storage tanks			Non-ventilated pit latrines	
		Roof catchment	Storage tanks with or without pumps	Provision by public, private business, or NGO	Public access	Public latrines	Public water closets; public VIP latrines; public pour-flush toilets; public non-ventilated latrines
	Informal access	Unprotected sources	Home treatment; home storage tanks				

Institutional and technical capacity

Another key factor in technology choice should be the availability of appropriate institutional and technical capacities for supervising design and construction stages of water supply and sanitation infrastructure, and for ensuring proper operation and maintenance of installed systems. In addition, there should be appropriate institutional arrangements for training and hygiene education to ensure proper use of installed facilities and to encourage behavioral changes aimed at inculcating regular hand washing and good personal hygiene. The technology should match the institutional and technical capacity that is likely to be available at every stage of installation and implementation of the water

Cost-reduction strategies help to stretch available funds and technologies

supply and sanitation infrastructure. Ideally, such capacity should be in place before technology is chosen and installed. In line with the recommendation on "learning by doing," however, it should be sufficient to determine what level of capacity needs to be developed and to take credible steps to put it in place during project implementation, rather than delay the intervention. Instruments to monitor performance and benchmark progress should also be put in place to create incentives for the necessary capacity building.

Cost-reduction strategies

Cost-reduction strategies help to stretch available funds and technologies to a much bigger population than is otherwise possible. Examples of cost-reduction strategies include:

- Widening technological options.
- Decentralization and unbundling.
- Using water-saving plumbing fixtures.
- Using appropriate design standards.
- Using multipurpose infrastructure.

Widening technological options

Through the work of a number of governments; private enterprise; and external support agencies, including the World Bank, donors, and nongovernmental organizations, a wide range of technological options are now available for water supply and sanitation. The use of a demand-driven approach requires that users, both women and men, should be provided with a range of technically feasible options, each with information on its attributes, benefits, and costs. It should be possible for consumers to use any of the choices presented to them, provided they want them and are willing to pay their portion of the cost, either in cash or in kind. At the same time, consumers should be free to use their own designs outside the choice-set presented to them, as long as the consumer choices are technically feasible and meet the test of sustainability, as already defined.

The use of a wider range of feasible technological options is important not only because it helps to satisfy the demand-orientation we are advocating, but also because it enables consumers to feel a sense of responsibility for what they perceive to be their best choice. It also forces cost comparison among options and thereby helps to reduce technology cost.

Decentralization and unbundling

The cost of sewerage is a function of the average sewer diameter, average depth, and total length. For large urban areas, unbundling a service area into parallel independent service zones, each with its own sewerage network, tends to result in a lower average diameter and average depth for the entire city. This leads to lower capital costs, thereby helping to stretch available funds to provide more coverage. The division of a large city into smaller decentralized areas

For large urban areas, unbundling a service area leads to lower capital costs

has three additional benefits. First, it allows investments to be made in phases in line with available funds. The normal alternative has been to wait until enough funds could be mobilized for the entire city. The use of this centralized approach has resulted in master plans that have not been implemented for 40 years or more in some instances. Such plans become obsolete by the time funds become available for their implementation.

The second feature of unbundling is that it is associated with management of smaller areas of service. This is much easier than management of an entire megacity. It is estimated that unbundling can reduced the cost of sewerage by as much as 30 percent (Wright 1997). Bangkok is a megacity where unbundling of sewerage is being successfully applied.

The third advantage is that it allows for market segmentation by getting away from the "one size fits all" approach and allowing differential service provision to different socioeconomic groups.

Use of water-saving plumbing fixtures
Water-saving plumbing fixtures reduce the quantity of water demanded and the quantity of wastewater produced, thus lowering the cost of water supply and sanitation infrastructure. Water-saving fixtures allow for reductions in the size and cost of water mains, water distribution network pipes, and sewers. Moreover, the use of such fixtures reduces water and sewer bills, thereby making such services more affordable to users. The pour-flush latrine and low-volume flush toilets are examples of water-saving devices in sanitation. The pour-flush toilet uses only about 2 liters of water per flush. The conventional water closet uses about 15 liters of water per flush. New low-volume flush toilets now mandated in the United States use only about 6 liters of water per flush. New standards in the United States require the use of automatic shutoff valves and other water-saving devices in a range of plumbing fixtures. The use of such devices in the pursuit of target 10 is highly recommended.

Use of appropriate design standards
One of the major problems in infrastructure design in developing countries is the adoption of technical design standards from developed countries without adaptation to local circumstances. Some of the design standards in place in developed countries, especially for sewerage, were established more than a century ago. Although sector professionals are anxious to update these standards to bring them in line with advances in theory and technology, local bylaws constrain them. For example, the maximum length of rods that are used to clean such sewers originally drove the spacing of manholes in sewerage. Today, the use of hydraulic sewer cleaning devices renders obsolete adherence to the old design standard for manhole spacing. With hydraulic cleaning devices, manholes can be spaced much farther apart, making the entire sewerage system more affordable, because manholes contribute significantly to the cost of

A welcome innovation in sanitation would be aesthetically acceptable compact sewage treatment plants

sewerage. Yet, many developing countries that do not have the constraints facing engineers in the developed countries continue to use, without modification, the design standards copied from the developed countries. Brazil and Australia have made significant advances in updating sewer design standards. "Simplified sewerage" is an example of new sewer design standards that give its users the same, if not better, standards of service at a fraction of the cost of using conventional sewerage design standards. The adoption of such progressive design standards, adapted as appropriate to meet local imperatives, is highly recommended.

Use of multipurpose infrastructure

In many rural areas, residents are more interested in access to water for agriculture than for drinking and sanitation, and typically much more water is needed for agriculture than for domestic purposes. Therefore, the marginal cost of increasing the quantity of water provided for agriculture to also meet domestic needs would be negligible in many instances. Opportunities for multiple uses of a water distribution system can thus reduce the cost of expansion of water supply and sanitation services.

The need for innovation

Some 30 years ago, it was thought that identifying a range of low-cost technological options would solve the problems in expansion of coverage of water supply and sanitation services. The World Bank undertook a worldwide two-year research project that identified such options and made information about them widely available. Nonetheless, repeated calls are made for innovation in water and sanitation technology. What is not clear are the gaps that such technological innovation should be designed to fill. While the absence of innovation in water and sanitation technology does not constitute an absolute constraint in the pursuit of target 10, innovation should be pursued in those areas that can make life-transforming changes in the expansion of access. In water supply, one example would be desalination of saline water. Several technologies are available for desalination (for example, reverse osmosis and distillation), and desalination methods are already competitive with other sources of water in some regions. The high cost of energy is the major constraint to the use of desalination as a means of bringing water to millions of people. Research is therefore needed to reduce the energy cost of desalination methods.

A welcome innovation in sanitation would be the development of aesthetically acceptable compact sewage treatment plants that could be used close to residential areas. The availability of such compact plants would facilitate the unbundling of sewerage systems. One such example has been developed for a form of sewage treatment known as the activated sludge system. Normally, such systems have a number of units arranged in a horizontal series. Consequently, they take up a lot of space, a requirement that makes them impracticable in

Innovations could speed progress toward the achievement of target 10

congested cities. Japan, Germany, the United States, and the United Kingdom are now experimenting with activated sludge treatment plants in which the units are stacked one above another, thereby saving a lot of space. Some of them have even been built under public garages. This innovative system works very well, but its cost puts it beyond the reach of many developing countries. Research is needed to make this approach affordable.

Another desirable innovation would be the introduction of incentives to stimulate the creativity of users in developing locally appropriate technologies for both water and sanitation. This is likely to happen if externally developed technologies are not imposed on developing countries or made a condition for receiving financial or technical support.

In sum, many technological options are already available to expand coverage of water supply and sanitation systems in a range of circumstances. At issue is the best way to make choices to meet specific local needs. The recommended criteria can be used to facilitate selection of appropriate technologies, and strategies are also available to reduce the cost of many technologies. Nonetheless, innovations could speed progress toward the achievement of target 10, for example, by reducing the cost of desalination or speeding the development of aesthetically acceptable compact sewage treatment plants and on-site methods, such as composting toilets that use little or no water.

Chapter 8

What would it cost?

What would it cost to meet the Millennium Development Goal for water and sanitation? Answering this question requires analysis at two levels: global and national. Global-level estimates are helpful in giving a sense of the magnitude of what is required. Global estimates are also useful for advocacy purposes, as comparisons between what would be required to meet the global water and sanitation goal and what the world as a whole is currently spending its money on can be effectively jarring.

For developing countries, however, the most useful question relates to the price tag of meeting the goal in their own countries. For this type of estimate, individual MDG-based needs assessments are required. Thus, after a brief discussion of global costs, this chapter will focus on a national needs assessment methodology developed by the UN Millennium Project.

Global estimates

Estimates at the global level vary. UNICEF has prepared preliminary estimates for meeting the water supply and sanitation target, based on the number of people to gain access and the unit cost derived from four different sources (UNICEF 2002b). The results are indicated in table 8.1; key assumptions used in arriving at these cost estimates are summarized in box 8.1.

As indicated, global financing costs range from $51 billion to $102 billion for water supply, and from $24 billion to $42 billion for sanitation for the period 2001–15. There is no "absolute" cost figure, as much will depend upon the technologies adopted and country-specific preferences and conditions. Taking an average would yield $68 billion for water and $33 billion for sanitation, for a total of $101 billion and an annual average of $6.7 billion. If this seems like a lot of money, these facts may put things in perspective: each year Europe and the United States spend $17 billion on pet food, Europe spends $11 billion

Table 8.1

Cost estimates for reaching the Millennium Development targets for water supply and sanitation, 2005–15

Billions of dollars

Source: UNICEF 2002b, based on sources cited there.

Source of estimate	Water target	Sanitation target
Vision 21	57	42
Joint Monitoring Programme	63	29
Nigam and Ghosh (1995)	51	24
Briscoe and Garn (1994)	102	37

Box 8.1

Assumptions used in arriving at the estimates in table 8.1

- Estimates are for a "minimum package" of services, in which low service levels (in terms of technologies and costs) were applied for rural populations and intermediate service levels were applied for urban populations. The vast majority of need was assumed to be in periurban areas and slums.
- To reach these low and intermediate service levels, costs of specific technologies were averaged.
- Estimated costs include only direct construction costs. Other program delivery costs necessary for ensuring sustainability (hygiene education, training, institutional development, and operation and maintenance costs) are not included. Nigam and Ghosh proposed an additional cost of 10 percent as being appropriate.
- While population growth over the 15-year period was accounted for, unit costs were assumed to be constant.
- Where sanitation costs are given on a per facility basis, each household sanitary facility is assumed to accommodate five people. Water costs are given on a per capita basis.
- The 100 million slum dwellers targeted in the Millennium Development Goal are assumed to be distributed over the regions by applying the proportion of urban populations unserved by region in 2000.

on ice cream; and the world as a whole spends $18 billion on makeup and $15 billion on perfume (Worldwatch Institute 2004).

National estimates: a method to assess needs

A needs assessment is required for countries to answer the basic question of what and how much is needed to meet the Millennium Development Goals by 2015. The UN Millennium Project has developed a comprehensive needs assessment methodology that countries can use to determine the magnitude of investments required to meet all the Goals.[1] This section explores in detail the way in which the methodology can be used to identify the specific water supply and sanitation investments needed to meet target 10. Since the importance of water for meeting the Goals extends beyond ensuring access to safe drinking water for domestic consumption, we argue for a broad-based, integrated approach to managing water resources and providing effective access to water supply and sanitation. The specific interventions for meeting target 10 fall into four broad categories:[2]

A needs assessment starts by identifying the necessary interventions

- Extension, rehabilitation, and operation of water supply and treatment infrastructure.
- Extension, rehabilitation, and operation of sanitation and wastewater treatment infrastructure.
- Promotion of hygienic behavior by households and proper use of water supply and sanitation facilities through hygiene education and behavior change programs.
- Extension of infrastructure for water storage and transport coupled with integrated water resources management (IWRM) to ensure adequate supply of water for domestic, agricultural, and industrial use, as well as ecosystem functioning.

The needs assessment for water and sanitation builds on existing work in this area, including studies carried out by the Cambridge Economic Policy Associates (Palmer and others 2003), the Global Water Partnership (GWP 2000), the Water Academy France (Smets 2003), WaterAid (Terry and Calaguas 2003), and the World Water Council (WWC 2000).

A needs assessment starts by identifying the necessary "interventions"—broadly defined as goods, services, and infrastructure. Whereas interventions, such as the provision of antiretroviral drugs to treat HIV/AIDS or the construction of new schools to achieve the primary education goal, are crucial for developing an investment plan for the Millennium Development Goals, they are quite distinct from the policies that need to underpin and deliver them, such as regulatory changes, decentralization of the health systems, or legislation to combat stigma. A simplified distinction between interventions and policies is that interventions describe *what to do* and allow us to specify *how much* of each activity is needed, while policies describe *how to do it*.

In a second step, targets for water and sanitation coverage to be achieved by 2015 are defined for each set of interventions. Using detailed investment models, countries can then project the human resource, infrastructure, and financial needs for meeting the water supply and sanitation target. These results can be refined iteratively to take account of synergies with interventions in other areas. Below we outline the specific assumptions made for the water and sanitation sector before reviewing results for a number of countries.

Our analysis differentiates between rural and urban areas, because they are so different in existing coverage, applicable technologies, and unit costs. To account for the need to gradually build up interventions and the human and organizational resources that deliver them, we tentatively project a linear scaling up of investments. The needs assessment model is flexible, so that this assumption can be easily modified. The costs for operation and maintenance are applied to the full stock of infrastructure. Finally, water supply and sanitation facilities for schools and hospitals have been included in the education and health sector analyses, respectively, with the exception of water supply for schools, which has been included in this section.

The data suggest considerable variation in coverage across countries and between urban and rural areas

Water supply and treatment infrastructure

Coverage data for access to water supply are based on the Joint Monitoring Programme estimates for 2002 (WHO/UNICEF JMP 2004). We have corroborated these revised estimates with national sources and have also included estimates of the percentage of existing infrastructure that is not functioning, assuming that these facilities will be gradually rehabilitated until 2015 at 50 percent of the replacement cost. Data from the most recent Demographic and Health Survey for each country are used to approximate the percentage of users having access to a particular technology.[3] The data suggest considerable variation in coverage across countries and between urban and rural areas. We have applied simple rules to project which technologies will be used for increasing access to water and sanitation.

For rural water supply, we estimate the relative shares of each technology according to the following principles:[4]

- Avoid an increase in the number of people depending on rainwater in those areas where rainfall is highly variable.
- Limit growth in public standposts (also known as public water taps) to the rate of population growth over the period to increase revenue collection.
- Assume that the share of household connections will reach the same proportion of the population as public standposts by 2015.
- Place the primary focus on water sources that require little or no treatment and impose minimal distribution costs, such as groundwater, spring water, upland water that reaches consumers by gravity, and rainwater.
- Increase the share of boreholes to half the share of improved dug wells, as defined by the Joint Monitoring Programme, subject to technical feasibility.

For urban water supply, we use the two basic principles:

- Improve revenues from user charges, shift from standposts to household connections.
- Limit growth in access to dug wells, boreholes, and public standposts approximately to population growth rates.

Capital costs for each type of technology vary across countries and have been collected from a number of sources, including WHO and UNICEF (WHO/UNICEF JMP 2000), national water ministries, project documentation from multilateral and bilateral organizations, and nongovernmental organizations. Unfortunately, data on capital cost tend not to be differentiated by urban and rural areas. Two opposing trends make it difficult to estimate the cost differential between urban and rural areas. On the one side, capital costs and salaries tend to be much higher in urban areas. On the other, lower population densities and longer distances can imply a higher cost of providing rural populations with access to water. On balance, we assume that rural capital costs for boreholes, rainwater collection, and dug wells are about 40 percent of the

Community mobilization and awareness raising can require substantial resources that must be included in the needs assessment

urban cost, while household connections and public standposts are assumed to be twice as expensive as in denser urban areas.

In addition to the resources required for water supply infrastructure, we include the cost of raw water provision and general operation and maintenance expenses. While some data exist on the price of water, mainly in urban areas, we have not been able to identify reliable data on the cost of providing water. The high variation in the cost of providing water locally was a complicating factor. A second problem is that many countries provide direct and indirect subsidies to the cost of drinking water, so that available cost data are insufficient for approximating the true cost of providing safe water. For these reasons, we have included the cost of treating and providing safe drinking water in overall operation and maintenance expenses.

Based on information provided by various members of the task force, the cost of maintenance and operation, including the cost of providing safe drinking water, ranges between 5 and 10 percent of the capital replacement cost.[5] Accordingly, this range has been applied to the different technologies, depending on the complexity of their maintenance.

Chapter 5 described how community mobilization and awareness raising need to accompany the provision of new water supply and sanitation infrastructure. These interventions can require substantial resources that must be included in the needs assessment. Typically, though, such programs for water supply and improved sanitation are combined into a single campaign. To avoid double counting, we have therefore estimated the resource needs of all community mobilization programs as part of the sanitation needs assessment described below.

Sanitation and wastewater treatment infrastructure

Coverage data for access to sanitation are based on the Joint Monitoring Programme's estimates for 2002 (WHO/UNICEF JMP 2004). In contrast to water supply, no reliable data were available on the extent of sanitation infrastructure that is not functioning. Based on interviews with experts, we assume conservatively that 15 percent of sanitation infrastructure is defunct. Just as for water supply infrastructure, we project that these facilities will be rehabilitated by 2015 at half the cost of construction.

In line with our analysis of water supply, the current coverage of sanitation technologies was derived from the most recent Demographic and Health Survey data.[6] The relative technology shares for rural sanitation were estimated based on the following assumptions:

- Make no additional public investment in the extension of conventional sewerage, simplified sewerage, or in septic tanks, except where such sewerage can be linked to high-density housing areas, residents from whom costs can be recovered, or effluent use for agriculture.

We assume conservatively that 15 percent of sanitation infrastructure is defunct

- Split the remaining service gap equally among pour-flush toilets, ventilated improved pit (VIP) latrines, and pit latrines.

For urban sanitation, the applied set of assumptions is:

- Limit the increase in connections to conventional sewerage to areas within the current sewerage boundaries, assuming that existing conventional sewerage has enough capacity for twice the current population coverage.
- Provide simplified sewerage for at least 50 percent of those with house connections to public water supplies.
- Discourage growth in septic tank use, and limit any such growth to no more than 10 percent of the current level;[7] all septic tanks should include two parallel sets of soakaway systems designed to be used one at a time for a year, after which the system in use would be rested while the other one is brought into service.
- Distribute the rest of the coverage gap equally among pour-flush, VIP latrine, and pit latrines.
- Provide properly attended and maintained public toilet facilities in congested public places, as done by Sulabh International in India.[8]

Capital costs have been collected from the same sources used to estimate costs for water supply. We distinguish between two sets of operating costs for sanitation systems: First, the resources required for maintaining the physical infrastructure, including local treatment of the excreta, such as emptying of pit latrines, VIP latrines, and septic tanks. Based on information provided by the task force, we estimate the total operation and maintenance costs of the first type to be between 5 percent and 10 percent of capital cost.

Second, operating costs are incurred from on-site education accompanying the rollout of infrastructure required to promote proper use, operation, and maintenance of sanitation facilities. Available estimates for these costs range from less than 10 percent of capital cost globally (Académie de l'Eau 2003) to 15 percent of capital costs in South Africa (Muller 2003) and 20 percent in India (Shekhar 2003). We have used the latter estimate for our calculations, which accounts for the full range of activities accompanying the installation of new sanitation facilities.

As described previously, some wastewater treatment may be required for sewered sanitation systems, particularly in densely populated urban and rural areas or in the vicinity of fragile freshwater ecosystems, such as shallow lakes. Our tentative target for wastewater treatment is to provide primary or secondary treatment to approximately 60 percent of all households with access to sewerage (conventional or simplified). We currently exclude tertiary and advanced industrial wastewater treatment from this analysis, assuming that these investments can and should be financed by the private sector, which generates wastewater requiring such treatment. It can, however, be argued that industrial wastewater treatment ought to be part of publicly provided infra-

We empha-size the importance of meeting needs for water storage infrastructure

structure to facilitate the creation of urban employment opportunities, while safeguarding the health of the population, as is the case in countries in Europe and North America. Evidence from India supports this argument: the Indian government is struggling to enforce its wastewater treatment program without driving small industries that cannot afford to pay the cost out of business (Cosgrove 2003).

Hygiene education and behavior-change programs

As in other areas, public education and behavior change programs can take a number of forms, including the deployment of community workers, the creation of mass media campaigns, and the formal integration of water and hygiene education into school curricula. The best approach typically comprises a mix of these interventions and will be time- and context-specific. Our needs assessment of hygiene education and behavior-change programs focuses on two core components: first, mass media campaigns to promote hygienic behavior and to discourage wasteful consumption of water and second, water and sanitation education at primary schools. These two sets of interventions complement community-based programs that precede and accompany the rollout of infrastructure.

In the absence of specific estimates for the water and sanitation sector, resource estimates for mass media campaigns and education components at primary schools are based on budgets for equivalent awareness campaigns and prevention programs against HIV/AIDS (UNAIDS 2002).[9] We assume conservatively that each country runs a mass media campaign once every two years.

Water storage, transport, and integrated management

The country needs assessments do not quantify countries' water storage needs for meeting the Millennium Development Goals. Doing so would require a more detailed country-specific analysis, taking into account appraisals of water consumption for productive and domestic use, economically viable storage potential, adverse impacts on the environment, and the need for resettlements. The World Commission on Dams highlights how difficult it is to reconcile economic, social, and environmental needs (World Commission on Dams 2000).

Nevertheless, we emphasize the importance of meeting needs for water storage infrastructure as part of a national Millennium Development Goals planning effort (as described further in part 2). Rough calculations suggest that countries in Sub-Saharan Africa might need to invest between $150 and $700 per capita to reach a level of water storage infrastructure equivalent to South Africa's (Grey and Sadoff 2002). Spread out over the 10 years between 2005 and 2015, these investments would amount to $15–$70 per capita. We do not know whether these figures represent the right order of magnitude of

The focus has been on developing a methodology for national needs assessments

investments required and what share of these investments might be amenable to private financing. Given the importance of water storage in the tropics of Africa, this area requires urgent attention and more analytical work.

Integrated water resources management (IWRM) in Ghana, Tanzania, and Uganda consists largely of improved policies and coordination mechanisms. While successful IWRM will require resources, these are difficult to quantify and have so far not been included. A draft study prepared by the Danish Ministry of Environment estimates that implementing IWRM in the Central Asian and Eastern European countries might cost between $0.03 and $0.35 per capita (Jønch-Clausen 2003). These results suggest that per capita investment needs for IWRM may be very modest.

Illustrative results

To reach the Millennium Development target for water and sanitation by 2015, planning should be carried out at the national and subnational level, with needs assessments at the national level as well. Because community preferences, applicable technologies, unit costs, technology standards, and so forth vary from country to country, the Millennium Project has not prepared a global estimate of the financing needs for water and sanitation. Instead the focus has been on developing a methodology for national needs assessments and then applying it in a number of countries. We emphasize that the results presented here are the product of an "outside-in" analysis and will need to be revised by a national-level planning process.[10] We do believe, however, that the results indicate the right order of magnitude of investments required in the sector.

A preliminary needs assessment for Ghana (using the methodology described here and in detail at the UN Millennium Project website) quotes total investment volumes for the years 2005, 2010, and 2015, underlining the gradual scaling-up of investments (table 8.2). The columns on the right provide total investment needs and averages over the period from 2005 to 2015. The lower table divides investments by the total population (not the population served) to obtain per capita estimates of the resource needs.

The analysis assumes that investments in water and sanitation are gradually scaled up over time to meet target 10 by 2015. Over time, operating costs, including maintenance, are generally higher than the initial capital costs; the magnitude of resources required for operation and maintenance are often grossly underestimated.

Results for other countries summarized in table 8.3 exhibit a substantial degree of variation, which results in differences in unit costs, service standards, and operation and maintenance expenditures (see the UN Millennium Project website for additional information on the methodology).[11]

We emphasize that these cost estimates are likely to understate the true investment needs for the water and sanitation sector that are required to meet the Millennium Development Goals. In particular, they do not yet fully

Table 8.2

Resource requirements for reaching target 10 in Ghana, 2005–15

Source: UN MIllenniium Project.

Total cost estimates in 2003 (millions of dollars)

Category	2005	2010	2015	Total 2005–15	Average 2005–15	Share of total over period (percent)
Water provision						
Rural						
Capital cost	10,026,715	6,327,163	7,639,544	74,871,750	6,806,523	3
Operating cost	15,944,164	15,012,887	14,650,132	166,297,043	15,117,913	5
Subtotal	25,970,879	21,340,050	22,289,676	241,168,793	21,924,436	8
Urban						
Capital cost	14,141,600	27,763,761	35,064,790	304,373,750	27,670,341	15
Operating cost	33,732,643	48,904,528	67,383,252	545,650,636	49,604,603	20
Subtotal	47,874,243	76,668,289	102,448,042	850,024,386	77,274,944	35
Total	73,845,121	98,008,339	124,737,719	1,091,193,179	99,199,380	43
Sanitation						
Rural						
Capital cost	3,735,093	7,970,192	24,860,156	114,308,051	10,391,641	4
Operating cost	3,083,993	5,126,261	9,535,140	61,225,914	5,565,992	3
Subtotal	6,819,086	13,096,453	34,395,296	175,533,965	15,957,633	7
Urban						
Capital cost	14,183,612	19,706,385	24,615,225	219,489,019	19,953,547	19
Operating cost	14,863,110	21,324,792	58,216,033	269,123,521	24,465,775	15
Subtotal	29,046,722	41,031,177	82,831,258	488,612,540	44,419,322	34
Total	35,865,808	54,127,630	117,226,554	664,146,505	60,376,955	41
Wastewater treatment						
Rural	10,304	3,051	1,361	35,587	3,235	—
Urban	1,883,716	6,910,847	11,063,001	76,981,097	6,998,282	4
Total	1,894,020	6,913,898	11,064,362	77,016,685	7,001,517	4
Hygiene education	5,305,757	7,285,891	9,776,081	81,199,248	7,381,750	4
Total cost	116,910,706	166,335,759	262,804,715	1,913,555,617	173,959,602	100

Per capita total cost estimates in 2003 (dollars)

Category	2005	2010	2015	Average 2005–15	Share of total over period (percent)
Water provision					
Rural					
Capital cost	0.5	0.3	0.3	0.3	4
Operating cost	0.7	0.6	0.6	0.6	9
Subtotal	1.2	0.9	0.8	0.9	13

Table 8.2

Resource requirements for reaching target 10 in Ghana, 2005–15

(continued)

Per capita total cost estimates in 2003 (dollars)

Category	2005	2010	2015	Average 2005–15	Share of total over period (percent)
Water provision (continued)					
Urban					
Capital cost	0.6	1.2	1.3	1.1	16
Operating cost	1.5	2.0	2.6	2.1	29
Subtotal	2.2	3.2	3.9	3.2	44
Total	3.4	4.1	4.7	4.1	57
Sanitation					
Rural					
Capital cost	0.2	0.3	0.9	0.4	6
Operating cost	0.1	0.2	0.4	0.2	3
Subtotal	0.3	0.5	1.3	0.7	9
Urban					
Capital cost	0.6	0.8	0.9	0.8	11
Operating cost	0.7	0.9	2.2	1.0	14
Subtotal	1.3	1.7	3.1	1.8	26
Total	1.6	2.2	4.4	2.5	35
Wastewater treatment					
Rural	0.0	0.0	0.0	0.0	0
Urban	0.1	0.3	0.4	0.3	4
Total	0.1	0.3	0.4	0.3	4
Hygiene education	0.2	0.3	0.4	0.3	4
Total cost per capita	5.4	6.9	10.0	7.2	100

Table 8.3

Resource requirements for reaching target 10 in five low-income countries, 2005–15

Source: UN Millennium Project.

Total cost estimates in 2003 (millions of dollars)

Period	Bangladesh	Cambodia	Ghana	Tanzania	Uganda
2006	689	50	133	160	63
2010	829	77	166	223	106
2015	1,178	151	263	545	336
2006–15					
Overall	8,719	882	1,797	2,764	1,467
Average per year	872	88	180	276	147
Average annual % of GDP, 2006–15	1.0	1.3	2.0	1.6	1.2
Per capita total cost estimates in 2003 (dollars)					
2006	4.4	3.3	6.0	4.1	2.2
2010	5.0	4.6	6.9	5.3	3.2
2015	6.5	8.2	10.0	11.9	8.6
2006–15 average per year	5.2	5.3	7.4	6.5	4.3

reflect all trunk infrastructure required for urban water supply and sanitation systems or required investments in water storage.

Identifying the required investments through the needs assessment methodology is a critical step toward meeting target 10. Developing a strategy for funding these investments is equally important, and to this topic we turn in the next chapter.

Chapter 9

Grappling with financing for the poorest

The previous chapter analyzed what it would cost to meet the Millennium Development Goals for water and sanitation at both global and national levels. This chapter analyzes the financial strategies that will be needed to cover these costs. Given the centrality of the financing issue—not to mention the passion that stakeholders on different sides of the debate bring to the table—this chapter tries to clarify several critical and often contentious issues related to the financing strategies needed to achieve a dramatic expansion of access to water supply and sanitation in the poorest countries of the developing world: What would it take? Who would foot the bill? And how could it be done?

This chapter focuses principally on the people living in absolute poverty in low-income countries, those most off-track in terms of reaching the goals. This focus on the poorest needs to be highlighted at the outset, because much of the debate on financing for water and sanitation revolves around a lack of clarity regarding the target group. Very little of the literature, in fact, distinguishes among the fundamentally different approaches needed to finance sustainable access to water and sanitation for different target groups. Of course, the target group on which this chapter focuses represents only a fraction of the more than 1 billion people without access to domestic water supply and the roughly 2.6 billion without access to sanitation. Those global figures include significant numbers of poor people in India, China, South Africa, Brazil, Indonesia, and other countries that have relatively sizable domestic resources for financing water and sanitation. The category of the unserved, particularly in the area of sanitation, also includes significant numbers of people who are *not* absolutely poor, both in the low-income and the middle-income countries of the developing world.

The chapter also addresses financing needs for meeting the Millennium Development Goal on water and sanitation within the context of a comprehensive financing analysis across all Goals for three reasons:

A simple typology illustrates four different target groups

- The larger goal is to meet the full set of Millennium Development Goals, rather than only the target for water and sanitation.
- Although the fact that poor people spend a lot of money on water is taken to show that the poor can afford to pay for water charges, in practice they may be compromising on essential expenditures for other basic needs, such as food, transport, energy, health, or education. Such expenditure is possible because the procurement is made a little at a time and at frequent intervals in response to unavoidable imperatives; it fails when payment should be made at longer intervals after the goods in question have already been used.
- This broader approach enables parallels to be drawn with approaches that work in other areas (especially in other service-related Goals, such as those for health and education).

Despite this cross-Goal analysis, the chapter focuses only on financing water infrastructure and services to meet the targets for domestic water supply and sanitation. It does not address financing for other kinds of water infrastructure and services—for example, financing for irrigation infrastructure projects to help address the targets on hunger. An important document that addresses this wider spectrum of water financing issues is the report of the World Panel on financing water infrastructure (World Panel on Financing Water Infrastructure 2003).

Principal target group: poor people in the poorest countries

A simple typology, represented in table 9.1, illustrates four different target groups within the overall population of people who currently do not have access to water or sanitation or both.

Two examples help to illustrate the approach:
- Indonesia, a middle-income country, has roughly 62 million people without access to sanitation, 44 million without access to water, and 14 million below the poverty line (UNDP 2003). If we assume that all people in Indonesia below the poverty line also do not have access to improved sanitation, then the figures that would go into the boxes for Quadrants 2 and 4 for sanitation would be:

  Quadrant 2: Unserved people living in absolute poverty: 14 million.

  Quadrant 4: Unserved people living above the poverty line:
      62 million – 14 million = 48 million.

Table 9.1

Unserved people: where are they?

	Low-income countries	Middle-income countries
Below poverty line	*Quadrant 1:* Unserved people living in absolute poverty in low-income countries	*Quadrant 2:* Unserved people living in absolute poverty in middle-income countries
Above poverty line	*Quadrant 3:* Unserved people living above the poverty line in low-income countries	*Quadrant 4:* Unserved people living above the poverty line in middle-income countries

Expanding water supply and sanitation coverage requires money

- Mali, a low-income country, has roughly 1 million people without access to sanitation, 4 million without access to water, and 8 million below the poverty line (UNDP 2003). If we assume that all people in Mali without access to improved water and sanitation are also below the poverty line, then the figures that would go into the boxes for quadrants 1 and 3 for sanitation would be:

  Quadrant 1: Unserved people living in absolute poverty: 1 million.

  Quadrant 3: Unserved people living above the poverty line: 0.

This chapter principally discusses strategies for countries such as Mali, where the lion's share of the unserved are living in absolute poverty.

A rough initial distribution of the global population of unserved people for which data were available across the four quadrants for both water and sanitation shows that the target group of unserved people living below the poverty line in low-income countries by no means represents the majority of the unserved, especially for sanitation (tables 9.2 and 9.3).[1] However, it is the target group most likely to be left behind if appropriate financial strategies are not urgently developed to reach them.

Financial constraints in low-income countries

Globally, expanding water supply and sanitation coverage requires many things, and one of them is money—whether from national and subnational government tax revenues, user charges, cross-subsidies from users who can afford to pay, private-sector investment, contributions from nongovernmental organizations and charity organizations, official development assistance, or a combination of some or all of these sources.

For deeply impoverished countries, none of those sources—not even all of them combined—currently provides sufficient resources to expand services as dramatically as would be required to meet target 10. Here the challenges are to mobilize the necessary resources from the international community, while

Table 9.2

Distribution of the global population without access to safe water supply

Millions

	Low-income countries	Middle-income countries	Total
Living below the poverty line	320	96	416
Living above the poverty line	30	259	289
Total	350	355	705

Table 9.3

Distribution of the global population without access to basic sanitation

Millions

	Low-income countries	Middle-income countries	Total
Living below the poverty line	540	93	633
Living above the poverty line	565	730	1,295
Total	1,105	823	1,928

The financing strategy needs to ensure that the poorest of the poor are not excluded

also working to ensure that budgetary processes, policies, and institutional arrangements within countries give priority to investment in basic water supply and sanitation services for the poor. Governments and donors alike often direct their resources not to poor communities where the needs for access are the greatest, but rather to areas where there is political capture by politicians or where the criteria for donor success, such as reforms, are in place.

Specific factors that inhibit the flow of resources required for the construction, operation, and maintenance of water supply and sanitation infrastructure and the delivery of services were discussed at length in chapter 5. Those particularly relevant to low-income countries include the following:

- Many towns and municipalities have poor access to loan financing facilities, their tax revenues are limited, transfers from central governments are unreliable, and local financial markets are weak.
- Water and sanitation utilities often have weak managerial and financial capacities and are unable, for a variety of reasons, to generate sufficient cashflow for recurrent expenditures.
- Financing water and sanitation facilities is unappealing to private investors for many reasons, including the "lumpiness" of necessary investments, payback periods of 20 years or more, and the political difficulties inherent in charging and collecting cost-recovering tariffs.
- Trends in official development assistance suggest that support for water supply and sanitation infrastructure is very modest—both in relation to support provided to other infrastructure sectors and in terms of what is necessary to meet target 10. In addition, the prerequisite condition normally prescribed for official development assistance—that certain reforms are in place to ensure effective and accountable use of funds—has been a severe constraint to the countries most in need of help to meet target 10.

Some basic principles

A sound financing strategy for meeting the water supply and sanitation Goal in the poorest countries is to compare total financing needs with the potential for domestic resource mobilization by households and governments and then, based on the gap between the two, identify external finance requirements. The financing needs for target 10 can be quantified through a needs assessment covering all capital and operating costs.

The financing strategy needs to ensure that the poorest of the poor are not excluded. Many households are too poor to afford even minimal amounts of clean water and therefore resort to consuming water from unimproved sources. The fact that many urban households spend high shares of their disposable incomes on water supply is often cited as evidence that they can "afford" high water prices. While an exclusive focus on water supply and sanitation might justify this conclusion, it becomes untenable in the context of the broader Millennium Development Goals. Since water is necessary for human survival,

Many low-income countries face large financing gaps

poor households are often forced to compromise on other essential expenditures—food, clothing, healthcare, clean sources of energy, transport—to finance their minimal consumption of water. As a result, these households may be malnourished or sick. For them water is not "affordable," even though they are currently paying more for it than the rich do. Besides, they are able to pay as much as they do in aggregate terms only because they make procurements only to meet immediate needs, and they do so at frequent intervals and in small amounts. However, they find themselves unable to make the same aggregate payments if the payment intervals are longer and the amounts they should pay at a time are significant.

Similar constraints operate at the level of national budgets, where countries may be able to finance the water and sanitation objective alone, but lack the resources required to meet the other Millennium Development Goals at the same time. This is part of the reason that water is often absent from poverty reduction strategies. Any sectoral financing strategy needs to be embedded in a financing strategy for *all* the Millennium Development Goals to ensure that sufficient resources are available to meet the full range of goals.

In addition to being affordable, a financing strategy needs to ensure that basic household needs for water are met without unduly wasting scarce water resources or depriving water utilities of revenues from households that can afford to pay. Several countries have used lifeline tariffs to reconcile affordability with the need to limit per capita water consumption and to generate water revenues. These tariffs charge no fees or minimal fees up to the minimum need of 20–50 liters per person per day and apply the full cost for any water consumption beyond this minimum need.

Where financing needs exceed the potential for domestic resource mobilization by households and governments, external financing will be required to fill the financing gap. Needs assessments for the full range of Millennium Development Goals suggest that many low-income countries, particularly in Sub-Saharan Africa, face large financing gaps on the order of 20 percent to 30 percent of their gross domestic product, or GDP (UN Millennium Project 2005). Given the magnitude of the investments required, the extreme poverty of the countries, and the fact that the investments are unlikely to yield a financial return in the near future, external finance for the poorest countries will need to be grant-based. These countries are too poor to afford loans, because they would not be able to service the repayments.

Donors often insist on "financial sustainability" for investments in infrastructure and social services, requiring that the users bear all operating costs. Ample experience across all sectors has shown that many poor countries are unable to finance operating costs on their own. For example, the 46 percent of Ethiopians living below the national poverty line[2] are unlikely to be able to finance the operation of rural water supplies or urban sanitation infrastructure. In addition, the country is too poor to either cross-subsidize nearly half its

The poorest countries need more aid if they are to meet the Goals

population or attract private investors, particularly in this sector. Clearly, if the Millennium Development Goals are to be achieved, bilateral and multilateral donors will need to fund substantial shares of operating costs.

The ability of low-income countries to finance the water and sanitation

In low-income countries, the financing for meeting the Millennium Development Goals needs to come from government revenues, household income, and external finance in the form of grants. The private sector can play an important intermediary role in financing infrastructure, but any loans need to be recouped from the users or the government. In countries that cannot service loan repayments on investments in basic infrastructure and social services, the private sector does not, therefore, provide a new source of financing. This is confirmed by recent experience in low-income countries, which suggests that the private sector can at best play a marginal role in financing the water and sanitation target in urban areas. Of course, the private sector can, and often does, assume a critical role in the provision and operation of water supply and sanitation infrastructure.

As argued above, a country's ability to finance the investments and operating costs of meeting a particular target needs to be assessed in the light of total financing needs for meeting all the Millennium Development Goals, which may amount to roughly $100 per capita per year for the poorest countries. It is impossible for low-income countries to finance investments of this order of magnitude—even if tax revenues are maximized and all opportunities for cross-subsidization within the country are exhausted. These countries need more aid if they are to meet the Goals.

As a general rule, poor countries are able to spend lower shares of their income on the Goals, compared with middle- or high-income countries, since a larger share of income must be devoted to meeting subsistence needs for food, clothing, shelter, and the like. Today, a typical very low-income country is able to devote between 5 percent and 7 percent of GDP to government expenditures on the Millennium Development Goals, in addition to perhaps 3 percent of GDP in household user fees. We project that government expenditures can be raised by four percentage points of GDP between 2005 and 2015, which represents a substantial reallocation and increase in government expenditures over a relatively short period of time. On the basis of this ambitious increase in domestic resource mobilization, the typical very low-income country may be able to afford between 12 percent and 14 percent of GDP by 2015. Averaged over this 10-year period, this corresponds to approximately $35–$50 per capita per year. This leaves an annual funding gap of approximately $50–$65, which cannot be closed using domestic resources (UN Millennium Project 2005).

In contrast, middle-income countries not only have higher per capita incomes, but are also able to devote larger shares of their GDP to meeting the Goals. As a result, their total domestic resource mobilization exceeds annual

Any financing strategy compatible with the Goals needs to ensure that the poor are not excluded based on their low incomes

financing needs for the Goals. The potential for domestic resource mobilization is significant in some representative countries (table 9.4). Some middle-income countries that right now may be able to devote as much as 15 percent of GDP to meeting the Millennium Development Goals do not require any external finance. However, even if low-income countries were to spend an unrealistically high 15 percent of their GDP on the Goals, they would still require substantial external finance to meet the roughly $100 per capita needed each year to reach the Goals. Moreover, since middle-income countries generally have better infrastructure, as well as better health and education outcomes, they are likely to require fewer public investments to meet the Goals—even after accounting for the higher salary levels relative to low-income countries.

What does this assessment of aggregate financing needs imply for poor households in each country? As discussed above, any financing strategy compatible with the Goals needs to ensure that the poor are not excluded from access to improved water supply and sanitation based on their low incomes. In practice, subsidies for capital and sometimes operating costs may therefore be required to ensure equitable access to basic infrastructure services. In particular, the capital cost for water supply schemes in rural areas, as well as infrastructure investments in urban agglomerations, may need to be partially or wholly subsidized. We tentatively assume that populations living below the national poverty line[3] are unable to contribute substantially to the capital costs of new water supply and sanitation infrastructure beyond providing labor or "sweat equity," and will require lifeline tariffs along the lines of the South African rural water-supply model. In the poorest countries, this would affect between 35 percent and 50 percent of the population who earn less than the national poverty line.

In contrast to middle-income countries, where the share of population unable to meet basic nutritional needs is of course lower, low-income countries

Table 9.4 Potential domestic resource mobilization for the Millennium Development Goals _US$ per capita_	GDP per capita, 2001	Mobilization of 12 percent of GDP per capita	Mobilization of 15 percent of GDP per capita
Group and country			
Middle-income countries			
Brazil	2,915	350	437
China	911	109	137
Indonesia	695	83	104
South Africa	2,620	314	393
Low-income countries			
Bangladesh	350	42	53
Cambodia	278	33	42
Ethiopia	95	11	14
Ghana	269	32	40
Tanzania	271	33	41
Uganda	249	30	37

A viable financing strategy requires a high degree of specificity for each country

do not have sufficient resources available to cross-subsidize capital and operating costs. While there may be potential for cross-subsidization at the margin, the balance of aggregate domestic resource mobilization and financing needs indicates clearly that countries such as Bangladesh, Ghana, and Tanzania will require substantial external financing if they are to meet the Millennium Development Goals. Improved mechanisms for domestic resource mobilization and financing, such as improved tariff schemes or public-private partnerships, are of course important, but alone they cannot solve the financing problem that these countries need to overcome to meet the Goals.

A financing strategy for low-income countries

What might a viable financing strategy for meeting target 10 in low-income countries look like? Clearly, it would need to maximize domestic resource mobilization while ensuring that capital and operating costs are adequately funded without excluding the poor.

We are fully aware that a viable financing strategy for water supply and sanitation requires a high degree of specificity for each country to ensure maximum compatibility with existing institutional arrangements, the degree of community involvement in decision-making, available economic and financial resources, prevailing social and cultural preferences, and so forth. For this reason we restrict ourselves to outlining key elements that we believe may help guide the development of financing strategies for individual countries.

In addition to the principles of affordability and incentive compatibility outlined above, a financing strategy for target 10 in low-income countries needs to satisfy the following five requirements:

- *Maximum scalability.* Meeting target 10 in the poorest countries, while still possible, requires progress at an unprecedented pace. For this reason, the financing strategy needs to be one that can be scaled up quickly and straightforwardly to allow for rapid increases in the population served.
- *Minimal transaction costs.* Low-income countries often have very limited institutional capacity and technical resources, which reduces their ability to implement complex financing schemes. For example, there will be institutional limits to countries' ability to implement cross-subsidization across households and communities, even where it may be financially feasible. Any viable financing strategy therefore needs to minimize transaction costs.
- *Full financial accountability.* Governments and local authorities need to ensure that domestic and external resources are used effectively and are not diverted away from meeting the Millennium Development Goals. Financing mechanisms for the water supply and sanitation target will therefore need to be transparent, which reinforces once more the importance of simple financing arrangements.

**The greatest
need for
subsidies
may be to
cover capital
costs of new
infrastructure**

- *Closed revenue cycle.* Financing mechanisms need to be financially viable in the sense that all capital and operating costs are fully covered—either through user fees, government subsidies, or external finance.
- *Technical feasibility.* Finally, available technologies for water supply and sanitation may impose technical constraints on the range of feasible financing mechanisms. For example, public standposts can make it difficult to levy user fees or to ensure that richer households contribute more to the operating costs.

The greatest need for subsidies may be to cover capital costs of new infrastructure. While some rural sanitation technologies, such as improved pit latrines, may not require any significant financial resources except for technological components that are unavailable at the local level and labor and locally available materials provided by the communities themselves, capital costs for most water supply and sanitation infrastructure typically need to be subsidized for the poorer segments of the population. A common approach is to invite communities to choose among a range of different technology options to identify the solution that is best adapted to local needs and means, financial or otherwise. To ensure that subsidies are targeted to the population most in need, the level of subsidies should decrease as levels of service increase (for instance, standpipes providing water supply to several previously unserved households might be subsidized, whereas individual household connections, the highest and most expensive level of service, would not be). In this way, wealthier households with a preference for higher levels of service will pay a higher share of the total cost.

It has often been found that trunk infrastructure is too expensive to be financed by communities in poor countries. The high cost, combined with the "public goods" nature of trunk infrastructure, its positive externalities, and the difficulty in aggregating financing from a large number of households lead us to conclude that basic trunk infrastructure should be publicly financed. This applies in particular to networked sanitation systems in urban areas, as well as wastewater drainage and treatment of both sewage and septage.

Lifeline tariffs have been used successfully to cofinance the operating costs of water supply. The experience in South Africa and other countries demonstrates that lifeline tariffs help ensure that even the poorest households enjoy effective access to sufficient amounts of clean water. Hence, we recommend that lifeline tariffs be applied wherever technically feasible and that new water supply systems be designed to facilitate the application of lifeline tariffs. This notwithstanding, technical and institutional constraints will likely make it difficult to introduce lifeline tariffs in many rural areas of low-income countries. In cases where the rural poor are unable to meet the full operating costs of water supply, flat subsidies may therefore be a viable option. Since their domestic consumption of water will remain low, environmental constraints on overall water availability should not be of major concern for the design of tariff schemes—except, of course, in arid regions.

Deep-rooted community ownership should attract favorable financing mechanisms and terms

As demonstrated above, many low-income countries will require substantial external finance to meet the Millennium Development Goals. While the modalities under which such aid should be provided go beyond the scope of this paper and have been discussed elsewhere by the Millennium Project,[4] three key principles can be summarized here:

- All official development assistance to the poorest countries that are significantly behind schedule for meeting the Millennium Development Goals should be provided in the form of grant or grant-like support.

- Low-income countries should develop Goals-based poverty reduction strategies, together with medium-term expenditure frameworks, that include explicit provisions for meeting the water and sanitation targets. Donor methodologies must be changed to allow countries to develop poverty reduction strategies that realistically address the challenges posed by the Millennium Development Goals; those countries whose poverty reduction strategies are technically, socially, and environmentally sound and focused on attaining target 10 should be afforded grant or grant-like financing to support their efforts in expanding access to services.

- Subsidies for capital (and, where necessary, for operating costs) should be established to ensure equitable access to basic infrastructure services. Capital costs for water supply and sanitation programs in rural areas, some small towns, and urban slums may need to be partially or wholly subsidized. Care must be taken to ensure that the particular strategies adopted (such as capital grants, lifeline tariffs) are targeted to poor households and are not merely benefiting wealthier consumers with network connections. Subsidies should focus on expanding access rather than consumption.

Critically, poverty reduction strategies need to incorporate mechanisms to ensure that funding for water and sanitation reaches the implementing authorities. In many instances this will require transfer mechanisms to make available funds from the national level to lower levels of government, such as local authorities. Setting up effective transfer mechanisms that ensure full transparency and financial accountability is extremely complex and may need to be carried out gradually.

Affordability, sustainability, and water conservation

As stated above, a viable financing strategy needs to be compatible not only with existing institutional arrangements and available economic and financial resources, but also with the degree of community involvement and ownership in the projects being financed. Thus deep-rooted community ownership and involvement should attract comparably strong and favorable financing mechanisms and terms. Lessons from experience suggest that such deep-rooted ownership and involvement is realized when communities recognize their own contribution to the situation in which they find themselves and resolve to assume

Water charges are powerful instruments for water conservation and demand management

the responsibility and a leading role in addressing the problem. It is this awakening that sparks corrective community-led actions and provides a foundation for strong community ownership and involvement.

The preceding discussion envisages that external financing becomes necessary when financial needs exceed the potential for domestic resource mobilization. Such financing is not inconsistent with local ownership and community involvement in water supply and sanitation projects. The use of grant-based budget support for both capital and operation and maintenance for communities that are most off track in meeting the Millennium Development Goals is the most robust way of making up the financing gap. In the United States, for instance, there was initially a 75 percent capital subsidy for sewage treatment plant construction.

The main domestic sources of financing are from households (in the form of tariffs) and government (which comes from general and selective taxes). Tariff levels have an impact on affordability, and therefore we strongly recommend lifeline tariffs, which help not only with affordability by the poor, but also in reconciling affordability with the need to limit per capita water consumption and generate adequate water revenues. Thus, water charges are powerful instruments for water conservation and demand management. They are also powerful instruments for making service providers responsive to user preferences and needs.

What about middle-income countries?

So far, this chapter has focused on outlining a financing strategy for low-income countries that require external finance to be able to meet the Millennium Development Goals. Financing strategies for water and sanitation objectives in middle-income countries will differ substantially from the strategy outlined above.

As noted earlier, since middle-income countries have higher per capita incomes and are able to devote larger shares of their GDP to meeting the Goals, their total domestic resource mobilization generally exceeds annual financing needs for the Goals—in fact, middle-income countries that are able to devote as much as 15 percent of GDP to meeting the Goals do not require any external financing. Moreover, middle-income countries are likely to require fewer public investments to meet the Goals. As the example from Indonesia illustrated, the number of unserved people in middle-income countries who are above the poverty line is often relatively significant, facilitating cost recovery from users.

Financing strategies and modalities for middle-income countries will therefore differ from those for low-income countries in at least two ways. First, middle-income countries do not require external financing to meet the Millennium Development Goals and can typically access private capital markets for incremental resources. Second, middle-income countries have greater opportunities to involve the private sector in financing the water supply and sanitation goals. Factors that facilitate the direct involvement of the private sector in financing water supply and sanitation include the higher per capita income of households, the higher rates of urbanization, the better trunk infrastructure, and of course the stronger capital markets. (In the absence of these conditions, the private sector is unlikely to play a significant role in financing the water supply and sanitation target.) Of course, even in middle-income countries, significant regional and community disparities exist, and the government has a critical role to play in facilitating national financial policies that ensure equal access to services even in traditionally neglected and economically depressed areas.

2

Water resources for all the Millennium Development Goals

Chapter 10

Why does water resources development and management matter?

Sound water resources development and management underpins attainment of *all* the Millennium Development Goals, not only the one dealing specifically with water supply and sanitation. Moreover, it can avert tremendous human suffering (box 10.1). In this chapter and the two that follow it, we discuss the links between water resources and the Goals (especially those on poverty, hunger, health, gender, and environmental sustainability) and the actions that countries will need to take to optimize the contribution of water resources to the achievement of the Goals.

We use the term "water resources development and management" to mean the actions required to manage and control freshwater to meet human and environmental needs. Such actions include investments in infrastructure for storage, abstraction, conveyance, and control, as well as for hydropower, flood control, irrigation and drainage, water harvesting, and so on; investments and actions undertaken to protect groundwater resources, control salinity, and promote water conservation; and an array of governance and management measures, including the development and strengthening of institutional and regu-

Box 10.1

Water-related disasters: facts from the World Health Organization

Source: WHO 2004a.

- Almost 2 billion people were affected by natural disasters in the last decade of the twentieth century, 86 percent of them by floods and droughts.
- Flooding frequently leads to contamination of drinking-water systems with human excreta from inadequate sanitation and with refuse and industrial waste from dumps.
- Droughts cause the most illness and death, not only by limiting adequate water supply but also by triggering and exacerbating malnutrition and famine.
- Droughts and floods have broad economic impact: the Zimbabwe drought of the early 1990s was associated with an 11 percent decline in GDP; the recent floods in Mozambique led to a 23 percent reduction in GDP; and the drought of 2000 in Brazil cut projected economic growth in half.

Water can act as a spur to economic development

latory systems and policy reforms to promote wise stewardship of freshwater resources.

Investments in water resources development and management can contribute to meeting the Millennium Development Goals as a whole both through broad interventions designed to promote sustainable development in an area—such as multipurpose river basin development and aquifer management—and through targeted actions addressing one or more particular goals in a specific location, such as watershed management within degraded areas farmed by poor families. Both types of interventions are important for making many of the Millennium Development Goals a reality; indeed, holistic approaches to water resources development and management can help to deliver the Goals more cheaply and sustainably.

Table 10.1 illustrates some of the many ways in which the development, management, and use of water affects the targets embodied in the Goals (see Goals on p. xvi). The role of water resources development and management in combating poverty and hunger, ensuring environmental sustainability, improving health, and reducing gender inequalities is analyzed in more detail below.[1]

Poverty and hunger

One in five people on the planet, two-thirds of them women, live in extreme poverty. Of the world's 6 billion people, 2.8 billion live on less than $2 a day, and 1.2 billion on less than $1 a day (DFID and others 2002). Chronic hunger, among the starkest and most absolute manifestations of poverty, affects 800 million people. In this era of progress and plenty, 17 percent of the world's people are on the brink of starvation, and 11 children under the age of five die from malnutrition every minute.

In addition to the role that improving access to domestic water supply and sanitation plays in reducing poverty, water can act as a spur to economic

Box 10.2
Improving water management to spur economic development

Source: World Bank 2003.

- Water infrastructure and sound water resources management can spur rural development. In Petrolina, in Northeast Brazil, water resources management and development has created a large number of high-quality, permanent agricultural jobs (40 percent of which are held by women). For every job in agriculture, two jobs have been created in the supporting commercial and industrial sectors. These opportunities have reversed the historic pattern of outmigration.
- Experience has shown that cooperative programs for water resources management have played an important role in regional integration and stability in Eastern Europe (the Baltic Sea), Southeast Asia (Thailand and Laos), and South Asia (the Indus Basin).
- Irrigation and drainage have contributed to past success in doubling food production, forestalling famine, and reducing global food prices. Globally, irrigated areas represent 17 percent of the cultivated area, but account for 40 percent of food production. In India, districts with little irrigation have a poverty incidence 2.5 higher than those with substantial irrigation.

Table 10.1	**Millennium Development Goal**	**Contribution of improved water resources management**
Contribution of improved water resources management to the Millennium Development Goals	**Poverty** To halve the proportion of the world's people whose income is less than $1/day	• Water is a factor of production in agriculture, industry, and other economic activities. • Investments in water infrastructure and services are a catalyst for local and regional development. • Reduced vulnerability to water-related hazards reduces risks in investments and production. • Reduced ecosystem degradation makes livelihood systems of the poor more secure.
	Hunger To halve the proportion of the world's people who suffer from hunger	• Water is a direct input to irrigation for expanded grain production. • Reliable water sources support subsistence agriculture, home gardens, livestock, and tree crops. • Reliable water sources support sustainable production of fish, tree crops, and other foods gathered on common property resources (also affects poverty when such goods are sold for income). • By helping to lower food prices, water management can reduce urban hunger.
	Primary education To ensure that children everywhere complete a full course of primary schooling	• Improved water management reduces the incidence of such catastrophic events as floods that interrupt educational attainment.
	Gender equality To ensure that girls and boys have equal access to primary and secondary education	• Community-based organizations for water management can improve social capital of women by giving them leadership and networking opportunities and building solidarity among them.
	Child mortality To reduce by two-thirds the death rate for children under five	• Improved nutrition and food security reduces susceptibility to diseases. • Well-managed water resources help poor people make a decent living and reduce their vulnerability to shocks, which in turn gives them more secure and fruitful livelihoods to draw upon in caring for their children. • Malaria is a leading cause of death among children, and better water management reduces mosquito habitats.
	Major disease To have halted and begun to reverse the spread of HIV, malaria, other major diseases	• Improved water management in human settlements reduces transmission risks of such mosquito-borne illness as malaria and dengue fever. 1.2 million people die of malaria each year, 90 percent of whom are children under 5. • Improved health and nutrition reduce susceptibility to and severity of HIV/AIDS and other major diseases.
	Environmental sustainability To stop the unsustainable exploitation of natural resources	• Improved water management, including pollution control and water conservation, is a key factor in maintaining ecosystems integrity. • Development of integrated management within river basis facilitates sustainable management of ecosystems and mitigates upstream-downstream effects. • Biodiversity conservation and combating desertification are furthered by sound water management.
	Slum dwellers To improve the lives of 100 million slum dwellers	• Improved flood control and drainage in urban areas can improve conditions in slum settlements, which are often built on sites particularly vulnerable to water-related disasters.

development (box 10.2), and its role as a resource for agriculture, energy, and industry is essential to fighting poverty and hunger. Water is an important factor of production in a variety of industries crucial to economic development and poverty reduction; it is also central to the livelihood systems of the rural poor. Meeting the Millennium Development Goal in this area will be

Three points of connection stand out: health, livelihoods, and vulnerability

impossible without better water management and a dramatic expansion of access to water for the world's poorest (box 10.3). Ensuring an adequate food supply, achieving aggregate progress against poverty at the national level, and relieving poverty at the community and household levels simply cannot occur in many parts of the world, given current water shortages. Clearly, therefore, insufficient water blocks overall economic growth.

For the poor much more than for the nonpoor, the fulfillment of humankind's most basic aspirations, such as living a long and healthy life, having sufficient resources to earn a living, and seeing one's children reach adulthood, is predicated on the state of the environment, including water resources. Environment is central to poor people's sense of well-being, empowerment, and control over their own lives. Three points of connection between poor people and their water environment stand out: health, livelihoods, and vulnerability.

- *Health.* The health of poor women and men is disproportionately affected by contaminated water and poor sanitation services, setting up a cycle of ill-health and further impoverishment that has severe financial and personal costs.

- *Livelihoods.* In rural areas, poor people's livelihood systems are rooted in the natural world and depend upon ecosystem health. Contamination of common property resources, such as lakes, rivers, and coastal areas, directly translates into less food, income, and time for the poor. Common property resources provide a significant share of food and household income for the poorest families.

- *Vulnerability.* Vulnerability is a critical dimension of poverty. Poor women and men are particularly at risk from environmental shocks and crises. Increasingly frequent and severe natural disasters (cyclones, hurricanes, floods, landslides, and droughts), as well as changes in rainfall patterns, shifting agricultural zones, and rising sea levels impact developing countries and the poor who live there disproportionately. The poor are the most affected by environment-based conflicts, which are

---

Box 10.3

Main water-related recommendations of the Millennium Project for meeting the poverty and hunger Goals

Target 1 on poverty
- Increase public investment in basic human needs, including water and sanitation, to foster a productive labor force that can participate effectively in a global economy.

Task Force on Hunger
- Increase agricultural productivity of food-insecure farmers, with a special focus on small-scale water management.
- Improve nutrition of the vulnerable (water-related diseases are a leading cause of diarrhea, which hinders the body's ability to absorb nutrients).
- Restore natural assets of food-insecure people, including water resources (lakes with fish, for instance).

Poor water management practices worsen the water shortages in many countries

also becoming more frequent. Extreme events can have a strong impact on the ability of many developing countries, especially in the tropics, to achieve the Millennium Development Goals. Damage caused by floods and droughts and other extreme climate events can undo, in a short period, many years of steady development and growth. Although such extreme events start with direct damage to infrastructure and crops, they often ripple through many areas of economic activity, leading to widespread macroeconomic, financial, and political consequences. In Kenya, for example, flooding during the El Niño event of 1997–98 is estimated to have cost some $880 million (10 percent of GDP) through the loss of roads, pipelines, and water treatment plants (Mogaka and others 2002).

The bulk of the world's poorest people, 800 million to 1 billion rural people, live in arid areas and depend directly on natural resources, including water, for their livelihoods (Dobie 2001). Many drylands people are subsistence farmers who also keep some livestock, while others are pastoralists, a nomadic way of life that is increasingly under threat. In dry, rural countries, such as Mali and Eritrea, most of the population lives this way, whereas in countries with both humid and dry regions, the dry areas are home to the poorest of the poor (Dobie 2001).

Retaining as much water as possible is a question of survival, but in arid areas a substantial amount of rainwater is lost through surface runoff, evaporation, and percolation. When the rains come and the water runs off, topsoil is carried away, gullies are formed, and the water is lost. People in drylands are uniquely vulnerable not only to drought and other natural disasters, but also to economic and social changes. Achieving sustainable development in the drylands has significant implications for reducing poverty and hunger globally.

Agriculture is now and will continue to be a key sector for low-income countries and the poor who live there. In developing countries, 80 percent of export earnings come from the agriculture sector. It is also the thirstiest sector: irrigated agriculture accounts for almost 70 percent of the global freshwater use. Limited and unreliable access to water is a determining factor in agricultural productivity in many regions, a problem rooted in rainfall variability that is likely to increase with climate change.

Today, underperforming irrigation systems and poor water management practices worsen the water shortages that already exist in many countries. Irrigation and poor drainage lead to salinization and waterlogging. Excessive extraction for irrigation has lowered water tables to critical levels in many places. The use of pesticides and fertilizers in agriculture pollutes groundwater. Invasive species have covered huge water areas throughout the world, clogging irrigation channels, threatening infrastructure, and leading to the collapse of fisheries.

Most irrigation systems are financially out of reach for poor smallholders

The return to water in food production, including the efficiency of agricultural water use, can be improved substantially through better water resources management—and provide "more crop per drop." Clearly this is necessary to meet the hunger target; it is also critical in terms of the contribution increased grain production can make to the economy as a whole, and thus to meeting the poverty eradication Goal.

Projected increases in the world's population will lead to greatly increased demands for food, primarily from developing countries. Currently, the 17 percent of the world's cultivated land that is under irrigation produces 40 percent of the world's food (FAO 2003). Much of the projected increased demand for food will have to come from improved and expanded irrigation, but this will be only a partial solution. Most irrigation systems are financially out of reach for poor smallholders. Most food demand for poor people will come from areas where investment in irrigation makes no sense, with too little return from the significant capital needed. The major part of the crops produced worldwide is still grown in rain-fed agriculture, and to improve the livelihoods of the farmers in the developing world more emphasis must be put on employing practices that ensure higher yields per water input.

Water is also a factor of production in industry and many other types of economic activity, including both large-scale activities and small, often home-based activities where the poor are entrepreneurs, such as food processing for vending in markets. Access to key factors of production, including water, is critical to the viability of activities that can serve as a ladder out of poverty. In some cases, investments in water infrastructure, such as dams and irrigation schemes, can act as a catalyst for local and regional development.

Water can be critical in supplying energy services to unserved poor women and men in rural areas, and safe, environmentally friendly, and affordable energy services are critical to poverty reduction. Energy services that allow for heating, cooking, and illumination are not only a boon to the activities of daily life; they are also critical inputs to agriculture and the types of small-scale productive activities that are a significant component of the rural economy in poor areas.

In sum, water is critical in achieving the Goals on poverty and hunger because:

- Agriculture is and will continue to be a key sector for low-income countries and the poor who live there.
- Water is a factor of production in industry and many other types of economic activity.
- Common environmental resources provide a significant share of food and household income for the poorest families, and the livelihood systems of poor women and men depend upon a healthy environment.
- Pollution of common resources, such as lakes, rivers, and coastal areas, directly translate into less food, income, and time for the poor.

**Water is
perhaps
the most
fundamental
of all
environmental
resources**

- Sound water management may reduce the incidence of a range of other diseases for which water is a vector.

Environmental sustainability

The overall Millennium Development Goal of ensuring environmental sustainability (Goal 7) has three specific targets:

- *Target 9:* Integrate the principles of sustainable development into country policies and programs; reverse loss of environmental resources.
- *Target 10:* Reduce by half the proportion of people without sustainable access to safe drinking water and basic sanitation.
- *Target 11:* Achieve significant improvement in the lives of at least 100 million slum dwellers by 2020.

Clearly, water is a key dimension in achieving each of these three targets.

Target 9 on sustainable development

Water is perhaps the most fundamental of all environmental resources and the most critical for the viability and long-term sustainability of the world's ecosystems (box 10.4). Ecosystem health, in turn, is critical for the quantity and quality of water supply. Human activities, such as infrastructure development, modification of river flows, land conversion (for example, deforestation), increased agricultural production, overfishing, introduction of exotic species, and release of pollutants, upset the delicate balance between water resources and environmental sustainability.

Several threats to overall ecosystem health, and consequently to the ability of ecosystems to provide the services upon which human life depends, are particularly relevant to water resources.

- Climate change and resulting alterations in weather patterns, water distribution, and fisheries will seriously affect marine ecosystems and small island developing states, and will also threaten poor populations unable to protect themselves from flooding, erosion, water shortages, and coral bleaching.

Box 10.4

**Main water-related
recommendations
of the Millennium
Project Task Force
on Environmental
Sustainability**

- Institute integrated water resources management using an ecosystem-based approach.
- Invest in improving the water efficiency of cropping systems.
- Invest in wastewater treatment—particularly in urban areas.
- Improve environmental monitoring, indicators, assessment, and use of information in decisionmaking.
- Remove environmentally damaging subsidies in water use and fisheries.
- Protect critical land and marine ecosystems.
- Strengthen institutional capacity for integrated ecosystem management.

Poor slum dwellers have little way to insulate themselves from threats

- Loss of species diversity and genetic diversity within species impacts the health of marine and coastal environments, as well as that of wetlands.
- Global fisheries, marine ecosystems, and coastal habitats are quickly degrading because of overfishing and contamination from land-based activities.
- Freshwater ecosystems are being damaged by runoff, silting, fertilizers, pollution, and invasive species.
- Drylands are further degrading as a result of desertification, dropping water tables, and overirrigation.

It is important to note that target 9 is intended to address the goal of "stopping the unsustainable exploitation of water resources by developing water management strategies at the regional, national, and local levels, which promote both equitable access and adequate supplies," which was clearly enunciated in the Millennium Declaration, but is not referred to explicitly or implicitly in any other of the eighteen Millennium Development targets.

Target 10 on water and sanitation

This is, of course, the Millennium Development target on water and sanitation that was discussed at length in previous chapters. Although clearly this target is much more than an "environment" target, given its implications for human health and poverty reduction, officially it resides with the overall Goal of ensuring environmental sustainability.

Target 11 on improvements for slum dwellers

For poor people living in slums, the water-related problems already discussed in relation to the other Millennium Development Goals—inadequate access to clean water and sanitation services; poorly managed water resources; and the resulting drain on human health, education, women's empowerment, and environmental sustainability—are magnified (box 10.5). The geographical concen-

---

Box 10.5

Living with urban environmental problems

Source: UN-HABITAT 2004.

"We are eight people living in a small one-room shack where we have to sleep in shifts. There is a public toilet down the lane, but we have to queue for two hours. The toilet is broken, sewage flowing everywhere. Several girls have been molested there, and some even raped, in broad daylight. My sisters and mum don't go there. We keep our "business" for the evenings. In the dark we wrap it into plastic bags and throw it as far away as possible. These are our flying toilets, and our neighbors do the same. We know it's not right, so we do this only at night. Our tummies sometimes hurt the whole day, since we just have to hold. When it rains, the flying toilets [together with the contents] get washed with the rainwater and accumulate on the door. The feces stay there for days. When the rains are heavy, it gets washed right into the house. We have no hope of leaving here. We don't have anywhere else to go."

—Halima, a Nubian girl from Kibera, Nairobi's largest slum, home to 700,000 people

Management of water resources more generally has significant health impacts

tration of people, production, and pollution in slums amplifies the biological pathogens and chemical hazards to which urban people are exposed. Poor slum dwellers, unlike their wealthier urban counterparts, have little way to insulate themselves from these threats. They are exposed to a host of environmental risks because they live in poor housing, often built in hazardous locations (such as industrial sites or flood-prone areas). Poor urban dwellers are also frequently outdoors, because they generally face long commutes, often work as laborers or street vendors, and frequently flee their overcrowded houses. As a result, morbidity and infant mortality rates are higher among slum dwellers than among urban people who do not live in slums, or among the rural population (UN-HABITAT 2003).

As the Bruntland Commission noted more than 15 years ago, "the future will be predominantly urban, and the most important environmental concerns of most people will be urban ones" (World Commission on Environment and Development 1987). Two-fifths of people in Africa, Asia, the Pacific, Latin America, and the Caribbean now live in urban areas, and every passing day further swells the ranks of city and town dwellers. UN-HABITAT estimates that more than 900 million people in the developing world live in slums. In least developed countries and Sub-Saharan Africa, more than 70 percent of the urban population lives in slums, a figure expected to increase (UN-HABITAT 2003).

Tackling urban environmental problems is critical to meeting the Millennium Development target of improving the lives of 100 million slum dwellers (box 10.6). The main challenge is addressing threats to health, livelihoods, and security stemming from hazardous living conditions and poor services; these threats include substandard housing, polluted water, lack of sanitation and solid waste systems, outdoor air pollution from industry and traffic, indoor air pollution from low-quality cooking fuels, and extreme vulnerability to environmental disasters (which are likely to increase with climate change). Many steps taken to reduce environmental hazards, such as building with better materials and ensuring adequate drainage systems, also contribute to disaster preparedness, as does improving urban planning and zoning so that the poor are not relegated to flood-prone or otherwise unsafe living sites.

Box 10.6

Main water-related recommendations of the Millennium Project Task Force on Improving the Lives of Slum Dwellers

- Promote citywide slum upgrading including the provision of infrastructure services for water and sanitation.
- Provide alternatives to slum formation by making land and basic infrastructure available for low-income housing.
- Invest in urban trunk infrastructure, including for water and sanitation.
- Ensure that water tariffs are affordable for poor people.
- Improve solid waste disposal and provide investments to lower the pollution of water and air.

Vector-borne diseases are becoming more difficult to treat

Health

Over and above the impact of domestic water supplies and sanitation on human health, the management of water resources more generally has significant health impacts in terms of vector-borne diseases and water contamination. World-wide, more than 160 million people are infected with schistosomiasis,[2] which causes tens of thousands of deaths each year; there is a 77 percent reduction in schistosomiasis from well-designed water supply and sanitation interventions (WHO 2004a). Human-built reservoirs and poorly designed irrigation schemes are the main drivers of schistosomiasis expansion and intensification. Malaria kills more than one million people each year, 90 percent of them in Africa, the great majority of them children. Along with HIV/AIDS, malaria is one of the major public health scourges eroding development in the poorest countries in the world, and costs Africa more than $12 billion annually. It has slowed economic growth in African countries by 1.3 percent a year, the compounded effects of which are a gross domestic product level now 32 percent lower than it would have been had malaria been eradicated from Africa in 1960 (WHO 2004b).

Vector-borne illnesses, which include malaria (box 10.7), dengue, and schistosomiasis, are passed to humans by insects and snails that breed in aquatic ecosystems (UN/WWAP 2003). Vector-borne diseases are becoming more difficult to treat because of the growing resistance of bacteria to antibiotics, parasites to other drugs, and insects to insecticides. Thus, improved water management practices are becoming an increasingly important tool in combating this category of disease. For instance, improving irrigation techniques to avoid standing or slow-moving water can have a big impact on the breeding of mosquitoes that carry malaria. Improved disposal of household wastewater can also eliminate a choice breeding ground for mosquitoes.

Persistent organic pollutants, or POPs, are another danger as a source of water contamination. POPs are produced and released into the soil, air, and water by human activity, such as irrigation, industrial discharges, and improper waste disposal. Derived from pesticides, other agrochemicals, industrial chemicals, and the byproducts of industrial processes, they can accumulate in living organisms to levels harmful to both human and environmental health. They include such substances as dioxin, PCBs, and DDT.

Box 10.7

Malaria: facts from the World Health Organization

Source: WHO 2004b.

- Some 1.2 million people die of malaria each year, 90 percent of whom are children less than 5 years old.
- There are 396 million episodes of malaria every year; most of the disease burden is in Sub-Saharan Africa.
- Intensified irrigation, dams, and other water-related projects contribute significantly to this disease burden, and better management of water resources reduces transmission of malaria and other vector-borne diseases.

Management of water resources has significant gender dimensions

Research suggests that the rural and urban poor, who are most exposed to environmental hazards, and especially women, children, and infants, are generally the groups most affected by POPs. Evidence points to links between human exposure to specific POPs and cancers and tumors, learning disorders and changes in temperament, immune system changes, reproductive disorders, birth defects, a shortened period of lactation in nursing mothers, and diseases such as endometriosis and increased incidence of diabetes, among others. These substances appear to become highly concentrated in human tissue and breast milk and can be passed to the developing fetus through the placenta. Even in small amounts (parts per trillion) these substances can have serious impacts on the development of the brain and reproductive system of children (CIEL website). These substances become integrated into the food chain, prolonging their damaging effects on ecosystem and human health.

Gender equality

In addition to the gender implications of improving access to domestic water supplies and sanitation, as described in part 1, the management of water resources more generally has significant gender dimensions (box 10.8). For example:

- Rural women produce 60 percent to 80 percent of food in developing countries, and their contribution to food security is likely to increase because of the "feminization of agriculture," which results when rural men migrate to urban areas in search of paid work and women remain to farm and care for family members. Women's role as farmers is frequently overlooked by agricultural extensionists, including those working for irrigation agencies; they often exclude women from access to water (for instance, by requiring land titles for access to irrigation systems). Explicitly involving women farmers in irrigation schemes and giving them a voice in decisionmaking processes related to water management is essential to fighting rural poverty. Also helpful would be including other ways women use irrigation water, such as in home-based cottage industries and home gardens, in water development and management plans (Molden and de Fraiture 2004).

Box 10.8

Main water-related recommendations of the Millennium Project Task Force on Education and Gender Equality

- Provide incentives to keep girls in primary and secondary school.
- Invest in gender-sensitive infrastructure such as girls' toilets, without which many girls drop out of school.
- Invest in "gender-responsive infrastructure," that is, infrastructure that reduces the time poverty of women and girls, such as infrastructure for water supply and sanitation.
- Protect women's property and inheritance rights, to which access to water is often linked.

There are positive reinforce-ments among the Goals, as well as downward spirals

- Social and economic analyses, including documenting natural resource uses, are incomplete without an understanding of gender differences and inequalities. With gender analysis, planners gain a more accurate picture of communities, natural resource uses, households, and water users. Understanding the differences between women and men (who does what work, who makes which decisions, who uses water for what, who controls which resources, who is responsible for the different family obligations) is part of a good analysis and can contribute to more effective initiatives.

- Without specific attention to gender issues, initiatives and projects can reinforce and even worsen inequalities between women and men. Although many initiatives are thought to be "gender neutral," they rarely are. Projects and programs often bring new resources, such as training, tools, and technology. Whether someone is male or female can influence whether he or she can take advantage of these opportunities, and even projects aimed at women can be "captured" by men when significant new resources are at stake.

- The involvement of both women and men in integrated water resources initiatives can increase project effectiveness. Experience shows that ensuring both women's and men's participation can enhance project results and improve the likelihood of sustainability. In other words, a project is more likely to achieve what planners hope it will achieve if women are active participants and decisionmakers.

In addition, even water-related environmental challenges affect women more negatively than men. For example, studies in Bangladesh show that women suffered most following the 1991 cyclone and flood. Among women ages 20–44, the death rate was 71 per 1,000, compared to 15 per 1,000 for men. The reasons: women were left at home by their husbands to care for children and protect property; their saris restricted their mobility; they were malnourished and thus physically weaker than men; and during the cyclone, the lack of *purdah* (partitions used to separate women from men or strangers) in public shelters may also have deterred women from seeking refuge (Baden and others 1994).

Exploiting potential synergies through combined approaches

There is a fundamental synergy between the various Goals.[3] It is difficult—if not impossible—to make progress on a few Goals without progress on the others. There are positive reinforcements among the Goals, as well as downward spirals. Malnourished people are more susceptible to diseases, such as diarrhea, and diarrhea in turn saps the body of calories and micronutrients. Healthy, well-fed people have more energy to escape from poverty. Safe drinking water near home keeps more girls in school, and educated girls have better nourished children, even without an increase in income. Poor, malnourished people are more likely to mine their natural resources for short-term benefits, regardless

Countries should avoid actions that focus single-mindedly on one target at the expense of another

of the long-term cost. Environmental degradation and polluted water affect the poor first. Healthy, well-nourished people with a decent income prioritize protection of their environment and natural resources. Conservation of natural forests provides "famine foods" to prevent malnutrition during periods of crop failure. Rehabilitation of degraded soil and water resources reduces the risk of crop failure and shortens the preharvest hunger period.

A critical challenge for meeting the Millennium Development Goals, therefore, is to define and promote strategies that will contribute to multiple Goals, and avoid strategies that create conflicts among them. Independent sectoral planning will increase the total cost of achieving the Goals, reduce effectiveness, and make it hard for communities to plan and manage multiple programs. Achieving the Goals will require political consensus and mobilization across many constituencies; integrated and synergistic strategies are more likely to generate enthusiasm and reduce costs of conflict. While exploiting all possible synergies, countries should also actively avoid water resource development and management actions that focus single-mindedly on one target at the expense of another.

Six key synergistic approaches that involve the planning, development, management, and use of water are:

- *Disseminate small-scale water technologies for livelihoods.* These technologies provide livelihoods to small and landless farmers, while addressing the hunger and environment goals (Rijsberman 2004). An array of technologies is available, appropriate to a variety of agroclimatic and socioeconomic conditions, ranging from rainwater harvesting in dry areas to the use of manual pumps to access shallow groundwater. What needs to be recognized is that successful adoption by a large number of people depends less on the exact nature of the technology itself than on: (a) the social marketing of the technology; (b) the availability of micro-credit programs; (c) the institutional support through nongovernmental networks or community-based organizations to provide training and technical support; and (d) the community and household preferences.

- *Reduce the vulnerability of communities to water-related natural disasters through land reform, infrastructure construction for water storage and flood protection, and improved land use planning, including slum upgrading.* These changes would address poverty, hunger, and health goals by increasing incomes and reducing the domestic and production risks faced by poor households.

- *Invest in water and sanitation systems, including new infrastructure for water management, in support of the nutrition, health, and environment Goals.* Investments in water supply and sanitation services will contribute to the achievement of public health, poverty, and hunger Goals. Infrastructure investment creates both temporary and permanent job opportunities, contributing to poverty alleviation.

Win-win approaches are highly desirable but not always possible

- *Invest in community-based natural resource management, including urban agriculture, for hunger, poverty, and environment Goals.* This might involve investing in community fisheries conservation strategies to reduce hunger in fisher and fish-consuming populations and to achieve marine conservation objectives; strengthening resource tenure and building the capacity of forest communities for joint conservation and rehabilitation, as well as sustainable commercial use; and investing in community herding systems that jointly address livestock, rangeland, and wildlife management with a view to protecting and enhancing the livelihoods of poor, rangeland-dependent communities. This might involve supporting urban and periurban small-scale agriculture, livestock, and forestry to jointly address tenure, water, food access, micronutrient malnutrition, and poverty goals.

- *Develop new sanitation technologies to use wastewater for periurban agriculture.* This development would address a key aspect of the sanitation Goal by turning the challenge of dealing with urban wastewater into an opportunity, a resource for generating additional livelihoods. It also addresses the poverty and malnutrition Goals for one of the most vulnerable groups of very poor people, those living in the periurban areas, the slums, of medium-to-large cities in developing countries. The Food and Agriculture Organization has estimated that 20 million hectare are directly or indirectly[4] irrigated with wastewater in 50 countries—close to 10 percent of the total irrigated area (UN/WWAP 2003).

- *Improve terms of agricultural trade.* Trade creates markets for agricultural products, thus enabling investment in more efficient water use. In an increasing number of developing countries, irrigated agriculture can be a key to export-led economic growth, as illustrated by the experience of Chile and South Africa. A change in global trade regimes and the opening up of markets by industrialized countries would greatly enhance the opportunities for such growth, which, if supported by appropriate macroeconomic policies, would also provide strong incentives for more efficient water use. Furthermore, trade in agricultural products and in "virtual water,"[5] as governed by the World Trade Organization, has important ramifications for the availability of water resources in many countries.

Although win-win approaches that advance more than one Millennium Development Goal simultaneously are highly desirable, they are not always possible. Indeed, there are many situations in which tradeoffs among the Goals are inevitable, particularly in the short term. Initiatives designed to spur economic development, for example, can come into conflict with the need to protect the quantity and quality of water. Cutting down trees for firewood or income-generating activities can contribute to deforestation, which eventually affects both rainfall and siltation of streams and rivers. Development of small dams to enable dry-season irrigation by smallholders can increase suitable breeding places for malaria mosquitoes and snail vectors of bilharzia or schistosomiasis. Pollution from industrial or agricultural activities designed to generate livelihoods and reduce poverty can greatly affect water quality. Irrigation and poor drainage can lead to salinization and waterlogging, negating the intended improvements in agricultural productivity. Excessive extraction of groundwater for irrigation can lower water tables to critical levels, which may deplete drinking-water supplies for the poor. Sewerage systems that "solve" environmental problems and avert health crises in one area can create environmental problems elsewhere, if the untreated sewage is dumped into another community's water source. As all these examples demonstrate, careful analysis and coherent management is called for to keep improvements in one area from having negative effects in another.

Chapter 11

What actions are needed?

Whereas investments in water resources development and management contribute in a variety of ways to meeting the Millennium Development Goals as a whole, the specific water-related interventions required to meet the Goals will vary across regions, countries, and even subnational areas. Context strongly influences the nature of the water resources actions that must be taken to meet the Goals.

The key determinant across virtually all regions and scales of analysis is the relationship between the availability of freshwater and the requirement for its use. Both availability and requirement are multidimensional notions, each having quantitative, qualitative, temporal, and spatial dimensions. Simply put, the actions needed to meet the Millennium Development Goals in a given case depend on the extent to which the availability of water resources—in its many dimensions—is adequate to meet the requirement for water resources to meet the health, poverty, gender, and environmental sustainability objectives of the Millennium Development Goals.

The availability of freshwater resources can be disaggregated into three principal dimensions: quantity, quality, and variability.

- The *quantity* of water available, from both surface and groundwater sources, is one fundamental aspect of availability. This amount is, of course, strongly related to rainfall and to the infrastructure already in place for water storage and abstraction. Availability comprises both physical access to sources wholly within a particular boundary (including fossil groundwater) and negotiated access to shared water sources, such as rivers, lakes, and aquifers.
- *Quality* is an aspect of freshwater availability that has become a major issue in some parts of the world, and that can also have a major impact on attainment of the health and environmental sustainability Goals. In

Tradeoffs will need to be made in the use of water resources to meet the various Goals

some cases, such as Bangladesh's problem with arsenic-contaminated groundwater, water quality problems are naturally occurring. Much more common, however, is the degradation of water quality by anthropogenic causes, such as pollution discharges into surface water bodies and leaching of contaminants into underground water sources.

- *Variability* in the availability of water, both in time and space, depends both on climatic variables and on the types of infrastructure and management arrangements already in place for water control. Surface waters often have highly seasonal regimes; this is particularly the case in the tropics, where most of the countries that are off-track in meeting the Goals lie. In addition to seasonal variability, there is often considerable variability from one year to another. Both seasonal and year-to-year variability create a need for diversification of water sources, early-warning systems, contingency plans for droughts and floods, and storage alternatives (both surface and subsurface).

The requirement for freshwater resources not only has quantity, quality, and (spatial and temporal) variability characteristics, but also goal-specific dimensions—which mean that the nature of the water resources actions needed to meet the Millennium Development Goals will vary from Goal to Goal. For example, to meet the poverty Goal, countries will need to use water for productive purposes to ensure livelihoods in water-dependent sectors, such as agriculture, industry, energy, transport, and fisheries; they will also need to control water variability, since households living at the brink of survival can easily be devastated by a single water-related extreme event, such as a flood or drought. Meeting the hunger Goal will require the use of water as an input to agriculture and to support productive activities that help ensure economic access to food (for example, through employment of landless labor in the dry season), as well as access to safe water and adequate sanitation to maintain the health conditions required for proper absorption of nutrients. Meeting the health Goals will require access to domestic water availability and sanitation, sound water management to limit vector-borne diseases, and appropriate levels of water quality. Meeting the gender Goal will require ensuring that women have a strong voice in decisionmaking processes related to water management. Meeting the environment Goals will require that sufficient amounts of water are reserved to ensure healthy ecosystem functioning. It is, however, important to note that the Millennium Development Goals will not be addressed in isolation. Typically, other uses—agricultural, municipal, and industrial—dominate water management activities and need to be addressed to ensure that the Millennium Development Goals receive priority.

All this will greatly affect the level and the nature of requirements for water, the stress on water resources, and the mechanisms for identifying and ensuring its best use—the actions needed to meet the Millennium Development Goals. Unfortunately, in many of the world's poorest countries, the quantity, quality, and variability of water resources is such that tradeoffs will need to be made in the

**Countries
that start
"from behind"
can overcome
these
constraints**

use of water resources to meet the various Goals, particularly between the hunger and environmental sustainability Goals. According to a recent study conducted under the Comprehensive Assessment of Water Management in Agriculture, sponsored by the Consultative Group on International Agricultural Research (CGIAR), more than 1.4 billion people already live in river basins where high water-use levels threaten freshwater ecosystems (Smakhtin and others 2004). Other studies have shown that in order to sustain ecosystems, irrigation withdrawals—vitally needed to meet the hunger Goals—will need to be reduced by 7 percent by 2025, in comparison with 1995 levels (Alcamo and others 2000). Clearly, innovative approaches will be required to reduce these inherent tradeoffs among the uses of water resources to meet the various Goals.

A quick picture of this situation is provided in map 11.1, which depicts water stress in major basins, taking into account environmental water requirements (Smakhtin and others 2004). The map uses a water-stress indicator that relates total withdrawals to the mean annual flow less an estimated amount for environmental flow. Much of the area under greatest stress, where people are already overexploiting rivers by tapping water that should be reserved for environmental flows, coincides with areas that are heavily developed for irrigation to provide water for food. Much of Sub-Saharan Africa and Latin America has low degrees of environmental water stress, raising the issue of whether these areas could be tapped for additional water to support livelihoods, if that could be done sustainably. Note that areas with high levels of water stress do not coincide with areas with low levels of access to safe drinking water or basic sanitation.

The preceding analyses suggest two important conclusions:

First, the specific actions that a particular country or region should take to improve water resources management depend on the relationship between the availability and requirement for water resources, as well as the socioeconomic, political, and historical circumstances of that area. Clearly, natural endowments give countries and regions different starting points for water resources development and management. But countries that start "from behind"—with high variability and low per capita freshwater availability—can overcome these constraints through appropriate investments and management arrangements.

Second, given the complex relationship between water resources and poverty, hunger, gender equity, and environmental sustainability, coordinated water management will have to be a fundamental component of any national strategy to attain the Millennium Development Goals. In particular, planning and policy development based on the Goals must be supported by an integrated approach to land, water, and ecosystems, one which conforms broadly to the recommendations from the Johannesburg Summit regarding integrated water resources management and water efficiency strategies. Meeting the Millennium Development Goals will therefore require investing in water resources development and management and adopting an integrated water resources management approach, as outlined below.

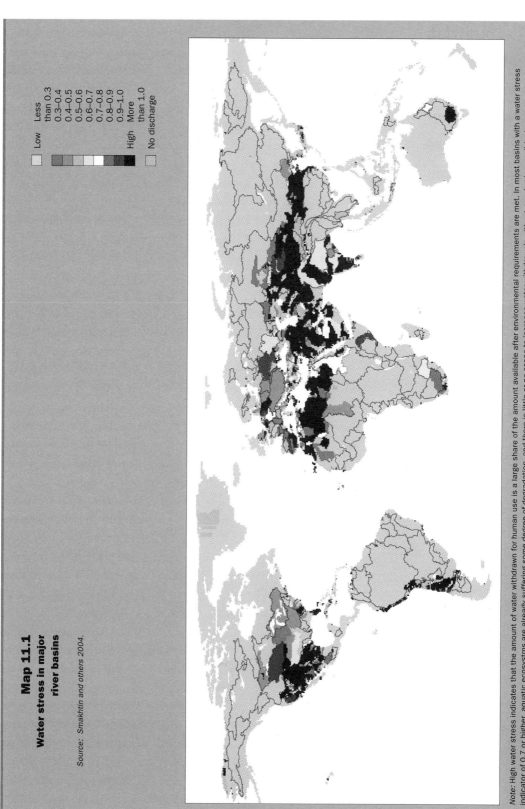

Map 11.1

Water stress in major river basins

Source: Smakhtin and others 2004.

Low Less
     than 0.3
     0.3–0.4
     0.4–0.5
     0.5–0.6
     0.6–0.7
     0.7–0.8
     0.8–0.9
     0.9–1.0
High More
     than 1.0
     No discharge

Note: High water stress indicates that the amount of water withdrawn for human use is a large share of the amount available after environmental requirements are met. In most basins with a water stress indicator of 0.7 or higher, aquatic ecosystems are already suffering some degree of degradation, and there is little or no scope to increase water withdrawals without causing irreversible damage

Countries will need to embark on a plan of action involving both supply and demand management

Investing in water resources development and management

As the challenges for sound water resources management vary within and among countries, so must the strategies for identifying and addressing water-related obstacles to achieving the Millennium Development Goals. In general, however, countries with high variability or low availability in relation to fresh-water requirements will need to embark on a plan of action involving both supply and demand management. A coherent approach to investing in water resources infrastructure and management to meet the Millennium Development Goals in a particular country might include:

- *Identifying intermediate water resource targets that support each of the key Millennium Development targets.* In the case of the hunger target, for example, a short-term water-related target might be an estimate of the land area that would need to be brought under irrigation or the degree of investment required to improve the efficiency of existing systems. For both the poverty and the hunger targets, an intermediate water target might be a calculation of the storage capacity and early warning systems that would be needed to effectively control floods and droughts. Intermediate targets for water resources should address both investment and management issues, taking into account the vast deficiencies in infrastructure endowments in the countries farthest from reaching the Goals, as well as the potential for demand management. Intermediate targets will need to include both a physical dimension—for example, the need for irrigation infrastructure in working order—as well as a concept of use—for example, whether communities and local governments are able to maintain a safe, reliable supply of water from a tube well.

- *Carrying out needs assessments for water resources development and management based on intermediate targets.* Governments should determine the infrastructure development, watershed management practices, demand management systems, and institutional and policy measures needed for meeting the Millennium Development Goals, as well as the human and financial resource requirements to achieve them. They should cost out these needs, including both capital and operation and maintenance costs. The water infrastructure considered should include all hydraulic infrastructure needed to align water supply with demand, from water storage and irrigation infrastructure to interbasin water transfers and infrastructure for industrial and other economic uses. Such costs should also include investments needed to ensure that infrastructure development does not negatively impact any of the Millennium Development Goals, especially the environmental sustainability targets. Equally important, estimates of the resources necessary to ensure proper, sustainable functioning of installed infrastructure—for example, through training and institutional capacity-building programs—should be included in such assessments.

Water resources development and management should be integrated

- *Developing a plan that outlines how to meet the needs identified in the assessment and how such actions will be integrated into a national poverty reduction strategy based on the Millennium Development Goals.* This would entail mapping out, with specific milestones at national and subnational levels, the year-to-year actions and investments required to meet the needs identified in the assessment. Such plans should not be stand-alone sectoral documents, but elements that will be integrated into overall strategies to reduce poverty and promote sustainable development in line with the Goals.

- *Defining and promoting strategies that will contribute to multiple Goals, and avoiding strategies that create conflicts among them.* A coherent national planning process should guide sectoral planning. The absence of coherence may increase the total cost of achieving the Millennium Development Goals, reduce effectiveness, and make it hard for communities and subnational governments to plan and manage multiple programs. Integrated and synergistic strategies that generate buy-in from all stakeholders and reduce costs and conflict should be given priority. This is not to advocate rigid central planning; what is recommended is a coordination of sectoral activities in such a way that promotes synergies among them, rather than attempts to plan entire national economies.

Adopting integrated water resources management

Because the Millennium Development Goals are interlinked, water resources development and management in support of the Goals should be pursued in an integrated manner, with priority given to actions that further multiple goals. Integrated water resources management (IWRM), as defined by the Global Water Partnership, is a process that "promotes the coordinated development and management of water, land, and related resources, in order to maximize the resultant economic and social welfare in an equitable manner without compromising the sustainability of vital ecosystems."[1] Integrated water resources management builds on three basic pillars: an enabling environment of proper water resources policies and legislation; an institutional framework of capable institutions at national, local, and river-basin levels; and a set of management instruments for these institutions. Of course, the form that IWRM will take must vary from country to country; in some cases, groups of neighboring countries may profitably engage in joint IWRM exercises.

IWRM focuses on development (investment), as well as management issues. This approach is particularly important for the poorest countries most at risk of failing to achieve the Millennium Development Goals, where deficiencies in infrastructure endowments are vast. The target set by the World Summit on Sustainable Development in Johannesburg for countries to develop IWRM and water efficiency strategies by 2005 provides an opportunity to

Integrated development will need to recognize the challenges of sharing water between countries

infuse planning processes based on the Millennium Development Goals with consideration of water resources (GWP 2004). If properly designed, these national IWRM strategies and processes can establish an enabling framework that encourages water management and services that benefit the poor, and thus advance the Goals.

At the same time, the 2005 IWRM target included in the Johannesburg Plan of Implementation should be interpreted as meaning the *initiation* of a robust water resource management process. For example, one meaningful measure of progress toward a national IWRM process would be that representatives of all stakeholder groups have had the opportunity to discuss the necessary compromises between competing interests in water. Such processes take time, and the IWRM activities initiated in anticipation of the 2005 milestone should be considered essential first steps in a much longer journey toward sustainable water resources management.

Experience in several countries suggests that IWRM is an effective way of coordinating development strategies across sectors and geographical regions. Uganda and Burkina Faso have gone through multiyear IWRM processes resulting in new national policies, strategies, and laws for their water resources development and management. China, India, Thailand, and Nicaragua refer to their policy reform processes as IWRM-based.

The integrated development and management of water resources in support of the Millennium Development Goals in countries sharing transboundary water resources will need to recognize the challenges of sharing water between countries. Transboundary considerations, however, should not be viewed simply as an additional level of integration; they can also be a potential catalyst for the development of more effective approaches to reaching the Millennium Development Goals.

Examples of context-specific actions

Ultimately, context should determine the specific actions and strategies a country should use to reach the Millennium Development Goals. Context includes the relationship between availability and requirement for freshwater resources, as well as the socio-economic circumstances of the country. Four examples will illustrate this point.

Regions with a tropical monsoon climate (ample water but high variability in time) and low levels of investment in water storage infrastructure.[2] In these situations, meeting the Millennium Development Goals may require:

- A significant investment in water storage capacity.
- Diversification of water sources.
- Development and implementation of early warning systems based on climate prediction tools.
- Development of contingency plans.

Areas where the impact of climate change on water resources is anticipated to be grave, leading to more frequent and severe floods, droughts, mudslides, typhoons, and cyclones.[3] Here, actions might include:

- Greater investments in storage capacity.
- Increased investment in technologies, capacity, and institutional structures to monitor and predict extreme weather events (early warning systems).
- Improved national disaster preparedness and planning.
- Zoning regulations (or improved enforcement of existing regulations) that keep people from living in areas regularly destroyed by floods.
- Long-term national water management plans that take into account the affects of climate change and focus on achieving the Millennium Development Goals.

Water-scarce regions, in which water is a limiting factor in the achievement of the hunger Goal.[4] Here, actions might include:

- Identifying new incentive structures for water use and conservation to influence unsustainable consumption patterns.
- Identifying unsustainable agricultural subsidies and trade barriers and assessing the degree to which trade can help solve regional food deficiency problems.
- Closing the productivity gap between what can be and what is produced by exploiting the potential for water productivity gains in rain-fed and irrigated areas through innovative agronomic, economic, and social interventions.
- Facilitating the diffusion and use of new technologies for increasing water productivity—whether low-tech or high-tech—in irrigated and rain-fed agriculture.
- Closing nutrient loops—making sure that nutrients are returned to agricultural lands and improving soil fertility through the reuse of urban domestic wastewater for periurban agriculture.

Regions in which current levels of economic and social activity impact on water resources, leaving them inadequate to meet the health and environmental sustainability Millennium Development Goals or where future depleting water use will further threaten aquatic ecosystems and the goods and services that they provide. In these situations, actions might include:

- Investment in infrastructure to reduce the environmental impact of urban and industrial activity, which may include both water-specific infrastructure (sewage treatment works) and broader investments (slum upgrading, may dramatically reduce "diffuse" pollution).
- Identifying minimum ecological service criteria for protection of aquatic ecosystems against water depletion.

- National-level monitoring of aquatic ecosystem health, public health, water quality and quantity, and biodiversity.
- Establishing national policies, strategies, and institutions and developing national environmental action plans.
- Using the tools of environmental economics for reflecting the true value of ecosystem services and the real costs of pollution.

Chapter 12

Monitoring and support systems

This chapter explores how the global community can help monitor the nature, quality, quantity, and current and projected uses of water resources for all the Millennium Development Goals, and how it can better support national governments in their efforts to address a range of water and sanitation questions. The following discussion and set of recommendations relates both to United Nations organizations and to their international partners.

Monitoring water resources

Monitoring is a critical component of planning and action. Monitoring change in situations over time is necessary to gauge the effectiveness of interventions and measure the impact of policy reforms and investment at the national and subnational levels. Monitoring is also critical to compare needs and prioritize action among countries at the international level, which implies a need for standardized approaches, data, and methods of gathering information. And at all levels, civil society's most powerful advocacy tool is accurate information, the end product of reliable monitoring efforts.

The challenges related to tracking progress in the development and management of water resources for all the Millennium Development Goals are very different from those involved in tracking progress in expanding access to domestic water supply and sanitation services as called for in target 10. Target 10 is in itself a measurable goal, whereas water resources management is not an end in itself, but rather an input to efforts to increase food production, reduce poverty and disease, and protect ecosystems. The international community has a fairly well-developed conceptual framework and institutional mechanism for monitoring target 10, but the frameworks and institutions for monitoring water resources management and development in relation to the Millennium Development Goals are still in their infancy. As a result, mea-

Three types of intermediate targets could be monitored: *process measures*, *output measures*, and *impact measures*

suring "success" in this area presents a host of issues that have not yet been resolved.

Conceptual framework

Although the international community does not yet have a conceptual framework for monitoring water resources for all the Millennium Development Goals, we present below what we believe to be four essential foundations on which such a conceptual framework might be built:

- *A framework for sorting out the ways in which the development, management, and use of water resources will affect the Millennium Development Goals.* Table 10.1 captures the specific parameters that need to be monitored to ensure that the development, management, and use of water is having the best possible impact on the achievement of the Millennium Development Goals. Meeting the poverty target (target 1), for instance, will require not only attaining equity in access to safe drinking water, but also reducing poor people's vulnerability to such water-related diseases and disasters as floods and droughts.

- *A set of intermediate targets that relate the development, management, and use of water resources to each of the relevant Millennium Development targets.* Following the concept of "nested systems frameworks" (Small and Svendsen 1992), the relationship between water and any one of the Millennium Development Goals can be described as a set of nested systems, each with its own particular set of intermediate objectives. The primary link between these systems is that the outputs from one system become part of the inputs into the next system. In this context, three types of intermediate targets could be monitored: *process measures*, which refer to the processes internal to any given system; *output measures*, which describe the quality and quantity of outputs at a point where they become inputs to the next higher system; and *impact measures*, which refer to the impact of these outputs on the Millennium Development Goals as a whole. This approach requires monitoring not only the inputs and outputs of any subsystem, but also the efficiency with which inputs to any subsystem are turned into outputs. In relation to the hunger target, for example, it is important to measure not only the water consumed in irrigated agriculture and the resultant food output, but also the relationship between the two—the "crop per drop" ratio.

- *For each intermediate target, an analytical system to define and measure the target.* As with target 10, this effort will require, for each intermediate target, terminology for defining precisely what we mean by the contribution of water resources management and development for that target, the operational meaning of the agreed terminologies, and survey instruments and indicators for assessing progress in water resources management and development toward the target. In the case of the hunger target,

Intermediate targets for water resources will need to give attention to both development and management

for example, an intermediate target might be the proportion of land area that is effectively irrigated in relation to the proportion of land area that would need to be irrigated if the hunger target is to be met. For both the poverty and the hunger targets, one parameter to monitor might be the degree to which the unequal distribution of water in time and space can be controlled, for example, by measuring the proportion of storage infrastructure (both surface and subsurface) and early warning systems that are effectively in place in relation to the infrastructure and management systems that would be needed to effectively control floods and droughts.

- *A system for monitoring the extent to which each country's vision of integrated water resources management is translated into tailored solutions as a base for achieving the Millennium Development Goals as a whole.* As noted earlier, there is increasing acceptance that the management of water resources must be undertaken with an integrated approach. Management decisions to alleviate poverty, to allow economic development, to ensure food security and the health of human populations, as well as preserve vital ecosystems, must be based on our best possible understanding of all relevant systems. From this point of view, the implementation of one of the task force's fundamental propositions—that countries should elaborate coherent water resources development and management plans that will suppport the achievement of the Millennium Development Goals as a whole (see chapter 13)—also needs to be carefully monitored. In the short term, this implies monitoring the implementation of the target set in Johannesburg, which requires countries to have formulated integrated water resources management strategies by 2005.

Clearly, these four essential foundations only begin to scratch the surface of the needed conceptual framework for monitoring water for all the Millennium Development Goals. In further developing this framework, a wide range of issues will need to be taken into account. Perhaps the most important is that, since the relationship between water and the Millennium Development Goals is enormously site specific, intermediate targets and milestones will need to be set and monitored at national and subnational levels. In addition, baseline dates will need to be set for all targets (1990 is recommended in all cases, unless special circumstances dictate otherwise). Finally, as with target 10, intermediate targets for water resources will need to give attention to both development and management issues, recognizing the key role of investment in infrastructure and the vast deficiencies in infrastructure endowments in the poorest countries most at risk of failing to achieve the Millennium Development Goals.

Institutional mechanisms

Within the overall reporting process referred to earlier, there is currently no global system in place to produce a systematic, continuing, integrated, and

The World Water Assessment Programme focuses on assessing the situation of freshwater throughout the world

comprehensive global picture of freshwater and its management in relation to the Millennium Development Goals. Designed to help close this gap is the World Water Assessment Programme (WWAP), which focuses on assessing the situation of freshwater throughout the world (WWAP website). Its primary output is the periodic *World Water Development Report* (UN/WWAP 2003). The current report, which came out in 2003, will be updated every three years; the next volumes are slated for 2006, 2009, 2012, and 2015. The program focuses on terrestrial freshwater, but links with the marine near-shore environments and coastal zone regions as principal sinks for land-based sources of pollution and sedimentation and as areas where the threat of flooding and the potential impact of sea level rise on freshwater resources is particularly acute.

The WWAP is undertaken by UN agencies working in concert under the auspices of UN-Water. The program is hosted by UNESCO and serves as an "umbrella" for coordination of existing UN initiatives within the freshwater assessment sphere. In this regard it links strongly with the data and information systems of the UN agencies.[1] Currently, the compilation and development of indicators are being undertaken in all key areas of water resources and reflected in the *World Water Development Report*. Organized in terms of the Millennium Development Goals, these areas include:

Goal 1: eradicate extreme poverty and hunger

- *Food security.* Food security, particularly of the poor and vulnerable, depends upon the more efficient mobilization and use of water and the more equitable allocation of water for food production.
- *Water and industry.* Industry needs and private-sector responsibility to respect water quality and take account of the needs of competing sectors has a significant impact on water quality and quantity.
- *Water and energy.* Water is vital for all forms of energy production, and there is a need to ensure that energy requirements are met in a sustainable manner.
- *Risk management.* There is tremendous need in developing countries to provide security from floods, droughts, pollution, and other water-related hazards, especially in light of climate change.

Goals 4, 5, and 6: reduce child mortality; improve maternal health; and combat HIV/AIDS, malaria, and other diseases

- *Meeting basic needs.* Because of its importance in the promotion and protection of human health, access to safe and sufficient water supply and sanitation is a basic human right and essential to health and well-being.

Goal 7: ensure environmental sustainability

- *Protecting ecosystems.* Safeguarding the integrity of ecosystems requires sustainable water resources management.

The *World Water Development Report* appears to be the most viable mechanism for periodically reporting on progress

- *Water and cities.* Urban areas are increasingly the focus of human settlements and economic activities, and they present distinctive challenges to water managers.

Integrated approaches to achieve all goals
- *The nature of the resource.* The availability of water (quantity and quality) from all sources and its variation through time affect all aspects of development.
- *Valuing water.* Managing water in a way that reflects its economic, social, environmental, and cultural values in all its uses and moving toward pricing water services to reflect the cost of their provision, taking account of the need for equity and the basic needs of the poor and the vulnerable, are important components of sound water management.
- *Governing water wisely.* Good water governance requires the involvement of the public and the interests of all stakeholders in the management of water resources.
- *Ensuring the knowledge base.* Good water policies and management depend upon the quality of knowledge available to decisionmakers.
- *Sharing water resources.* Promoting peaceful cooperation and developing synergies among different users of water at all levels within and between states through sustainable river basin management or other appropriate approaches is critical.

Clearly, much needs to be done to help the *World Water Development Report* system become an effective process to monitor water resources for the Millennium Development Goals. In addition to conceptual problems, enormous measurement challenges remain to be tackled. Just to take one example, data and information collection is not done in a systematic and consistent fashion at any level, and thus it is difficult to compare data over time or between countries. In addition, there are problems of definition. Despite these challenges, the *World Water Development Report* appears to be the most viable mechanism currently available for periodically reporting on progress made in the area of water resources development and management toward achieving the Millennium Development Goals as a whole.

In addition to monitoring the larger question of water resources for all the Millennium Development Goals, the international community should support and track progress on the development of plans and strategies for integrated water resources management and efficiency by 2005, as called for in the Johannesburg Plan of Implementation. The information gathered through these monitoring processes can be used by the international community during the second Water Decade, "Water for Life," which runs from 2005 to 2015, to mobilize international awareness and political commitment to water resources planning, development, management, and use to meet the Millennium Development Goals (UNESCO website).

UN organizations need to play a strong supporting role

Global institutional support structures

Direct action to manage and develop water resources to meet the Millennium Development Goals should take place as close as possible to where the problems and opportunities lie—principally at national and subnational levels. Nevertheless, UN organizations with their international partners (including international water and sanitation networks and partnerships) need to play a strong supporting role. In particular, they need to assist countries to meet the water supply and sanitation target and to manage water resources through technical support and capacity building, objective analysis and knowledge sharing, global monitoring, and advocacy functions. The need for these types of support was one of the key lessons of the International Drinking Water Supply and Sanitation Decade (see box 1.2). These functions need to be effectively aligned toward the achievement of the Millennium Development Goals, and they need to be accompanied by international leadership and strategic guidance through a clear mechanism that builds on each organization's strengths and comparative advantages and reduces duplication.

The way in which UN organizations and their partners (including international water and sanitation networks and partnerships) presently support national water and sanitation efforts could be substantially improved. The current system has two characteristics that both contribute to its weaknesses and set it apart from the way in which the international community addresses other Millennium Development Goal issues, such as hunger or health.

First, some 24 UN system organizations and a number of international water and sanitation networks and partnerships are involved in water resources and sanitation. There is no single "lead agency" (as, say, FAO is for agriculture and WHO is for health). With so many actors involved in water and sanitation, ensuring coordinated and effective action that is aligned with the Millennium Development Goals is a challenge; indeed, organizations sometimes compete with one another, and "turf battles" occur. The United Nations System Chief Executive Board for Coordination endorsed UN-Water in November 2003 as the new official United Nations systemwide interagency mechanism for follow-up of the water-related decisions reached at the World Summit on Sustainable Development 2002 and the Millennium Development Goals (box 12.1). The new terms of reference of UN-Water respond to the need to increase coherence and coordination at inter-agency and country levels and also to the needs described earlier concerning coherent and coordinated leadership (UN DESA website). Nevertheless, the task force is concerned that UN-Water does not have adequate budget or staff to execute these functions at the scale required, especially in light of the policy prominence of water and sanitation in the forthcoming decade.

Second, in the past 15 years, most UN system organizations have experienced pressure to respond to emerging issues. Declining contributions to many organizations coupled with these increased demands have tended to reduce core funds and increase reliance on financing tied to pre-defined areas of work. The

Box 12.1

The evolution of interagency coordination in water resources and sanitation

Cooperation and coordination among UN agencies in the area of water resources started with the Intersecretariat Group for Water Resources, which was established in 1977 following the UN Water Conference at Mar del Plata, Argentina. The intersecretariat defined areas where interagency collaboration would be important, such as in the implementation of the International Drinking Water Supply and Sanitation Decade, which extended from 1981 to 1990. After the Earth Summit in 1992, the intersecretariat was integrated into the former Administrative Committee on Coordination as the ACC Subcommittee on Water Resources. In 2000 the subcommittee started a long-term project called the World Water Assessment Program, the main product of which is the World Water Development Report (UN 2003). Following the recent restructuring of the ACC, the members of the UN system entities dealing with water formed "UN-Water," the United Nations Inter-Agency Committee on Water Resources. In late 2003, the United Nations System Chief Executive Board for Coordination (CEB) formally established UN-Water as the interagency mechanism for follow-up of the water-related decisions coming out of the 2002 World Summit on Sustainable Development and the Millennium Development Goals concerning freshwater.

overall effects of these trends vary among organizations, but have included a reduced emphasis on water and sanitation, wide gaps between mandated responsibilities and delivery capacity, and a resulting inability to provide intellectual and practical leadership. In parallel, several international networks and partnerships have emerged and are active in technical analysis, knowledge sharing, and advocacy. These entities include the Water Supply and Sanitation Collaborative Council (WSSCC website), the Global Water Partnership (GWP website), and the World Water Council (WWC website), as well as nongovernmental organizations such as WaterAid. This diversity of actors contributes much to the strength of international water and sanitation support and advocacy, but also creates new challenges to coordination to ensure effective coherent action.

Recommendations for the international community

To reach the Millennium Development Goals, the problems identified above need to be addressed forthrightly and urgently.

- United Nations system organizations and their member states must ensure that the UN actors engaged in technical support and capacity building, objective analysis and knowledge sharing, global monitoring, and advocacy have, both individually and collectively, the organizational capacity, mandate, staffing, and resources needed to carry out these functions.
- At the country level, UN Country Teams must strengthen their efforts to provide technical and capacity-building support to governments, including in the preparation of national strategies for water supply and sanitation based on the Millennium Development Goals, as well as strategies for integrated water resources management and water efficiency. Likewise, development banks and bilateral donor agencies must

The provision of leadership and strategic guidance to the international community is essential

effectively coordinate their actions at the country level, including harmonization of procedures and joint programs.

- The WHO/UNICEF Joint Monitoring Programme must be strengthened as the key global mechanism for monitoring access to water supply and sanitation and provided with greater funding. WHO and UNICEF should ensure that arrangements increasingly enable contribution to and participation in the JMP. Bilateral agencies should both provide more funding and refrain from setting up parallel structures. UN-Water should be mandated to periodically report, through the *World Water Development Report*, on progress in water resources development and management for the Millennium Development Goals, including progress on the development of strategies for integrated water resources management and efficiency by 2005. UN-Water and *World Water Development Report* must be strengthened and provided with greater funding to fulfill these roles successfully.

At the global level, provision of leadership and strategic guidance to the international community is essential. UN organizations and key operational actors and others involved in water and sanitation must be involved in this effort through a clear mechanism that should build on each organization's strengths and comparative advantages and reduce duplication. The recently defined mandate and widened participation of UN-Water correspond closely to this need, but this mechanism presently has neither the necessary funds nor staff. Several options exist:

- A multiagency entity (such as the Global Fund to Fight HIV/AIDS, Tuberculosis and Malaria or UNAIDS) could be created to act as the main advocate for global action on water and sanitation and to lead, strengthen, and support national scaling-up efforts. Such a mechanism would need to include the key operational actors in water and sanitation, build on the various organizations' strengths and comparative advantages, and have a clear joint strategy, designation of roles and responsibilities, a program of action, and accountability for results. UN Water, which has recently been reconstituted to include broader representation from non-UN bodies, could be transformed into a body with this responsibility; at present the entity has neither the funding nor staff to take on this role, but with a concerted capacity-building effort over the next year, it might be possible for it to assume that responsibility within a reasonable timeframe.

- A second option would be to establish a truly operational group and program on water and sanitation with the key operational bodies in and outside the UN system. The program would need to be well funded and staffed, with a clear mandate to act on achieving the targets and possibly a sunset clause in 2025.

**The global
networks and
the funding
agencies
supporting
them must
strengthen
and
rationalize
their efforts**

- A third option would be to assign UN system task managers for the various aspects of water resources and water supply and sanitation. WHO and UNICEF, for example, could take the lead in sanitation; UNESCO or UNEP in the management of freshwater resources.

In addition, the recently established Secretary General's Advisory Board on Water and Sanitation must focus on providing high-level policy commentary on progress toward the water and sanitation target, advising on strategic direction, identifying critical obstacles to progress, and making recommendations for overcoming them. It should independently and boldly comment on developing country, donor country, and UN system practices, and produce a periodic, brief, focused, high-profile report that would eschew advocacy in favor of pointed recommendations aimed at improving progress within the sector and at advancing the sector's position in the development arena.

Finally, the global networks engaged in water and sanitation and the funding agencies supporting them must collectively strengthen and rationalize their efforts to provide technical support, capacity-building, objective analysis, knowledge-sharing, and advocacy functions, and align those functions towards the achievement of the Millennium Development Goals, while at the same time taking steps to ensure they are accountable to the communities of the developing world.

3

Achieving the Millennium Development Goals

Chapter 13

How to make the Goals a reality

Expanding water and sanitation coverage is not rocket science. It requires neither colossal sums of money nor breakthrough scientific discoveries or dramatic technological advances. Although reaching the water and sanitation target will by no means be easy, particularly in the very poorest parts of the world, and worldwide the sanitation challenge is indeed daunting, achieving target 10 is possible.

The critical question is, how? This chapter focuses on the answer. Based on the analyses presented in the previous chapters, what do we, as a task force, think it will take to meet the water and sanitation target and to optimize water resources management for the entire set of Millennium Development Goals? More specifically, what are the key actions that we have identified as essential to meeting the Millennium Development Goals?

A call to action

We would like to set the stage by first identifying five critical guiding principles without which the Millennium Development Goals simply cannot be achieved.

The task force is unanimous in its belief that the water and sanitation target (target 10) will not be reached unless:

- *There is a deliberate commitment by donors both to increase and refocus their development assistance and to target sufficient aid to the poorest low-income countries.*
- *There is a deliberate commitment by governments of middle-income countries that do not depend on aid to reallocate their resources so that they target funding to their unserved poor.*
- *There are deliberate activities to create support and ownership for water supply and sanitation initiatives among both women and men in poor communities.*

Local, subnational, and national governments have the primary responsibility for expanding access

- *There is a deliberate recognition that basic sanitation in particular requires an approach that centers on community mobilization and actions that support and encourage that mobilization.*

Furthermore, our group is convinced that the Millennium Development Goals as a whole will not be met unless:

- *There is deliberate planning and investment in sound water resources management and infrastructure.*

Without these five preconditions, the poorest countries will miss target 10; the poorest people in on-target middle-income countries will be left behind; many of the gains that are made will not be sustained; the sanitation crisis will continue unabated; and, in many countries, water scarcity, variability, and contamination will hamstring progress toward all the goals.

Our starting points are thus clear: *poor people and poor countries must get priority,* and *resources and policies must be focused on spurring and supporting community-led action.* The key to reaching the targets will be to mobilize and support people themselves, country by country, particularly in slums, rural areas, and other marginalized communities where access to services is lowest.

Consistent with this focus on ground-level action, we believe that local, subnational, and national governments have the primary responsibility for expanding access to water supply and sanitation services. National governments must stand by their commitments to the Millennium Development Goals by making them priority national development goals, preparing strategies and action plans for their achievement, opening doors for community action, and mobilizing public awareness and support, especially for sanitation and hygiene. Though governments need not engage directly in service delivery, they do need to set standards for service providers (including public utilities and the private sector), and they must intervene, if necessary, to make things happen.

To make the Millennium Development Goals a reality for everyone, countries must focus their efforts and resources where needs and challenges are greatest, particularly among concentrations of very poor people in urban slum areas, periurban areas, and rural areas. They must ensure that the financial burden of serving the poor is not borne by the poor alone. For upper low- and middle-income countries, this commitment principally means that existing resources must be used more effectively. To make subsidies for the poorest possible, governments must end subsidies for the nonpoor. This reallocation of resources will require significant political will and commitment, since ensuring basic services for all rather than subsidizing "luxury" service for some will challenge powerful interests and create a new set of winners and losers.

That said, there is clearly a critical supporting role for international agencies, international nongovernmental organizations (NGOs), and, most importantly, donor countries, which have also committed to the Millennium Development Goals. Most of the countries with the lowest levels of human development and that have made the least progress over the past ten years are stuck in poverty

Official development assistance should be targeted within countries to programs that benefit the poorest

traps, bypassed by economic development because of structural impediments like geography, climate, the burden of disease, rapid population growth, heavy debt burdens, dependence upon primary commodity exports, and the inequities of the global current trade regime. For these countries, all the governance reforms, enabling policy environments, and social mobilization efforts in the world will not address the fact that domestic resources are simply inadequate to support a meaningful expansion of services. Without more official development assistance, these countries simply cannot meet the water and sanitation target; they do not have and cannot generate sufficient resources from any other source. To meet the Goals, donor countries must fulfill their side of the Monterrey compact to provide more aid, as well as increase the efficiency of aid through better coordination.

At present, there is often an inherent tension in the process: Should countries outline in a serious way what it would truly take to meet the Millennium Development Goals or should they outline what they believe they can achieve *within likely levels of development assistance?* For the poorest countries most off-track for meeting the Millennium Development Goals, it is crucial to make transparently clear the gap between what they could achieve with likely levels of development assistance and what they really need in order to achieve their goals—and for the international community to step in with the necessary funding. In the water sector, donors and developing countries alike have become accustomed to identifying what can be done *within the confines of existing aid allocations and national budgetary limits.* To meet the Goals, this process must be turned on its head, with identification of needs and demands coming first and appropriate allocations being made second.

To ensure inclusion of and priority for the poor, the vulnerable, and the remote in improved services, official development assistance should be targeted within countries to programs that benefit the poorest. Subsidies should focus on access rather than consumption and should help to attract rather than take the place of community and private resources. Grant-based aid should never go to projects that will primarily benefit the middle- and upper-income groups. For low- and middle-income countries, actors at the international level can play a pivotal role as advocates, catalysts, mobilizers of international support, and sources of additional resources. The framework for this support must be national development planning and budgeting processes that focus on achieving the Millennium Development Goals. There is also a particular need for financial instruments that protect countries from risks, such as adverse currency movements.

Ten critical actions

Meeting the water and sanitation target and optimizing water resources for the Millennium Development Goals by 2015 will require a dramatic scaling-up of efforts—dramatic in terms of both the extent of action required and the speed with which these actions must be undertaken. The financial, governance, and

Scaling-up service delivery in the poorest countries will require unprecedented short-term action

capacity constraints low-income countries face will make this a complicated challenge. Scaling-up service delivery in the poorest countries will require unprecedented short-term action, as well as a focus on building the management systems needed to implement large-scale programs over the medium term and to sustain the gains made over the long term. It will also require a departure from "business as usual" on the part of all key actors, and new approaches that center on decentralization, transparency in budgetary allocations, and massive capacity-building efforts right down to the village level. This dramatic scaling-up of efforts that meeting the ambitious Millennium Development Goals and targets entails will require very significant investments, both in infrastructure and in institutional strengthening and reform, as well as at least ten complementary actions necessary to underpin them. These ten actions can be crystallized as follows:

Action 1. Governments and other stakeholders must move the sanitation crisis to the top of the agenda.

"Water supply and sanitation," occasionally joined by "hygiene," are words that often appear together in speeches and pronouncements, and indeed this trio belongs together as a cornerstone of public health, as well as social and economic well-being. Sanitation and hygiene, however, somehow disappear during the planning, policymaking, budgeting, and implementation phases, while the lion's share of effort and resources are allocated to water supply. This needs to change: sanitation and hygiene promotion need to move "front and center" rather than continuing as add-ons to water supply. They are key to development with dignity.

Fundamentally, advocates and sector professionals must not be afraid to tell the plain, ugly truth about what really happens—namely, open defecation. That 42 percent of the world's people lack what virtually all readers of this report take for granted—a toilet—is a travesty with devastating impacts on peoples' daily lives, health, and self-respect; we should not be afraid to say so. Here, lessons from the successes in galvanizing global support for the HIV/AIDS epidemic are important; only when policymakers, civil society groups, and the woman and man on the street started speaking openly about how HIV spreads (mainly sexual contact) and how to stop it (condoms, monogamy) did rates of new infection start to decline.

In many cases, countries must approach the challenge of improving sanitation service with different strategies than those employed to expand access to water supply. Expanding sanitation depends not just on building latrines, but also on understanding what motivates people to act in certain ways, and then finding ways to capitalize on those motivations. Mobilization, education, communication, and social marketing, aimed at households, communities, schools, and public authorities are key. The focus needs to be on decisions and investments made at the household and community levels, rather than on

Having a leadership role in community management of water supplies can increase women's social capital

installation of hardware. More and different types of people need to be pulled into this effort, including NGOs, women's groups, religious organizations, schools, youth groups, small-scale service providers, and local entrepreneurs; indeed, many "traditional" sanitation service providers will need to create space for more actors to enter, influence, and support the market.

Innovation, pragmatism, and, above all, community solidarity and mobilization must be brought to bear to find local solutions that respond to local needs in an affordable and effective manner. Design of sanitation facilities must respond to user preferences, beliefs, and practices; demand for different technical options; motivations for change; and capacity to maintain facilities in the long term. As in all sound marketing practice, sanitation promotion should take into account the distinct needs and preferences of different consumer groups, such as women and children.

Given the enormous ground to be covered to meet the sanitation target, the hallmarks of sanitation strategies should be maximum scalability, minimum transactions costs, full financial accountability, and closed revenue cycles, along with technical feasibility and operational and environmental sustainability.

Action 2. Countries must ensure that policies and institutions for water supply and sanitation service delivery, as well as for water resources management and development, respond equally to the different roles, needs, and priorities of women and men.

Gender differences and inequalities are fundamental to all efforts aimed at improving water supply, sanitation, and water resources management. Because they shoulder the lion's share of domestic responsibilities, women and girls suffer disproportionately when water supply and sanitation services are deficient. Across virtually all cultures, women have a greater need than men for facilities that are safe, private, and near their homes. In water resources management and development, women and men often have different priorities; women, for instance, often prioritize water for domestic use and household gardens, while men want water for irrigating cash crops. Women's relative access to and control over water (and other key resources linked to water, such as land, credit, and extension services), as well as gender biases within public institutions, greatly affect the degree to which women can take part in and benefit from water management and development schemes.

Addressing this reality is critical for the effectiveness and sustainability of water and sanitation interventions. In addition, community action and social mobilization around the provision of basic social services like water have been shown to be a valuable entry point for promoting women's empowerment. Having a leadership role in community management of water supplies, for instance, can increase women's social capital as well as their bargaining power within the household. Priority should be given to policies that capitalize on the potential synergy between the water and sanitation target and the gender equality Goal.

This focus on service delivery should also extend to monitoring systems

Action 3. Governments and donor agencies must simultaneously pursue investment and reforms.

Meeting the water and sanitation target by 2015 will require a dramatic scaling up of efforts—dramatic in terms of both the extent of action required and the speed with which these actions must be undertaken. Waiting for reforms to be implemented before making the necessary investments will make it impossible to meet the 2015 deadline. Over the past decade, donors have often made funding for infrastructure and service delivery contingent upon capacity building and institutional reform. However, in a number of cases, the acquired skills atrophied before the investments materialized, or the "reforms" were merely cosmetic. In other cases, expected official development assistance or funding from private-sector investment in service delivery following institutional reform never appeared. Allowing reforms and investments to take place simultaneously, which some call "learning by doing," will help address the tension between the desire to have reforms in place before investments and meet the Millennium Development Goals by the deadline of 2015. It will also ensure that reforms are grounded in reality. This parallel approach could be made contingent upon a credible program of investments and a commitment (at the highest level) to simultaneous reforms.

Action 4. Efforts to reach the water and sanitation target must focus on sustainable service delivery, rather than construction of facilities alone.

The Millennium Development Goals necessarily focus on measurable targets, such as the proportion of people without access to water supply and sanitation. It is important to remember, however, that water supply and sanitation are services, not simply facilities. The former is a process—requiring the sustained involvement of government, service providers, and households—while the latter is a product that can be delivered in a one-off project. Adopting a service orientation requires attention to financial flows and institutional arrangements for operations and maintenance, as well as incentives for providing safe, reliable services to all customers (including the poor) on a continuing basis. This approach is being contemplated in Brazil, where government has proposed subsidizing service for the poor contingent not on the provision of physical infrastructure, but rather on the supply of reliable service.

This focus on service delivery should also extend to monitoring systems. Monitoring and assessment systems for access to water supply and sanitation services need to be active and adequately resourced from the sub-national to the international level. These systems need to employ valid and reliable measures of access to water supply and sanitation services. More specifically:

- Access to services, rather than to infrastructure, should be at the center of monitoring efforts. The parameters that matter most to users—including the convenience, reliability, sustainability, and adequacy of water supply and sanitation services—should be measured over time, as should equity of access by women and the poor.

Water supply and sanitation service delivery should be managed at the lowest appropriate level

- Monitoring systems should employ a sample survey approach.
- Collected data should be shared in user-friendly formats with NGOs, civic groups, and the public at large, as well as with national and international institutions.

Action 5. Governments and donor agencies must empower local authorities and communities with the authority, resources, and professional capacity required to manage water supply and sanitation service delivery.
Water supply and sanitation service delivery should be managed at the lowest appropriate level; however, this devolution of responsibility must be accompanied by corresponding devolution of financial resources and authority, as well as the provision of technical and managerial support to build local capacity.

Decentralization of authority and responsibility to local institutions that lack the requisite technical, managerial, or financial capacity and authority for planning and service delivery can hinder, rather than accelerate, the expansion of sustainable services. Partnerships with local businesses, women's organizations, and other NGOs can be used to help build capacity in local governments and move the service-expansion agenda forward. Civic organizations can help promote accountability through facilitation of information dissemination and citizens' exercise of voice and demand for services. Also important is the careful balance of authority between local institutions and the center—for example, with respect to setting standards and subsidy policies—so that the interests of low-income households are protected. Central governments should take explicit measures to ensure that decentralization of service provision is not captured by local elites; it should rather create incentives for local governments to serve the poor.

There are strong links between local government reform and reforms in water supply and sanitation sectors. The provision of water supply and sanitation services can, in some instances, be pivotal for strengthening local governments. It can also provide an effective entry point for women's participation (action 2) in local political processes, particularly when the equal representation of women in water management is a design feature of programs and policies. An emphasis on service provision (action 4) implies a greater focus on ongoing management, which depends upon effective local institutions.

Action 6. Governments and utilities must ensure that users who can pay do pay in order to fund the maintenance and expansion of services—but they must also ensure that the needs of poor households are met.
Only service providers that have adequate funds can operate and maintain present systems properly and establish the creditworthiness needed to support service expansion. Closing the revenue gap depends both on reducing costs and increasing revenues. Improving revenue collection can often be achieved simply by charging for what is delivered and collecting bills in a timely manner. Households and communities are capable of making responsible decisions

The financial burden of serving the poor cannot be borne by the poor alone

about investments in sustainable water supply and sanitation, and will pay for them if service providers can be held responsible and accountable for the quality of the service they provide. In fact, willingness to charge by governments and service providers is often the limiting factor for adequate revenue generation and resource mobilization. Governments must set an example in their communities by paying their own water bills promptly and in full.

At the same time, governments must recognize that the financial burden of serving the poor cannot be borne by the poor alone. Some poor families and communities simply cannot pay for water supply and sanitation services; carefully targeted subsides for this group are essential. Where the needs of the poor are not being met because available public resources are being captured by the rich and powerful, appropriate reforms must be implemented. Community-based financing or microfinancing may be a starting point, building a domestic financing system in the process. Governments can also develop financial models for support to nongovernmental and community-based organizations, which can often deliver services at lower costs.

In many areas without access to improved services, however, the financial resources for meeting the Millennium Development Goals must come from outside the communities concerned. Part of the additional funding must come from those already served, using appropriate cross-subsidies; part may come from national income redistribution mechanisms; and part from international donors. In general, subsidizing access (connections in network systems, for example) has proved to be a more transparent way of targeting the poor as compared to subsidizing consumption (for example, monthly bills). In addition, even in the poorest communities beneficiaries can typically contribute to the costs of improved service through various forms of in-kind contributions. Such contributions engender a sense of ownership necessary for sustainability.

It is also critical to recognize that financial sustainability for water supply and sanitation systems requires discipline within national-level budgeting processes. No system should be built unless it is known how it will be financed—not just the initial capital investment, but also the costs of operation and maintenance. Budgeting processes in general also need to become more transparent. Reduction of corruption at all levels, including in the donor organizations and international agencies, is key.

Action 7. Within the context of national poverty reduction strategies based on the Millennium Development Goals, countries must elaborate coherent water resources development and management plans that will support the achievement of the Goals.

Acting on this recommendation clearly requires that there is a coherent poverty reduction strategy in place from which a water resources development and management plan can be derived. Ideally, an integrated water resources management strategy based on the Goals will entail:

Innovation in institutional and financial mechanisms could accelerate progress

- An assessment of the nature of a country's freshwater supply from all sources (both surface and groundwater), taking into account such key factors as the infrastructure already in place for water abstraction, the water available from shared sources, variability in time and space, and water quality.
- An assessment of the nature of the demand for water resources to meet poverty, hunger, health, and environmental sustainability Goals.
- A coordinated process to reconcile the supply and demand for water resources, one which conforms broadly to the recommendations from the Johannesburg Summit regarding the preparation of integrated water resources management and water efficiency plans by 2005.
- A coherent strategy for the implementation of such plans.

Action 8. Governments and their civil society and private sector partners must support a wide range of water and sanitation technologies and service levels that are technically, socially, environmentally, and financially appropriate.

Supporting a broad range of technological choices allows communities to install the water supply and sanitation infrastructure that they want, are willing to pay for, and can maintain in the long term; it can also lower per capita costs, thus permitting limited resources to bring service to more households. Hand pumps, improved wells, rainwater harvesting, locally designed latrines, installations using volunteer labor, community maintenance, and the promotion of small-scale independent service providers are examples of "lower-tech" approaches that may be particularly relevant and cost-effective for many rural and periurban areas. In some urban settlements, small, locally operated water supply and sanitation systems may be less expensive to construct and maintain than large, centralized systems.

Encouraging the development and use of a range of technologies and services levels helps to resolve the tension between the need for a swift scaling-up of services to meet the 2015 target and the aim of sustaining the gains made over the long term. One-size-fits-all approaches necessarily mean that some households and communities end up getting the "wrong" services, namely, those that are not technically feasible, socioculturally appropriate, or affordable for users, or that are simply not the types of services that users want. A failure to respond to user preferences and circumstances all but guarantees an eventual failure of the services themselves.

Action 9. Institutional, financial, and technological innovation must be promoted in strategic areas.

Innovation in institutional and financial mechanisms, as well as technological advances in key areas, could accelerate progress toward the water supply target, the sanitation target, and the Millennium Development Goals as a whole.

Innovation in financing systems, policies, institutions, and technologies is also needed to accelerate progress

To meet the water supply and sanitation targets, innovation is particularly needed in the financial, policy, and institutional arenas—such as service delivery systems that help service providers to ensure effective relationships with households and communities, to work with communities, households, local civil society, and private-sector partners, and to build capacity to innovate and adapt solutions. While most experts agree that a full complement of technologies is now available for safe, reliable water supply in almost any setting, progress toward the sanitation target is still constrained by the lack of technologies that are reliable and affordable enough to implement on a wide scale without having negative impacts on the environmental sustainability target. Technical advances in such areas as effective, affordable, and simple-to-operate sewage treatment plants that can be located close to residential areas; drainage and solid waste disposal; and urban wastewater treatment and management in large urban agglomerations should therefore be promoted and accelerated.

Innovation in financing systems, policies, institutions, and technologies is also needed to accelerate progress toward the Millennium Development Goals as a whole. Win-win technical and institutional systems that advance more than one Goal simultaneously, rather than achieve one goal at the expense of another, are particularly needed. Examples include mechanisms to improve crop per drop and thus both spur progress toward the hunger Goal and reduce the demand for water; and programs for the reuse of waste water in agriculture, which could contribute to both the sanitation and hunger targets.

Action 10. The United Nations system organizations and their member states must ensure that the UN system and its international partners provide strong and effective support for the achievement of the water supply and sanitation target and for water resources management and development.

UN organizations, together with their international partners (including international water and sanitation networks and partnerships), must strengthen both their ability to assist and the level of their assistance to countries to meet target 10 and to optimize water resources management and development. This will contribute to the corresponding goal and targets directly and also to all other Millennium Development Goals. Doing so will require that financing, technical support, capacity building, objective analysis, knowledge-sharing, global monitoring and evaluation, and advocacy functions are effectively aligned toward the achievement of the Millennium Development Goals. United Nations system organizations involved in water and sanitation and their Member States must therefore ensure that the UN system organizations engaged in such functions have, both individually and collectively, the organizational capacity, mandate, staffing, and resources needed to carry out these functions, and to provide leadership and strategic guidance to the international community in these areas.

UN organizations must strengthen their ability to assist and the level of their assistance

The United Nations system organizations and their member states involved in water supply and sanitation and in water resources development and management should take the following actions:

- *At the country level,* the UN Country Teams should strengthen their efforts to provide technical and capacity-building support to governments, including in the preparation of national MDG-based strategies for water supply and sanitation and for integrated water resources management and water efficiency. UN organizations, development banks, and bilateral donor agencies must also effectively coordinate their actions at the country level, including harmonization of procedures and joint programs.

- *At the global level,* provision of leadership and strategic guidance to the international community is essential. UN system organizations and key operational actors and others involved in water and sanitation must be involved in this through a clear mechanism, which should build on each organization's strengths and comparative advantages and reduce duplication. UN-Water—with its recently defined mandate and widened participation—should be developed to this end. The WHO/UNICEF Joint Monitoring Programme should be strengthened as the key global mechanism for monitoring access to water supply and sanitation and provided with greater funding. WHO and UNICEF should ensure that arrangements increasingly enable contribution to and participation in the JMP. Bilateral agencies should both provide more funding and refrain from setting up parallel structures. UN-Water should be mandated to periodically report, through the *World Water Development Report* (WWDR), hosted by UNESCO, on progress in water resources development and management for the Millennium Development Goals, including progress on the development of strategies for integrated water resources management and efficiency by 2005. UN-Water and WWDR must be strengthened and provided with greater funding to fulfill these roles successfully.

The recently established Secretary-General's Advisory Board on Water and Sanitation should focus on providing high-level policy commentary on progress toward the water and sanitation target, advising on strategic direction, identifying critical obstacles to progress, and making recommendations for overcoming them. It should independently and boldly comment on developing country, donor country, and UN system practices; and produce a periodic, brief, focused, high-profile report that would eschew advocacy in favor of pointed recommendations aimed at improving progress within the sector and at advancing the sector's position in the development arena.

The global networks engaged in water and sanitation with the funding agencies supporting must collectively strengthen and rationalize their efforts to provide technical support, capacity-building, objective analysis, knowledge-sharing, and advocacy functions, and align those functions towards the achievement of the Millennium Development Goals, while at the same time, taking steps to ensure they are accountable to the communities of the developing world.

Chapter 14

An operational plan

The 5 guiding principles and 10 actions presented in chapter 13 represent, in broad strokes, the vital conditions needed both to achieve the Millennium Development Goals for water supply and sanitation and to ensure that sound water resources development and management underpins the broader effort to reach all of the Millennium Development targets. These principles and actions are further elaborated in this chapter within an operational plan that specifies the steps that each actor—national and subnational governments, donors, civic and community organizations, and research institutions—must undertake in support of the goals. Although the operational plan focuses only on actions by actors in the water sector, investments in other sectors, such as health and education, are crucial to the achievement of the water and sanitation targets. As stressed in previous chapters, progress in eradicating extreme poverty and hunger, achieving universal primary education, promoting gender equality, empowering women, and ensuring environmental sustainability will all help in advancing progress toward the Millennium Development targets for water and sanitation.

Operational plans for national and subnational governments, donors, civic and community organizations, and research institutions, respectively, are outlined in tables 14.1–14.7. In each table, entries in the action plan have been categorized into immediate priorities, short-term priorities, and medium-term priorities.

- *National and subnational governments.* National governments have principal responsibility for initiating the planning procedures and policy reforms, as well as for committing the financial and human resources, necessary to achieve the Millennium Development Goals. In addition, efforts by other stakeholder groups are often contingent upon strong initial action by national governments. The proposed operational plan should therefore be spearheaded by the actions that have to be taken by national governments, as outlined in table 14.1. Since some actions,

There is still time for the world as a whole to meet target 10— but only just

such as setting of standards for water and sanitation technologies, are carried out at the national level in some countries and at the subnational level in others, we have grouped these actions together in this table, on the assumption that they would be assigned to the responsible parties within a given country. Actions that are typically exclusive to national governments, such as the carrying out of national planning processes, have been noted with an asterisk.

- *Bilateral and multilateral development assistance agencies, regional development banks, and donor agencies and countries.* As stressed in chapter 13, the task force is unanimous in its belief that target 10 will not be reached unless there is a deliberate commitment by donors to increase and refocus their development assistance and to target sufficient aid to the poorest low-income countries. If the target is to be reached, therefore, fundamental changes by the bilateral and multilateral development agencies, regional development banks, and donor agencies and countries will be required, as detailed in table 14.2.
- *The United Nations system.* As emphasized in previous chapters, the United Nations system organizations and their member states must ensure that the UN system with its international partners provide strong and effective support for the achievement of the water supply and sanitation target and for water resources management and development. The actions that have to be taken by the United Nations system organizations and their member states are outlined in table 14.3.
- *Other national and international actors.* The actions to be undertaken by other key actors—service providers, civic and community organizations, international networks and partnerships, and research organizations—are outlined in tables 14.4–14.7.

Other important actions that should be undertaken by all actors on a continual basis—both during the Millennium Development process and beyond—are identified in table 14.8.

The task force recommends that all organizations engaged in the effort to achieve the Millennium Development Goals—from national and subnational governments to donors and NGOs—should themselves prepare an operational plan to focus their support on the achievement of the Goals. The Water Supply and Sanitation Collaborative Council, for instance, has undertaken such an exercise.

There is still time for the world as a whole to meet target 10—but only just. 2005 is a critical year; it must be the start of a decade of bold action and swift progress. If the global community fails to act urgently, target 10 will be nothing more than a broken promise, another missed opportunity. But if stakeholders at the community, national, and international levels can join together in this common cause, the heartbreakingly simple dream of safe water to drink and private, clean sanitation to use can become a reality for literally

Table 14.1

Priority actions for national and subnational governments

To reach target 10

Immediate priority actions	Short-term priority actions	Medium-term priority actions
• Ensure that water supply and sanitation are included in national planning processes, especially poverty reduction strategies. • Undertake assessments of water and sanitation infrastructure endowments and deficits. • Create a national-level "institutional home" for sanitation. • Obtain current, accurate information about the characteristics of unserved households, so that appropriate policies to expand access to these households are pursued. • Review and modify subsidy policies as necessary to ensure that improved water and sanitation services are affordable to the poor, and subsidies are provided only to low-income households. • Prioritize activities and programs that raise the profile of and demand for improved sanitation.	• Monitor changes over time to gauge the effectiveness of interventions and the impact of policy reforms and investments at national and subnational levels. • Ensure that appropriate, flexible standards for water, sanitation, and wastewater treatment technologies are in place. • Initiate policy reforms that improve the financial and technical sustainability of water and sanitation service provision, such as tariff reforms, "ring fencing," and adequate support for ongoing operations and maintenance. • Initiate policy reforms to attract financing to and facilitate efficient use of human and financial resources in water and sanitation service delivery. • Initiate policy reforms that improve the accountability of service providers, such as the establishment and funding of credible regulatory institutions, reform of civil-service legislation, and limiting political interference in decisionmaking.	• Monitor changes over time to gauge the effectiveness of interventions and the impact of policy reforms and investments at national and subnational levels. • Remove barriers to service provision in unregularized areas. • Shift principal control over water and sanitation planning and service delivery to local administrations, including budgetary authority. • Support decentralization by retaining strong oversight and support functions, particularly with respect to ensuring access to services by poor households. • Provide funding to support community mobilization and organization for actions towards the water and sanitation targets.

To improve water resources management for all the Goals

Immediate priority actions	Short-term priority actions	Medium-term priority actions
• Support Goals-based planning and policy development by an integrated approach to land, water, and ecosystems. • Use the action target set by World Summit on Sustainable Development in Johannesburg for countries to develop integrated water resources management and water efficiency strategies by 2005 as an opportunity to infuse Goals-planning processes with consideration of water resources. • Develop a coherent approach toward deciding on the investments in water resources infrastructure and management needed to meet the Millennium Development Goals.	• Monitor changes over time to gauge the effectiveness of interventions and the impact of policy reforms and investments at national and subnational levels. • Define and promote strategies that will contribute to multiple Goals and avoid strategies that create conflicts among them.	• Monitor changes over time to gauge the effectiveness of interventions and the impact of policy reforms and investments at national and subnational levels. • Disseminate small-scale water technologies to provide livelihoods to small and landless farmers, while addressing the hunger and environment Goals. • Reduce the vulnerability of communities to water-related natural disasters by land reform, infrastructure construction for water storage and flood protection, and improved land-use planning, including slum upgrading. • Invest in community-based natural resource management, including urban agriculture, for hunger, poverty, and environment Goals.

Table 14.2 Priority actions for bilateral and multilateral development assistance agencies	Immediate priority actions	Short-term priority actions	Medium-term priority actions
	• Increase current aid in the water and sanitation sector to levels commensurate with the costs of attaining the water and sanitation target in the poorest countries. • Redirect aid to the poorest countries and, within countries, toward programs that provide basic services for poor households. • Prioritize investments in basic sanitation and hygiene. • Reform aid procedures, so that aid supports policy reforms and infrastructure investment simultaneously, thereby enhancing institutional and policy frameworks while expanding services. • Increase funding to Joint Monitoring Programme and refrain from setting up parallel structures.	• Substantially accelerate the process for making aid available, and simplify the procedures for allocating aid. • Prioritize investments in programs that help "crowd in" community and private resources to benefit the poor, as well as initiatives that have the potential to yield results at scale. • Use the upcoming second Water Decade, 2005–15 ("Water for Life"), to mobilize international awareness and political commitment to sound water resources management and expansion of water and sanitaiton services to meet the Millennium Development Goals.	• Support initiatives that seek to encourage more open and frank discussion of sanitation needs and practices. • Promote and finance research and development that fosters innovations in appropriate technologies, social marketing, and institutional arrangements that improve access to water and sanitation services by the poor. • Promote initiatives that address multiple Millennium Development Goals. • Support, where useful, the creation of new, regional-level multilateral donor mechanisms such as the African Water Facility.

Table 14.3 Priority actions for the United Nations system	Immediate priority actions	Short-term priority actions	Medium-term priority actions
	• Strengthen UN country team efforts to provide technical and capacity-building support to governments. • Effectively coordinate actions at the country level, including harmonization of procedures and joint programs, both within the UN system and with development banks and bilateral donor agencies. • Support the Joint Monitoring Programme as the key global mechanism for monitoring sustainable access to water and sanitation and provide it with the necessary resources to carry out its work.	• Expand monitoring efforts to include information on the actions and investments undertaken by the international community toward meeting the Goals, as well as on the impacts of those activities. • Use the upcoming second Water Decade, 2005–15 ("Water for Life"), to mobilize international awareness and political commitment to sound water resources management and expansion of water and sanitation services to meet the Millennium Development Goals. • Ensure the independence and adequate funding of the Advisory Board on Water and Sanitation as a means of achieving high-level strategic focus among the international community. • Focus the Secretary-General's Advisory Board on Water and Sanitation on providing high-level policy commentary on progress toward the water and sanitation target. • Ask the Secretary General's Advisory Board on Water and Sanitation to comment independently and boldly on developing country, donor country, and UN system practices, and produce a periodic, brief, focused, high-profile report with pointed recommendations.	• Develop clear mechanism to provide leadership and strategic guidance to the international community. • Mandate UN-Water to periodically report through *World Water Development Report* on progress in water resources development and management for the Goals, including progress on the development of integrated water resources management strategies by 2005. • Strengthen UN-Water and *World Water Development Report* and provide with greater funding to fulfill these roles successfully. • Reform monitoring systems such that they measure access to sustainable services, rather than the presence of particular infrastructure. • Support the use of scientific sampling and household surveys for water and sanitation monitoring. • Ensure that data collected in global monitoring are widely disseminated in "user friendly" formats. • Support initiatives that seek to encourage more open and frank discussion of sanitation needs and practices.

Table 14.4 Priority actions for service providers	Immediate priority actions	Short-term priority actions	Medium-term priority actions
	• Support and lobby for policy reforms in water and sanitation subsidies, so that benefits are targeted to poor households. • Support and lobby for policy reforms in water and sanitation tariffs, so that service provision becomes financially sustainable.	• Seek out opportunities for partnerships with civic organizations that can improve access to water and sanitation services by poor households. • Revise budgets and institutional incentive structures, so that sustainable operations and maintenance of installed infrastructure receives sufficient priority and resources.	• Pursue innovative strategies, including lower cost appropriate technologies, to expand services to unregularized settlements.

Table 14.5 Priority actions for civic and community organizations	Immediate priority actions	Short-term priority actions	Medium-term priority actions
	• Prioritize activities and programs that raise the profile of and demand for improved sanitation. • Use accurate information—the end product of reliable monitoring efforts—as a powerful advocacy tool for change.	• Develop strategies for encouraging more open and frank discussion of sanitation needs and practices. • Seek out opportunities for partnerships with service providers that improve access to water and sanitation services by poor households. • Share information and experiences with service providers, as well as with subnational and national governments, seeking to better understand the characteristics of and obstacles faced by unserved households.	• Help to hold service providers and governments accountable for expanding and improving water and sanitation services to the poor through audits, public information campaigns, etc. • Help to identify strategies for ensuring access to services by poor households while also maintaining financial sustainability for service providers.

Table 14.6 Priority actions for international networks and partnerships	Immediate priority actions	Short-term priority actions	Medium-term priority actions
	• Raise public awareness of the deficits in coverage and quality of water supply and sanitation services through public statements, articles, events, celebrity endorsements, and other innovative strategies. • Test, refine, and publicize effective strategies for water and sanitation service delivery to the poor that have the potential to yield results at scale. • Collectively strengthen and rationalize efforts and align them towards the achievement of the Goals while at the same time taking steps to ensure accountability to the communities of the developing world. • Use accurate information— the end product of reliable monitoring efforts—as a powerful advocacy tool for change.	• Use the upcoming second Water Decade, 2005–15 ("Water for Life"), to mobilize international awareness and political commitment to sound water resources management and expansion of water and sanitation services to meet the Millennium Development Goals. • Publicly support policy reforms that better target subsidies to poor households, promote sustainability of service delivery, and heighten accountability of service providers to households. • Support initiatives that seek to encourage more open and frank discussion of sanitation needs and practices.	• Help to hold service providers and governments accountable for expanding and improving water and sanitation services to the poor through audits, public information campaigns, etc. • Package and disseminate information collected in national and international monitoring efforts such that it is accessible to community organizations, the media, and the general public. • Explore ways to use the new UN ECOSOC affirmation of the Right to Water to influence national policy on water and sanitation.

Table 14.7	Immediate priority actions	Short-term priority actions	Medium-term priority actions
Priority actions for research organizations	• Better document and communicate the economic benefits of improved water and sanitation services.	• Support the development of appropriate technical standards for water supply, sewerage, and sewage treatment.	• Carry out research and development of appropriate, affordable sanitation technologies.
	• Conduct research and disseminate findings on effective strategies for providing sustainable water supply and sanitation services in persistently challenging settings (unregularized urban communities, small towns, poor rural villages).	• Increase research and development on technologies and institutional innovations aimed at meeting several Goals simultaneously and reducing tradeoffs among the uses of water resources to meet the various Goals.	
		• Develop new sanitation technologies to reuse wastewater for periurban agriculture.	
		• Develop a conceptual framework for defining and measuring the contribution of water resources development and management to the Millennium Development Goals.	

Table 14.8	
Priority actions for all actors throughout the Millennium Development process and beyond	• Prepare an operational plan that outlines what they will do during the period 2005–15 to help achieve target 10 and the development and management of water resources for the Millennium Development Goals.
	• Maintain a focus on sustainability to ensure that gains made in expanding access to water and sanitation services and improving water resources management during the Millennium Development process will be maintained in the long term.
	• Incorporate gender considerations into policy recommendations and program design; address gender biases within their own institutions. Take measures to reduce corruption at all levels, whether in donor organizations, international agencies or companies, or public, private, or civic institutions in developing countries.
	• Take measures to reduce corruption at all levels, whether in donor organizations, international agencies or companies, or public, private, or civic institutions in developing countries.

Insights from case studies

This appendix briefly describes some case studies that have been mentioned in the report to guide the strategies for achieving target 10. These case studies demonstrate a variety of approaches that appear to be working. They include community management of rural water and sanitation projects, improvements in service for the urban poor, and increasing urban coverage for both the poor and the nonpoor. We will, however, start with a case that shows what is being done to reach the water target.

Turning the "right to water" into a reality: the South African experience

This case study illustrates the importance of political will in introducing a radical policy of free access to basic water supply, thereby helping South Africa to make rapid progress toward the Millennium Development target for water (drawn from World Bank 2002).

In 1994, 15.2 million out of South Africa's population of 40 million lacked access to basic water supply (defined as 25 liters per person per day of water of acceptable quality within 200 meters from home). Of these, 12 million lived in rural areas. In addition, 20.5 million lacked access to basic sanitation (defined as a ventilated, improved pit latrine or its equivalent). South Africa has used a combination of instruments to turn things around. These include introduction of policy reform with an accompanying legislative framework; devolution of responsibility for water supply and sanitation from the national level to local governments, using community-based approaches; launching of a capital works program that has provided infrastructure to meet the needs of more than 7 million people; and the introduction of free access to basic water supply, through which water has been provided for some 27 million people as of July 1, 2002. As a result, South Africa hopes that within seven more years all residents would have access to basic water supply.

This remarkable success in increasing access to basic water supply has been underpinned by a strong political leadership and support from the national government, which made it possible to devote so much funds to support the capital works program and the free basic water policy. An important contributory factor has been the existence of a very substantial institutional and technical capacity that was already in place before 1994. The existence of an appropriate institutional framework facilitated the introduction of legislation needed for the program. Finally, the level of economic development in South Africa supported the policy of free access to basic water. This case is not necessarily applicable to less developed countries, unless they benefit from new and creative concessional funding from external sources.

Community-led total sanitation with no subsidies: a spreading revolution

Community-led total sanitation is a revolutionary low-cost approach to rural sanitation, which relies on hands-off facilitation and community appraisal, analysis, and action, without any subsidy for hardware. In a matter of often only weeks, communities transform themselves from open defecation to total sanitation. Community-led total sanitation is spreading in Bangladesh, India, and Cambodia, and is starting in Indonesia, Mongolia, Nepal, Uganda, and Zambia. It shows potential to become an exponentially self-spreading movement.[1]

The methodology of community-led total sanitation by rural communities was pioneered in 2000 by Kamal Kar and colleagues with WaterAid and VERC, a nongovernmental organization (NGO) in Bangladesh. It spread there with support from CARE, PLAN, World Vision, other NGOs, and the government. The Water and Sanitation Program of the World Bank has been supporting and promoting community-led total sanitation in South and Southeast Asia. By mid-2004 community-led total sanitation had spread to more than 2,000 communities in Bangladesh, to several hundreds in India through the government of Maharashtra, and to Cambodia through Concern Worldwide. Starts had also been made in Indonesia, Mongolia, Nepal, Uganda, and Zambia. The impact has been dramatic drops in diarrheas and medical expenditures and major gains in well-being for women, children, and men.

In community-led total sanitation community members are facilitated to do their own appraisal of open defecation. Facilitators do not teach, educate, advise, criticize, preach, or tell people what they should do. They simply convene and facilitate appraisal and analysis. Community members together map their households and where they defecate. They then stand, smell, and discuss in their defecation areas; calculate the amounts of feces produced; analyze pathways of contamination through dirt, flies, and animals; and estimate how much each person ingests each day. Disgust, shame, religious precepts for cleanliness, and self-respect then commonly combine in a decision that open defecation must stop. People dig holes and construct homemade pit latrines according to local designs. To achieve total sanitation quickly, some latrines are shared. Those who are better off often help the poorer and landless with space and materials. Communities put up boards at the entrances to their villages proclaiming proudly that they are totally sanitized. The resulting social solidarity provides a base for further collective action. Communities evolve their own systems of monitoring and penalties for default. A social ratchet effect evidently sustains total sanitation once it has been established through such a process.

There are no standard designs. An explosion of innovative, low-cost models designed by community engineers has taken place. Many people start with very simple temporary structures of bamboo, sacking, and the like. In Bangladesh the cost of purchased materials can be less than $1. Progressive improvements then follow. Some start higher on the sanitation ladder and construct toilets in their houses. Local traders meet new demands for pans and accessories. Latrines are evacuated when full or are covered over and planted with trees, and new latrines are dug or constructed.

For community-led total sanitation to ignite, two conditions admit no compromise. First, there must be no policy, practice, or even rumor of subsidies for hardware. Community-led total sanitation has been inhibited and slowed by a national survey of sanitation, which led to expectations of subsidy. Community-led total sanitation cannot spread well, if at all, when there is hope of hardware subsidies. Second, facilitation by outsiders must be hands-off, enabling community members to do their own appraisal, calculations, and analysis, not prescribing but at most, when asked, telling them about practices in other communities. To ensure these behaviors requires careful hands-on training and mentoring.

Community-led total sanitation has been spread by not just by NGO facilitators but increasingly, with light external support, by community consultants and communities themselves. Community consultants have their own effective ways of facilitating, drawing on their experience of total sanitation in their own villages. Communities themselves have become lead institutions: CARE Bangladesh has pioneered a low-cost approach, also adopted by the government of Maharashtra, in which a community is rewarded for every other community totally sanitized through its efforts. Following the lead of Maharashtra, the government of India has changed its guidelines from providing an up-front hardware subsidy to households to offering a fiscal incentive of a lump sum to villages in which open defecation is assessed to have ended. Innovations such as these can be expected to continue as the approach expands in scale.

Community-led total sanitation presents many challenges. It demands shifts of mindset and policy as well as behavior:

- From teaching and educating to facilitating the communities' own analysis.
- From "we must subsidize the poor" to "communities can do it."
- From "we persuade and motivate" to "it's up to you, you decide."
- From top-down standardization to bottom-up diversity ("they design").
- From bigger budgets to lower budgets to allow more to be achieved.

For community-led total sanitation to realize its huge potential demands changes in mindsets and behaviors away from the standard philanthropic ("subsidize"), professional ("set high standards"), and bureaucratic ("demand big budgets") approaches. Instead, supporters concentrate on lower-cost training, facilitation, and support for community facilitators. If there are vested interests and ingrained practices, they have to be confronted. The challenge to those working in aid agencies, governments, and NGOs is to be consistent in making these big switches and to support sharing and learning across and within organizations and countries. It remains to be seen which organizations and who within them will have the vision, realism, and guts required. Continuous learning is needed about how and where spread occurs and how it can and should be supported. But enough is already known to see that if community-led total sanitation can become exponentially self-spreading, the scale of gains in well-being, for tens or hundreds of millions of rural people, will be enormous, and can make a major contribution to all the Millennium Development Goals.

From central to local government and community-based approaches to rural water supply: the experience in Ghana

This case study involved a shift from a supply-driven central government approach to a demand-driven approach to rural water supply and sanitation. It also involved a shift in the role of central government, from that of an implementer to that of a facilitator, with greater involvement of the private sector, thereby introducing competition with consequent improvement in performance and reduction in the cost of service provision (drawn from World Bank 2002).

It all started in 1990. Up to that time, one national public authority, the Ghana Water and Sewerage Corporation (GWSC), was responsible for water and sewerage services for both urban and rural areas throughout Ghana. During that period, most rural communities were served by boreholes equipped with hand-pumps. The boreholes were drilled by the GWSC, donors, or NGOs that also maintained them. There was only one private drilling company. The drilling market was characterized by lack of competition. As a result, the average cost of boreholes in Ghana was $9,000, compared with $3,000 in the United Kingdom or the United States. Mobile crews were responsible for the maintenance. In these circumstances, only about 40 percent of handpumps worked at any given time. There was no sense of ownership by the communities that were served by handpumps. So when handpumps broke down, people simply waited for them to be repaired when the mobile repair crew reached their communities. The situation was no better for piped systems that suffered long periods of supply interruptions because of breakdowns and maintenance neglect.

Beginning in the late 1980s, a number of institutional and policy reforms were introduced. New legislation was introduced under which the GWSC was replaced by the Ghana Water Company Limited (with responsibility for urban water supply) and the Community Water and Sanitation Agency (with responsibility for rural water and sanitation services). A new national water and sanitation policy was also introduced to shift the approach to service provision from a supply-driven one to a demand-responsive approach.

Under the new national policy, certain core functions were transferred from central government to the local government and the communities. Ownership of water supply was transferred to the local governments and the communities. The private sector became increasingly involved in various aspects of service provision. In one $20 million World Bank-financed community water and sanitation project implemented in 26 of the 110 districts in the country, district assemblies constructed 1,200 water points and 29 piped systems. There was a lot of private-sector and NGO involvement in the project. This included four drilling companies and 32 NGOs and community-based organizations. Several national and international NGOs were commissioned to train and build the capacities of the district-level NGOs and community-based organizations. The success of this project has led to a follow-up $80 million, nine-year World Bank-supported project. One of the aims of the new project is to shift from individual donor-supported water supply projects to a sectorwide approach under which all external support agencies would be encouraged to pull their resources into a single national water-sector program.

Several factors have helped to make this reform successful. Foremost was the speed of implementing the reform process. It was not rushed. Instead, a gradual approach was followed in the transfer of responsibility from the central level to the local government and community level. The transfer rate was matched to the rate of technical capacity building and support from the central level in the areas where local capacity was deficient. Second, the involvement of the private sector was accompanied by an incentive structure under which contractors were paid for their outputs rather than their inputs. Finally, the decentralization of service provision was facilitated by the general process of decentralization taking place within the country at the time.

Unbundling between different zones in an urban area: experience from Thailand

This case study shows how unbundling of service facilities can be used as an instrument for reducing the constraints of technologically complex, large-scale urban sewerage projects. The project in Bangkok also reduced the lumpiness of investments in urban sanitation, thereby removing barriers to access to urban sanitation services.

Bangkok, the capital of Thailand, is a city of 10 million people. In 1968, the Bangkok Metropolitan Administration prepared a wastewater master plan for the entire metropolitan area. Though technically sound, the plan was found to be prohibitively expensive and was shelved for 16 years. In 1984, the master plan was revised under a Japanese (JICA) technical assistance program. Instead of a single centralized program, the inner city was divided into ten sewerage zones, each with an independent collection and treatment system. The revised approach is an example of horizontal unbundling between different zones of an urban area. Sanitation investment in each of the ten zones is lower than the investment for a single project in the whole city. Each zone project is also technically simpler than the citywide project. These two impacts of unbundling have made it possible for the Bangkok Metropolitan Administration to implement various sanitation projects in different zones of the city, using a more affordable, phased investment program.

Unbundling, coupled with greater responsiveness to demand, helps to remove major barriers to the expansion of coverage. Yet they still do not address the question about where the boundary between public and private infrastructure should be drawn. Demand for improved sanitation is almost always based on perceived private benefits. These are much lower than the total benefits from citywide sanitation investments, which are known to include externalities or benefits that are realized beyond the boundaries of the direct user of sanitation services. Experiences in Pakistan and Brazil show how these issues have been addressed.

Reaching the urban poor with improved sanitation: the experience in Pakistan

This case study illustrates a tripartite partnership between community, government, and an NGO in the provision of improved sanitation services to a low-income urban fringe community. It also illustrates a stepwise approach to urban sanitation, in which the technology is adapted to the technical capacity and financial means of the beneficiary community. Its salient features include the use of such instruments as unbundling, community management with social intermediation, and internalizing the financing of community infrastructure for sanitation.

Orangi is a large *katchi abadi* (or low-income informal settlement) in Karachi. It has a population of more than 1 million. The Orangi Pilot Project (OPP) is a nongovernmental organization, and sanitation is one of four projects the NGO is undertaking in Orangi.

After years of research and learning by doing, the OPP has developed a model of low-cost sanitation in which government, the community, and the NGO are treated as partners, and sanitation development takes place at two levels: an "internal component" level and an "external component" level. The internal component has three sequential sanitation subcomponents: an in-house sanitary latrine or toilet, a lane sewer that collects sewage from houses along a lane in the community, and a neighborhood sewer that collects sewage from the lane sewers in a neighborhood. The last two subcomponents together are equivalent to what is known as a feeder sewerage system. The external component has two subcomponents: trunk sewers that collect sewage from neighborhood sewers and a sewage treatment plant for treatment and final disposal of the sewage from the trunk sewerage system. These two subcomponents may together be regarded as a trunk sewerage system.

The OPP sanitation project started with the NGO approaching the community and urging residents to form lane organizations and to elect a lane manager. Once this was done, technical support was provided to the lane organization to construct a lane sewer to collect waste from their houses. It had been hoped that the government would then step in and provide a sewer network to collect the sewage from the lane sewers. This did not happen. So the lane managers from each neighborhood came together and pooled their human and financial resources to construct neighborhood-level sewers to collect the wastes from the lane sewers.

Initially, the sewage from the neighborhood sewers was discharged into nearby natural drains. But eventually, the Karachi Municipal Corporation and the District Municipal Corporation agreed to finance the construction of a trunk sewer to collect the waste from the neighborhood sewer. This meant that there was a transitional period during which the untreated sewage from the Orangi community polluted the local environment. However, this was corrected when the public component of the sewerage system was installed. Without the price of the transitional environmental pollution, the community would not have gained access to basic sanitation, and the environmental pollution would have continued all the same through other means.

According to S. Akbaar Zaidi, the OPP model has been replicated in 59 settlements in 11 cities (Zaidi 2000). It has also been reported that the principles of the model are being applied to projects in Nepal, Central Asia, South Africa, and Sri Lanka (Hasan 2000).

The OPP model allows for vertical unbundling between the internal and the external sewer components, as well as horizontal unbundling between parallel neighborhoods. A feature of the OPP model is that the normal boundary between private and public provision is extended from the household level to embrace the entire neighborhood. That is to say, the neighborhood sanitation infrastructure is a public facility that is privately and collectively owned by those in the neighborhood. Thus, its ownership is private, but its use is public. Under this arrangement, investment and operational responsibility within the neighborhood is now treated as internal development and is left to the community. The responsibility for investment, operation, and maintenance beyond the neighborhood is treated as an external responsibility and is assigned to the public utility.

This definition of what is private and what is public has a number of attractive features. The entity that expresses demand to the public utility is not the household; it is the community. This reduces the number of respondents for demand assessment, thereby reducing the transactions cost for such assessments. Furthermore, this definition makes it possible for the neighborhood to be used as the channel for expressing the "voice" of households, thereby giving the households bargaining powers. In addition, the definition expands the responsibility for financing of private infrastructure beyond the household level. Financing of infrastructure within the neighborhood is thus internalized.

Another feature of the approach is that it defines a clear set of target groups that would serve as partners, along with social intermediaries, in the internal development of sanitation projects. A similar definition of the private-public boundary has also been used in the Brasilia condominial model.

A community-based approach to urban sanitation: the condominial model in Brazil

This case study illustrates a shift from conventional sewerage technology to a technically equivalent, lower-cost alternative known as the condominial system. The lower cost arises from the use of sound technical standards based on current scientific and technical research, as well as current experience and innovation, rather than a reliance on the 100-year-old concepts inherent in conventional sewerage. Community participation is an integral part of the project, as is the joint ownership of community resources, such as the sewerage system within a condominial block. This feature of unbundling is analogous to ownership of neighborhood-level sanitation infrastructure in the OPP model.

Brasilia's model for supplying sanitation services to its 2 million residents is the latest version of the condominial sewerage system. Developed in the 1980s in the state of Rio Grande do Norte by Jose Carlos Melo for low-income communities, the system has now become a standard solution for entire urban areas in Brazil, irrespective of residential income. The Water and Sewerage Company of Brasilia has been using this version of the condominial system for more than 10 years. Within the first 8 years, 121,000 homes were linked to the condominial system, using 1,300 kilometers of condominial branches and more than 660 kilometers of public networks at average costs per person of $27 and per meter of sewer network of $16.

The basic planning unit in this model is the condominium. It is defined as the urban block, square, or its equivalent. The residents of a condominium define its boundaries. They do so through an informal community organization. It is this block or condominium that is connected to the public sewer. This is in contrast to conventional sewerage systems, where connection to the public sewer is made directly to the individual house, a more costly approach.

The connection in the condominial system is made through the condominial branch sewer. Thus, the network within the condominial block is treated as private infrastructure, and its investment costs are borne by the residents of the condominial block, just as is the case for the OPP model in Pakistan. The infrastructure beyond the condominial branch sewer, up to the treatment plant, is treated as public infrastructure, and its investments are the responsibility of the public service provider. The cost of this system is, however, recovered from the sanitation charge.

The public network is divided into two parts, namely, a number of parallel microsystems and a citywide system. The microsystems are defined by subdividing or unbundling the urban area into small natural drainage basins, each with its own independent sanitation system, from collection to treatment and disposal. The microsystems receive wastes from the condominial blocks and either purify them within the corresponding microdrainage basin or feed them into a citywide sanitation network. The microsystems can therefore be operated as independent systems permanently or until such time that local or citywide development imperatives make it necessary that they should be connected to the citywide system. The citywide system receives flows from parallel independent microsystems. In much the same way, there could be a regional system that receives wastes from a number of parallel independent citywide systems.

Community participation is an integral part of the condominial model, just as it is in the OPP model. Community participation in decisionmaking and in community activities is viewed both as a right and as a duty of citizenship. It is viewed as a way of helping to find solutions for the common interest within the block. Participation is also considered a process of negotiation among interested parties to reduce costs, mobilize resources, and stimulate community actions, including monitoring of jointly owned resources such as the condominial sewerage.

The Brasilia example illustrates both horizontal and vertical unbundling. The city sanitation system is subdivided horizontally into a number of parallel microsystems. Each of these microsystems is subdivided horizontally into a number of parallel condominial blocks. In addition, the boundary for the private component of the sewerage system extends to cover the block, square, or equivalent. With this arrangement, sewage flows from households into a sewer network within the condominium area and from there into a network of micro-systems and eventually into a citywide system.

The Brasilia condominial model thus gives rise to a decentralized sanitation system with the possibility of interconnection into an integrated citywide network of clearly identifiable subsystems. The model has a lot of flexibility; it is demand-responsive and lends itself to service differentiation within different condominial blocks and within different microsystems. It has good prospects for overcoming most of the barriers to sustainable expansion of coverage in an urban area. It is being replicated in a number of countries in Latin America.

Its use, together with the concepts in the OPP model, holds very good promise for achieving the Millennium Development target of improving access to basic sanitation in many urban areas, large and small.

Tapping the strengths of spiritual organizations: the experience in India

Religious organizations tend to have motivational and organizational skills that make them highly effective in mobilizing followers and changing entrenched mindsets and habits. However, these strengths are not often appreciated or tapped for community-based water and sanitation programs. This case study illustrates the successful use of these skills in a rural sanitation project in the Medinipur District of West Bengal, India (drawn from Chowdhry 2002; Sengupta 2001; UNICEF 1994, 2002a).

The Medinipur District rural sanitation project, also known as the Intensive Sanitation Project (ISP), was launched in 1990. It involves a partnership among UNICEF, state and district governments in West Bengal, a religious NGO (the Ramakrishna Mission), and voluntary grassroots community organizations. It is implemented by the Ramakrishna Mission, a development-oriented religious organization established in 1897, with its headquarters at the outskirts of Calcutta, but heavily involved in social development and rehabilitation works in India and abroad.

The project is designed to motivate people to move away from the age-old practice of open defecation. Paradoxically, the practice of open defecation in the area was based on the belief that defecation is unhygienic, and hence it is best done far away from the home. As people used the open field, however, they were exposed to outbreaks of cholera and other excreta-related diseases that occurred during rainy seasons. The project implementation strategy was thus driven by a need to change mindsets and habits toward not just in-house sanitation, but also a clean and hygienic living environment. Thus, hygiene education was an integral part of the project.

The project has a three-tier organizational structure, with the Ramakrishna Mission interacting both with state and district governments at the top and also with cluster organizations, voluntary youth clubs, and beneficiaries at the community level. The organizational unit for the project implementation is the community development block. There are 54 such community development blocks in the project area, each with a population of about 150,000. Within the community development blocks are voluntary youth clubs, more than 1,000 in the project area. These are aggregated into a number of groups known as cluster organizations. There are 11 such cluster organizations in the project area.

The mission involves the local community in each stage of the program, especially in the delivery of sanitation messages, and strives to mobilize the community and develop local human resources. Community mobilization is done through trained motivators from the target communities. Its primary goal is to create awareness of the importance of health and hygienic practices through home visits, motivational camps, exhibitions, and such communication materials as flash cards, calendars, motivational kits, and audiovisual materials. Sanitation messages are conveyed through writings on walls, video and slide shows, and song squads. Training, especially the training of trainers, is given a high priority in the project. All categories of workers are given appropriate training related to their work.

In 1990, barely anyone in the villages of West Bengal's Medinipur District had household latrines. But just a decade later, roughly 80 percent of the families in Medinipur possess latrines—reducing exposure to communicable diseases of excretal origin and making Medinipur a role model for other parts of India.

Local involvement was also critical in the physical development of the latrines. Each component of the latrine was produced at production centers where local women were trained to manufacture the sanitary wares. A range of cheap and effective sanitation technologies, such as single-pit latrines, were made available. To help persuade reluctant villagers to switch to latrines, representatives of the production centers were enlisted to motivate and prepare households for such a change. These representatives received an incentive for every household they could motivate.

To date, approximately 1.2 million latrines have been delivered through the program throughout West Bengal, and another 1.5 million have been built through other programs. The impact of widespread latrine development has been accompanied by a remarkable reduction in illnesses and deaths associated with diarrheal diseases. The Intensive Sanitation Project in Medinipur has proved to be a successful people's movement and has helped develop a sense of pride and belonging among the villagers.

The Sulabh sanitation movement in Indian communities

This case study outlines a successful, low-cost sanitation approach developed and implemented by a nongovernmental organization, Sulabh International Social Service Organisation. The program, named "Sulabh Shauchalaya," means "easy access to sanitation." [2]

Sulabh's approach to improved sanitation is twofold: innovative modifications of an existing low-cost technology, and equally innovative institutional and social programs, combining sanitation objectives with social reform. Sulabh popularized the use of the pour-flush system in India, first as a domestic latrine and second as a public "pay-for-use" facility. Both have been very successful as a result of the institutional arrangements used by the organization.

The pour-flush technology has many advantages. It is affordable, even by the poorer members of society, as there are designs to suit different levels of income. Flushing requires only 2 liters of water, instead of the 10 liters needed by other flush toilets. It is never out of commission since, with the twin-pit option, one pit can always be used while the other one is being rested to allow its contents to decompose. The latrine can be built with locally available materials and is easy to maintain. It has a high potential for upgrading because, while it is a stand-alone, on-site unit, it can easily be connected to a sewer system if and when one is introduced in the area. The toilet is also culturally acceptable, inasmuch as it is flushed by the water used for ablution, and its water seal makes it odorless and insect-free.

So far, more than 1,000,000 units have been constructed (or substituted for existing unhygienic latrines) in houses, and 5,500 have been installed in pay-for-use public toilets since the organization's beginnings in 1970. A key aspect of Sulabh's program is its inclusion of facilities for bathing and doing laundry. Their public toilets are staffed by attendants 24 hours a day and supply powdered soap for hand washing, bathing, and laundry. Free services are offered to children, the disabled, and the poor. This is very important for the homeless and the very poor, who live under crammed conditions. More than 10 million people use the complexes every day. Some special facilities have also provided telephone services and primary healthcare. Another technological aspect of the program is the modification of the pour-flush toilets for the production of biogas from human excreta for electricity generation, cooking, and lighting. Sulabh's research and development activities are geared to practical solutions for solid and liquid waste disposal, including recycling and resource recovery.

Despite the virtues of the technology, the Sulabh program might not have been so successful had not public awareness and community participation been considered critical aspects in the goal of improving sanitation. Among isolated populations, unlikely to feel responsible for wider environmental conditions, the Sulabh International Social Service Organization has undertaken educational efforts to help reverse this frame of mind and instil strong community awareness. The approach includes door-to-door campaigns by Sulabh volunteers and workers who persuade people to convert from bucket latrines. Once approval is gained, the organization takes responsibility to relieve the beneficiary of the bother of constructing the twin-pit, pour-flush toilet. Sulabh also educates people on use and maintenance of their new latrine and promises to fix construction defects and solve technical problem at no cost. After construction, service is provided, and problems in use and maintenance are resolved by locally posted Sulabh workers.

The program includes technical training to local people to enable them to construct more latrines themselves. In rural areas, latrine builders are also trained in such fields as hand-pump repair, brick laying, social forestry, and biogas production. The organization estimates that 50,000 employment opportunities have been created through the Sulabh Shauchalaya program. Sulabh also helps local communities set up, operate, and maintain the community toilet complexes.

Another key institutional aspect of Sulabh's program is that the NGO has, in some municipalities, taken over these complexes from the city officials for a contracted period of 30 years, relieving the municipal authorities of the task of operating and maintaining them. This has vastly improved the quality of facilities available to users. Often these comfort stations are the cleanest ones in town, even in major cities such as Delhi, Bombay, Calcutta, and Madras. Sulabh's experience shows that, where financial resources are constrained by central administrations, functions can effectively be delegated to grassroots and community organizations.

Financing rural water supply and sanitation in China

Financing for rural water supplies and sanitation in China comes from many sources, including users, township enterprises, village committees, and national and provincial governments, as well as foreign loans and grants. Users, the largest source of financing, are expected to pay a significant share of capital costs and all operation and maintenance costs, including servicing of World Bank project loans.[3]

The Chinese government has made it a priority to invest in water and sanitation, aiming for 95 percent of the rural population to have access to improved water supplies, 70 percent to have piped water supplies, and 65 percent to have sanitary latrines by 2010. China is well on its way to meeting these goals with significant gains in coverage over the past 15 years. World Bank and other assistance have aided these efforts. The World Bank China Rural Water Supply and Sanitation Program has initiated projects aimed at serving about 23 million people in 18 provinces. China differs significantly from most developing countries in that there is little history of the central government providing large subsidies for the financing of rural water supply. Instead, there is greater emphasis on cost-sharing by provincial, county, and community institutions. This context proved to be compatible with the World Bank's development of a significant cost-recovery model, where capital, operation, and maintenance costs, including repayment of loans, are ultimately repaid by the rural beneficiary.

One concern regarding cost-recovery programs is that those served are often not the very poorest, whose needs are greatest. In China, the national policy is to use government funds for increasing coverage through providing basic levels of service to those in greatest need and to use external funds, such as from the World Bank, to provide greater levels of service, through piped water supply systems, where demand exists. Within the World Bank-assisted projects, however, the more remote and scattered areas are also provided water supply systems similar to the ones covered under the government programs: handpumps, rainwater collection systems, and small tube wells. The cost-recovery policy for the basic level of schemes in both World Bank-assisted and government programs is the same: full labor contribution and full responsibility for operation and maintenance costs. Debt servicing is not passed on to the consumers of these schemes with lower service levels.

The functional level of project management is the township water-supply plant. The cost of running the water plant, as well as the debt servicing cost, is met from those benefiting from higher-service-level schemes. The water plant collects water fees from households, each of which has a metered connection. Water tariffs are set by the plant management and the County Price Bureau, and prices are raised when necessary to cover increased operating costs. The tariff calculation is comprehensive and includes the cost of electricity, salaries, water-source fees, depreciation, debt servicing, interest on debt, overhead, and taxes.

To protect consumer's interests, China has developed an effective price regulatory system at the county level. Once the proposed tariff has been calculated at the water plant, it is sent through the County Project Office (CPO) to the County Price Bureau (CPB) for approval. The CPB reviews the calculation, holds discussions at the water plant and CPO levels, then visits the concerned villages and holds public hearings with the consumers to determine the affordability of the new tariff. In some cases, the Price Bureau asks the water plant to revise its tariff.

Cost-sharing by users promotes financial sustainability of water-supply systems, but many observers worry that poor households may not be able to afford cost-recovering tariffs. In most cases, the costs appear to be affordable. As an example, households supplied with water from the project typically consume 3 cubic meters a month. At a tariff of 2 yuan per cubic meter, the annual water bill comes to 72 yuan. Assuming an annual per capita income of about 2,000 yuan in rural China, this works out to 3.6 percent of annual income.

In 2002, 868 million Chinese rural residents—92 percent of the total—had access to improved water supplies. Of these, 57 percent had access to piped water systems, a 43 percent increase over 1985. In addition, 49 percent of rural households had sanitary latrines, 41 percent more than in 1993. Government programs have dramatically increased awareness of health care and hygiene issues among rural populations. Such progress has greatly improved the lives and health of rural residents and promoted rural economic and social development.

The scaling up and achievements of rural water supply and sanitation in China are closely linked to the country's political willingness to charge—and users' willingness to pay—cost-covering water tariffs. There are other factors, as well, including the country's stable political situation, rapid economic growth, commitment to rural residents, and the fact that external funding is only a small percentage of China's financial resources. The question of whether China's financing policy can be replicated is not an easy one to answer, but there are lessons to be learned in the government's willingness to price rural water supply services at financially sustainable levels, a condition that is not met in many other countries. Perhaps this case can help demonstrate to decisionmakers in other countries that cost recovery in rural water supply and sanitation can be realized.

Notes

Preface

1. These definitions of sustainable access to domestic water supply and basic sanitation are considerably broader than those used by the Joint Monitoring Programme for Water Supply and Sanitation, which is administered by the World Health Organization and the United Nations Children's Fund. The United Nations has charged the Joint Monitoring Programme with monitoring progress toward target 10.

Chapter 1

1. UN Millennium Project www.unmillenniumproject.org.

2. World Summit on Sustainable Development www.Johannesburgsummit.org.

3. Some text in this section and the section that follows titled, "The institutional context," was drawn directly from the annex of UN WEHAB Working Group 2002.

4. UN Millennium Development Goals www.developmentgoals.org.

5. Much of this section was drawn directly from UNDESA 2002b. Special thanks to task force member Manuel Dengo of UNDESA for allowing us to incorporate sections of this text verbatim.

Chapter 2

1. The remainder of this section draws extensively on *Water Governance for Poverty Reduction* (UNDP 2004). Special thanks to task force member Ingvar Andersson of UNDP for allowing us to incorporate sections of this text verbatim.

2. All dollar values in this report are U.S. dollars unless otherwise indicated.

Chapter 3

1. A survey instrument being prepared by the WSSCC task force gives further elaboration of the meanings of these two aspects of improved water supply.

2. Defined as domestic wastewater resulting from bathing and washing of dishes and clothes in the home.

3. For example, the Public Affairs Center (PAC) in India has conducted a survey of 36,500 households regarding basic services. Their data indicate a gap, sometimes wide,

between the availability of a service and its satisfactory functioning (for example, water pumps installed in villages, but not functioning).

4. WHO/UNICEF JMP www.wssinfo.org.

5. If possible, coverage estimates are based on all available national household surveys and censuses. All available surveys and censuses are plotted on a time scale. A linear trend line, based on the least-squares method, is drawn through these data points and determines the estimates for 1990 and 2000. In case household surveys and censuses are not available, coverage data given through the GWSSA 2000 questionnaire is used. In the future the linear trend line might be replaced by a curvilinear trend line. For a more detailed description of the methodology, please refer to WHO/UNICEF JMP 2000.

6. To be used in the calculation of coverage data for a country, surveys must meet certain criteria: The survey needs to be representative of the entire country; it needs to be well documented; and details about the data should be available. In the JMP approach, coverage data are based on the type of services used, so if a survey only gives one total figure for people with *access*, this survey cannot be used to calculate the coverage estimates because it is not clear whether this access meets the JMP standard of *improved*. However, details of surveys, even those not used, have been included in the country files and are visible in the graphs for purposes of comparison. Examples of valid surveys are the Demographic and Health Survey of ORC-Macro (funded by USAID) (see www.measuredhs.com), UNICEF's Multiple Indicator Cluster Survey (see /www.childinfo.org/MICS2/MICSDataSet.htm) and some of the World Bank's Living Standard Survey (see www.worldbank.org/lsms/). Many censuses have also been used, but sometimes their data are given with insufficient detail.

7. The Technical Advisory Group is made up of individual experts from academic institutions and civil society, plus representatives of organizations involved in water and sanitation and data collection, including UN-HABITAT, ORC Macro, the UN Environment Programme, the Environmental Health Project of the U.S. Agency for International Development, the World Bank, the Water Supply and Sanitation Collaborative Council, and the Millennium Project.

Chapter 4

1. Progress in Bangladesh must be evaluated in the context of the significant problem the country is currently facing with arsenic contamination of groundwater supplies.

2. Special thanks to task force member Jennifer Davis, who devised the community typology outlined in this section and who wrote the text that follows.

3. It should be noted that freshwater scarcity is one supply issue that receives limited attention in the typology. The International Water Management Institute estimates that 30 percent of the world's population lives under conditions of physical water scarcity (that is, without enough water to meet minimum industrial and domestic needs and provide for present levels of food production). Scarcity is also an important explanation for lack of access to water supply in many local-level analyses. Overall, however, the association between physical water availability and coverage is not as strong as, for example, the (inverse) association between poverty and access.

4. Water quality is, of course, a concern when households use water primarily intended for irrigation. Installing handpumps along irrigation canals as described above is just one strategy for improving the quality of water to levels needed for domestic purposes; the water is drawn through a natural sand filter before being pumped and captured. Point-of-use treatment technologies may be another option for households wanting to treat irrigation water for domestic use.

5. See, for example, Tendler's (1997) discussion of the importance that centralized functions had in development projects across several sectors in Ceará, Brazil.

6. These costs may be particularly high in urban settings where water supply and sanitation agencies are subject to technical standards that are often excessively stringent or inappropriate. Many former colonies in Africa, for example, use construction standards that were adopted without modification from Western Europe.

7. Some information was also supplied by task force cochair Albert Wright, based on his personal knowledge of the program.

8. For instance, the technical standards for sewers in some African countries include pipe specifications intended to allow networks to withstand snow loadings—clearly an artifact of the European climates in which the standards were developed.

Chapter 5

1. For example, most of the world's poorest countries did not include target 10 among their priority objectives in their Poverty Reduction Strategy Papers (PRSPs). See Mehta (2002).

2. Ring-fencing refers to the compulsory reservation of funds for use within a specific limited sector or department, such as a specific agency, utility, or division of a company. It implies, for instance, that income a utility gains from providing water supply would then remain with that utility to cover operation and maintenance costs, to pay salaries, or to fund expansion of services.

3. The term "institutional constraints" refers to obstacles developing countries face in a wide range of areas required for effective development policy-making and implementation, such as human resources, managerial skills, monitoring and evaluation systems, work processes, organizational cultures and norms, and legal frameworks.

4. We use the term "capacity building" as defined in Agenda 21 (chapter 37): "capacity building encompasses the country's human, scientific, technological, organizational, institutional and resource capabilities. A fundamental goal of capacity building is to enhance the ability to evaluate and address the crucial questions related to policy choices and modes of implementation among development options, based on an understanding of environment potentials and limits and of needs perceived by the people of the country concerned" (UNCED 1992).

5. The Orangi Pilot Project in Pakistan is a well-known example of this type of "bottom up" capacity building that led to a locally planned and implemented sanitation project.

6. In nominal terms, official development assistance for water and sanitation has declined since 1995, fluctuating between $18 billion in 1996 and $13.5 billion in 1999. These commitments were about $16 billion in 2002.

7. Calculated based on Silva and others (1998) as quoted in Annamraju and others (2001).

Chapter 6

1. For example, improved sanitation services are far more effective than improved water supply in reducing the incidence of such diarrheal diseases as cholera, thereby reducing public health costs, improving the productivity of workers, and underpinning higher academic attainment for children. While beneficial to individuals and households, these effects also have substantial macroeconomic impacts on the economies of their countries as well. (See, for example, Evans and others 2004.)

2. Of course, along with consumer demand for sanitation, it is important to recognize several other factors that can influence the likelihood that improved facilities will be constructed. These include access to water supply; security of land tenure; awareness of various technological options; availability of materials and personnel (for example, masons)

needed for construction; and such technical considerations as availability of sufficient space to construct a latrine or bathroom, or proximity to a feeder sewer.

3. While many countries have already achieved this type of decentralization, others have not; many centralized water and sanitation agencies still take full responsibility for all aspects of sanitation service delivery.

4. There is a pressing need for more analysis of the most effective ways of utilizing public funds to leverage increased access. The success of approaches such as that adopted by ZimAHEAD in Zimbabwe, and the total sanitation campaign in Bangladesh, certainly point to the need to focus on and support local decisionmaking. A recent evaluation of hygiene promotion programs also suggested that their impacts are robust and long lasting (Bolt 2004; Cairncross and Schordt 2004). Further work is needed, however, to evaluate the conditions under which different approaches work best.

5. The role of public funding in urban sanitation is crucial. In congested urban areas, shared infrastructure or systems of waste disposal are essential if household actions are to result in a cleaner and healthier living environment.

6. It is important to note, however, that progress toward the environmental sustainability goal is still constrained by the lack of sanitation technologies that address waste management adequately. Technical advances in such areas as effective, affordable, and simple-to-operate sewage treatment plants that can be located close to residential areas; drainage and solid waste disposal; and urban wastewater treatment and management in large urban agglomerations should therefore be promoted and accelerated.

7. Whereas the community-led total sanitation approach explicitly prohibits subsidies for the construction of sanitary facilities, there may be cases in which cross-subsidies among households or direct subsidies to poor households are justified. Given the wide range of socioeconomic characteristics, technical challenges, and costs of providing improved service found across unserved communities, blanket principles regarding subsidies are inappropriate.

8. Various tools exist for promoting dialogue on sanitation. The construction of simple latrine acquisition curves, for example, can force professionals into a discussion with households about what has changed over time, and the reasons some households have made investment and behavior decisions about sanitation and hygiene while others have not.

Chapter 8

1. The full needs assessment methodology can be found at www.unmillenniumproject.org/html/mpmethodology1.shtm. Special thanks to Guido Schmidt-Traub, who conducted the analysis outlined in this section and wrote the text that follows.

2. The water and sanitation needs assessment does not include the following interventions: soakaway pits for treating and disposing of sullage; large-scale infrastructure for water storage and transport; infrastructure for flood management and control; upgrading of existing water and sanitation infrastructure; advanced wastewater treatment for industrial effluents and other chemicals; or integrated water resources management (IWRM), including hydrological monitoring systems.

3. Macro International website www.measuredhs.com.

4. Albert Wright, a coordinator of the task force, has kindly provided us with these principles. They should, however, not be misinterpreted as rules. Instead, countries must develop their own coverage targets based on local needs and preference.

5. Estimating human resources, administrative capacity, and related costs pertaining to the maintenance of water and sanitation is extremely difficult. For example, staff requirements for water and sanitation systems can vary between 2 and 10 employees per

10,000 users, depending on the complexity of the system, its efficiency, and the extent to which automation or labor-intensive approaches are used (Muller 2003).

6. Macro International website www.measuredhs.com.

7. The reason is that, although septic tanks are a very good means of disposing of human excreta if properly maintained, experience has shown that systematic maintenance and regular emptying are difficult to ensure.

8. www.sulabhinternational.org.

9. UNAIDS is an innovative joint venture of the United Nations family that brings together the efforts and resources of 10 UN system organizations. It has been successful in putting AIDS on the global agenda, which has generated additional funds for the sector from the Bill and Melinda Gates Foundation to create the Global Fund. See www.unaids.org.

10. The UN Millennium Project is working with a number of governments to revise the preliminary estimates.

11. www.unmillenniumproject.org

Chapter 9

1. The number of people below the poverty line has been calculated by multiplying the national poverty headcount ratio by the population. National poverty headcount ratios are taken from the World Development Indicator database (World Bank 2004). Countries for which no poverty or water and sanitation data are available are not included in the calculations, which is why the totals are less than the total number of unserved people, for both water and sanitation. We are grateful to Michael Krause and Alice Wiemers of the Millennium Project Secretariat, who carried out this analysis.

2. The Ethiopian national poverty line is substantially below the $1 a day standard used by the World Bank.

3. National poverty lines are typically defined as the income equivalent required to meet minimum caloric food requirements as well as basic essential expenditures. In most countries, households living below the national poverty line have insufficient resources to provide sufficient food for all household members.

4. For example, aid modalities are discussed in some detail in UN Millennium Project (2004b).

Chapter 10

1. Table 10.1 and the following four sections (on poverty and hunger, environmental sustainability, health, and gender equality) draw extensively on UNDP 2004 and on material prepared by John Soussan of the Stockholm Environment Institute at the request of the task force coordinators. Special thanks to task force member Ingvar Andersson of UNDP for allowing us to incorporate sections of the UNDP report verbatim.

2. Schistosomiasis, also known as bilharzia, is a disease caused by water-borne flatworms or blood flukes that spend part of their development in human intestines or in their urinary tracts; the second part of their development takes place in small water snails (that act as intermediate hosts of the flatworms) when they are discharged into surface waters through feces or urine. The disease is endemic in 74 developing countries, affecting people in agricultural and periurban areas. It is a disease of great public health and socioeconomic significance. Those with the urinary types of the disease discharge blood in their urine and sometimes develop bladder cancer.

3. The material in this section is drawn from Scherr 2004.

4. Direct irrigation refers to wastewater streams being applied directly, undiluted, and often untreated, to agricultural land. Indirect irrigation with wastewater takes place when

wastewater is discharged in streams or irrigation canals, mixed with freshwater and used for irrigation diluted.

5. Virtual water is the amount of water that is embedded in food or other products needed for its production. Trade in virtual water allows water-scarce countries to import high water-consuming products, while exporting low water-consuming products, and in this way make water available for other purposes.

Chapter 11

1. Global Water Partnership www.gwpforum.org.

2. These are the areas that have been dubbed "economically water scarce" by the International Water Management Institute.

3. These events will in turn impact hydropower, dilution capacity, transport, flood control, and agricultural production and thus threaten gains made toward the poverty, hunger, health, and environmental sustainability Goals.

4. An IWMI study projects that about a quarter of all the population in 2025 live in countries that do not have sufficient water resources to meet reasonable needs without relying on high food imports (Seckler and others 1998).

Chapter 12

1. For example GRID; GEMS-Water; the Global International Waters Assessment (GIWA) of the UN Environment Programme; the Global Runoff Data Center (GRDC) of the World Meteorological Organization (WMO); AQUASTAT of the Food and Agriculture Organization; the International Groundwater Resources Assessment Centre (IGRAC) of WMO and UNESCO, the water supply and sanitation databases of the World Health Organization and UNICEF; and the databases of the World Bank Group.

Appendix 1

1. Special thanks to Robert Chambers and Kamal Kar for preparing this case study.

2. This case study is based on WSSCC (2000). Some information was also supplied by task force co-chair, Albert Wright, based on his personal knowledge of the program.

3. This case study is based on Water and Sanitation Program (2002). Additional information provided by Mi Hua, task force member and UN Millennium Project water and sanitation specialist.

References

Académie de l'Eau. 2003. "Sensibilisation, information et éducation des publics aux problèmes de l'eau." Paris.

Alcamo, J., T. Henrichs, and T. Rosch. 2000. "World Water in 2025: Global Modeling and Scenario Analysis." In F. R. Rijsberman, ed., *World Water Scenario Analyses*. London: Earthscan Publications.

Annamraju, S., B. Calaguas, and E. Gutierrez. 2001. "Financing Water and Sanitation, Key Issues in Increasing Resources to the Sector." Policy Briefing Paper. WaterAid, London.

AQUASTAT. [www.fao.org/waicent/faoinfo/agricult/agl/aglw/aquastat/main/index.stm].

Baden, Sally, A.M. Goetz, C. Green, and M. Guhathakurta. 1994. "Background Report on Gender Issues in Bangladesh." BRIDGE Report 26. University of Sussex, Institute of Development Studies, Brighton. [www.bridge.ids.ac.uk/reports/re26c.pdf].

Bartlett. S. J. 2003. "Who Pays for Water? Cost Recovery and User Fees in Boston's Public Water Infrastructure, 1849–1895." Master's thesis. Massachusetts Institute for Technology, Cambridge, Mass.

Bolt, Eveline. 2004. "Are Changes in Hygiene Behavior Sustained?" *Waterlines* 22 (3): 2–3.

Briscoe, John, and Mike Garn. 1994. *Financing Agenda 21: Freshwater*. Washington, D.C.: World Bank.

Cairncross, S., and K. Schordt. 2004. "It Does Last! Some Findings from a Multi-Country Study of Hygiene Sustainability." *Waterlines* 22 (3): 4–7.

Chaplin, S.E. 1999. "Cities, Sewers and Poverty: India's Politics of Sanitation." *Environment and Urbanization* 11 (1): 145–58.

Chowdhry, Kamla. 2002. "Ramakrishna Mission: Service and Salvation." Vikram Sarabhai Foundation, New Delhi.

CIEL (Center for International Environmental Law). "Impacts of Persistent Organic Pollutants." Washington, D.C. [www.ciel.org/POPs/popsimpacts.html].

Collignon, B., and M. Vezina. 2000. "Independent Water and Sanitation Providers in African Cities: Full Report of a Ten-Country Study Water and Sanitation Program." Water and Sanitation Program, Washington, DC. [www.wsp.org/pdfs/af_providers.pdf].

Cosgrove, W.J. 2003. Email correspondence with task force co-chairs on wastewater treatment. President, World Water Council. August.

Cosgrove, W.J., and F.R. Rijsberman. 1998. "Creating a Vision for Water, Life and the Environment." *Water Policy* 1 (1): 115–22.

Davis, J. 2003. "Corruption in Public Service Delivery: Experience from South Asia's Water and Sanitation Sector." *World Development* 32 (1): 53–71.

———. 2004. Email correspondence on urban development authorities and water and sanitation agencies. Professor of Development Planning, Massachusetts Institute of Technology. September.

Davis, J., S. Tankha , A. Ghosh, P. Martin, T. Samad, B. Zia, and G. Prunier. 2001. *Good Governance in Water and Sanitation: Case Studies from South Asia.* New Delhi: Water and Sanitation Program.

DFID (U.K. Department for International Development), EC (European Commission), UNDP (United Nations Development Programme), and World Bank. 2002. "Linking Poverty Reduction and Environmental Management: Policy Challenges and Opportunities." Special paper for the World Summit on Sustainable Development, August 26–September 5, Johannesburg.

Dobie, Philip. 2001. *Poverty and the Drylands.* Nairobi: United Nations Development Programme, Drylands Development Centre.

ECOSOC (Economic and Social Council). 2002. "General Comment No. 15." E/C.12/2002/11. www.unhchr.ch/html/menu2/6/gc15.doc.

Ensink, J.H.J., W. van de Hoek, Y. Matsuno, S. Munir, and M. Rizwan Aslam. 2002. "Use of Untreated Wastewater in Peri-Urban Agriculture in Pakistan: Risks and Opportunities." Research Report 64. International Water Management Institute, Colombo.

Evans, B., G. Hutton, and L. Haller. 2004. "Closing the Sanitation Gap: The Case for Better Public Funding of Sanitation and Hygiene Behaviour Change." Paper prepared for the Organization for Economic Co-operation and Development Roundtable on Sustainable Development, March 10, Paris.

FAO (Food and Agriculture Organization). 2003. *The State of Food Insecurity in the World 2003.* Rome.

GEMS (Global Environment Monitoring System) Website. www.gemswater.org.

Ghosh, G. 2004. Email correspondence with task force secretariat.

GRID (Global Resource Information Database) Website. www.grid.unep.ch.

Grey, David and C. Sadoff. 2002. "Water Resources and Poverty in Africa: Essential Economic and Political Responses." Paper presented at the African Ministerial Conference on Water, April 30, Abuja.

GWP (Global Water Partnership) Website. www.gwpforum.org.

———. 2000. "Towards Water Security: A Framework for Action." Paper prepared for the Second World Water Forum, March 17–22, The Hague, Netherlands.

———. 2004. "Catalyzing Change: A Handbook for Developing Integrated Water Resource Management (IWRM) and Water Efficiency Strategies." Stockholm.

Hasan, Arif. 2000. "Scaling Up of the Orangi Pilot Project Programmes: Success, Failures and Potential." Orangi Pilot Project–Research and Training Institute, Karachi, Pakistan.

Hunt, C. 2001. "How Safe Is Safe? A Concise Review of the Health Impacts of Water Supply, Sanitation and Hygiene." A WELL (Water and Environmental Health at London and Loughborough) study produced by Task 509. London School of Hygiene and Tropical Medicine. [www.lboro.ac.uk/well/resources/well-studies/full-reports-pdf/task0509.pdf].

IGRAC (International Groundwater Resource Assessment Center) Website. www.igrac.nl.

IWMI (International Water Management Institute) Website. www.iwmi.cgiar.org.

Jønch-Clausen, Torkil. 2003. Personal communication with task force co-chairs on costs of IWRM. October. Glen Cove, Long Island, N.Y.

Kayaga, S. 2003. "Public–Private Community Partnerships for the Poor: The Case of Small Towns Water Supply in Uganda." Paper presented at the Third World Water Forum, March 16–23, Kyoto, Shiga, and Osaka, Japan.

Kingdom, B., and M. Van Ginneken. 2004. "From Best Practice to Best Fit: Reforms to Turn Around and Institutionalize Good Performance in Public Utilities." Briefing note prepared by the World Bank for joint World Bank–WaterAid workshop, Modes of Engagement with the Public Sector Water Supply, Royal College of Nursing, August 23–24, London.

Kleemeier, E. 2002. "Rural Water Sector Reform in Ghana: A Major Change in Policy and Structure." Blue Gold Field Note 2. Water and Sanitation Program, Nairobi.

Kolsky, P., E. Bauman, R. Bhatia, J. Chilton, and C. van Wijk. 2000. "Learning from Experience: Evaluation of UNICEF's Water and Environmental Sanitation Programme in India 1966–1998." Swedish International Development Cooperation Agency, Stockholm.

Lovei, Laszlo, and Dale Whittington. 1993. "Rent-Extracting Behavior by Multiple Agents in the Provision of Municipal Water Supply: A Study of Jakarta, Indonesia." *Water Resources Research* 29 (7): 1965–74.

Macro International DHS (Demographic and Health Surveys) website. www.measuredhs.com.

Mehta, M. 2002. "Water Supply and Sanitation in PRSP Initiatives: A Desk Review of Emerging Experience in Sub-Saharan Africa." Water and Sanitation Program, Washington, D.C.

Mitter, Anjali. 1999. "Water for the Urban Poor: Côte d'Ivoire's Experiment with Private and Informal Sector Cooperation." Master's thesis. Massachusetts Institute of Technology, Department of Urban Studies and Planning, Cambridge, Mass.

Mogaka, Herzon, Samuel Gichere, Richard Davis, and Rafik Hirji. 2002. "Impacts and Costs of Climate Variability and Water Resources Degradation in Kenya: Rationale for Promoting Improved Water Resources Development and Management." World Bank, Washington, D.C.

Molden, David, and Charlotte de Fraiture. 2004. "Investing in Water for Food, Ecosystems and Livelihoods." Blue Paper discussion draft. Comprehensive Assessment of Water Management in Agriculture, Columbo. [www.iwmi.cgiar.org/Assessment/files/pdf/BluePaper.pdf].

Mukherjee, N. 2001. "Achieving Sustained Sanitation for the Poor: Policy Lessons from Participatory Assessments in Cambodia, Indonesia, and Vietnam." Water and Sanitation Project for East Asia and the Pacific, Jakarta.

Muller, Mike. 2003. Email correspondence on use, operations, and maintenance of sanitation facilities. Director-General, Department of Water Affairs. September. South Africa.

———. 2004. Personal communication with task force co-chair.

Nigam A. and G. Ghosh. 1994. "Costs and Resources for WES in the 1990s." *WaterFront* Special Issue.

———. 1995. "A Model of Costs and Resources for Rural and Peri-Urban Water Supply and Sanitation in the 1990s." *Natural Resources Forum* 19 (3): 193–202.

OECD–DAC (Organization for Economic Co-Operation and Development–Development Assistance Committee). 2004. "Aid for Water Supply and Sanitation." Report from the International Water Academy Seminar "Water for the Poorest" at World Water Week, August 19, Stockholm.

Palmer, K., M. Cockburn, D. Storer, and D. Hulls. 2003. "Funding Johannesburg—Beyond the Rhetoric; Delivering the Water and Sanitation Targets." CEPA Discussion Paper. Cambridge Economic Policy Associates, Cambridge, U.K.

Rijsberman, F. R. 2004 (in press). "The Water Challenge." In B. Lomborg, ed., *Global Crisis, Global Solutions.* Cambridge, U.K. Cambridge University Press.

Roche, R., C. Revels, and M. Amies. 2001. "Franchising in Small Town Water Supply." Water and Sanitation Program, Washington, D.C. www.wsp.org/publications/smv_franchising_doc.pdf.

Rosegrant, Mark W., Ximing Cai, and Sarah A. Cline. 2002. "Global Water Outlook to 2025: Averting an Impending Crisis." A 2020 Vision for Food, Agriculture, and the Environment Initiative. International Food Policy Research Institute, Washington, D.C., and International Water Management Institute, Colombo.

Scherr, Sara. 2004. "Pursuing Rural Synergies to Meet the Millennium Development Goals." Paper prepared for Millennium Synergy Initiative, Earth Institute, Columbia University, New York. www.forest-trends.org/trendlines/0604/initiative.htm.

Seckler, D., U. Amarasinghe, D. Molden, R. de Silva, and R. Barker. 1998. *World Water Demand and Supply, 1990 to 2025: Scenarios and Issues.* Research Report 19. International Water Management Institute, Colombo.

Sengupta, Chandan. 2001. "Our Challenge: Latrine for All." Paper presented at the 27th Water Engineering and Development Centre Conference, Lusaka.

Shekhar, Susmita. 2003. Personal email correspondence with the task force co-chairs on use, operations, and maintenance of sanitation facilities. Senior Vice President, Sulabh International Social Service Organisation. September.

Smakhtin, Vladimir, Carmen Revenga, and Petra Döll. 2004. *Taking into Account Environmental Water Requirements in Global-Scale Water Resources Assessments.* Comprehensive Assessment of Water Management in Agriculture. Research Report 2. International Water Management Institute, Colombo. [www.iwmi.cgiar.org/Assessment/index.asp?nc=7459&id=393&msid=260].

Small, Leslie, and Mark Svendsen. 1992. "A Framework for Assessing Irrigation Performance." Working Paper on Irrigation Performance 1. International Food Policy Research Institute, Washington, D.C.

Smets, H. 2003. "The Cost of Meeting the Johannesburg Target for Drinking Water." Water Academy France, Paris.

Silva, G, Tynan, N and Yilmaz Y. 1998. "Private Participation in the Water and Sewerage Sector—Recent Trends." Public Policy for the Private Sector Note 147. World Bank, Washington, D.C. [http://rru.worldbank.org/Documents/PublicPolicyJournal/147silva.pdf].

Solo, T. 1999. "Small-Scale Entrepreneurs in the Urban Water and Sanitation Market." *Environment and Urbanization* 11 (1): 117–31.

Sulabh International. Social Service Organization website. www.sulabhinternational.org.

Tendler, Judith. 1997. *Good Government in the Tropics.* Baltimore, Md.: Johns Hopkins University Press.

Terry, G. and B. Calaguas. 2003. "Financing the Millennium Development Goals for Domestic Water Supply and Sanitation." Report for the Water and Poverty Dialogue Initiative, WaterAid, London.

UN (United Nations). 2000. *We the Peoples: The Role of the United Nations in the 21st Century.* New York. [www.un.org/millennium/sg/report/ch0.pdf].

———. 2001. *Road Map towards the Implementation of the UN Millennium Declaration.* Report of the Secretary-General. New York. [www.un.org/documents/ga/docs/56/a56326.pdf].

———. 2004. "Millennium Indicators Database." [Retrieved on November 12, 2004, from http://millenniumindicators.un.org/unsd/mi/mi_goals.asp].

UNAIDS (Joint United Nations Programme on HIV/AIDS). 2002. "Financial Resources for HIV/AIDS Programs in Low and Middle-Income Countries over the Next Five

Years." Prepared for the 13th Meeting of the Programme Coordinating Board, December 11–12, Lisbon.

UNCED (United Nations Conference on Environment and Development). 1992. "The Dublin Statement on Water and Sustainable Development." Rio de Janeiro, Brazil. [Retrieved on November 12, 2004, from www.wmo.ch/web/homs/documents/english/icwedece.html].

UNDESA (United Nations Department of Economic and Social Affairs), Division for Sustainable Development website. www.un.org/esa/sustdev/.

———. 1992. "Agenda 21." Adopted at the United Nations Conference on Environment and Development, June 14, Rio de Janeiro, Brazil. [Retrieved on November 10, 2004, from www.un.org/esa/sustdev/documents/agenda21/english/agenda21chapter37.htm].

———. 2002a. "Plan of Implementation of the World Summit on Sustainable Development." Division for Sustainable Development, New York. [www.un.org/esa/sustdev/documents/WSSD_POI_PD/English/WSSD_PlanImpl.pdf].

———. 2002b. "Preliminary Analysis of WSSD Outcomes on Water, Natural Resources, Natural Disasters and SIDS." Division for Sustainable Development, Water, Natural Resources, and SIDS Branch, New York.

UNDP (United Nations Development Programme). 1981. *International Drinking Water Supply and Sanitation Decade 1981–1990: Decade Dossier.* New York.

———. 1988. *Water of Ayole.* VHS cassette. Produced by Sandra Nichols. New York.

———. 2002. *Human Development Report 2002: Deepening Democracy in a Fragmented World.* New York: Oxford University Press.

———. 2003. *Human Development Report 2003: Millennium Development Goals: A Compact among Nations to End Human Poverty.* New York: Oxford University Press.

———. 2004. *Water Governance for Poverty Reduction: Key Issues and the UNDP Response to the Millennium Development Goals.* New York. [www.undp.org/water/pdfs/241456%20UNDP_Guide_Pages.pdf].

UNESCO (United Nations Educational, Scientific, and Cultural Organization) website. www.unesco.org.

UN General Assembly. 2000. "Resolution 55/2 United Nations Millennium Declaration." 8th Plenary Meeting. September 8. [Retrieved on 12 November 2004 from www.un.org/millennium/declaration/ares552e.htm].

———. 2004. "Resolution 58/217. International Decade for Action, 'Water for Life', 2005–2015." In the Report of the Second Committee (A/58/485). February 9.

UN-HABITAT (United Nations Human Settlements Programme). 2003. "Guide to Monitoring Target 11: Improving the Lives of 100 Million Slum Dwellers." Nairobi. [www.unhabitat.org/programmes/guo/documents/mdgtarget11.pdf].

———. 2004. "Unheard Voices of Women in Water and Sanitation." Water for Asian Cities Program, Manila and Nairobi.

UNICEF (United Nations Children's Fund). 1994. "Sanitation: The Medinipur Story: Intensive Sanitation Project." UNICEF-Calcutta, India.

———. 2002a. "Invest in Children, Advance Sustainable Development: In India, Success in Improving Sanitation." Press Release. [Retrieved on November 12, 2004, from www.unicef.org/events/wssd/india.html].

———. 2002b. "Financing the International Goals for Water and Sanitation." Unpublished paper drawn from WSCC 2000; WWC 2000; WHO/UNICEF JMP 2000; Nigam and Ghosh 1994; Briscoe and Garn 1994. New York.

UNICEF MICS (Multiple Indicator Cluster Survey) website. www.childinfo.org/MICS2/MICSDataSet.htm.

UN/ISDR (United Nations Inter-Agency Secretariat of the International Strategy for Disaster Reduction). 2004. *Living with Risk: A Global Review of Disaster Reduction Initiatives.* [Retrieved from www.unisdr.org/eng/about_isdr/bd-lwr-2004-eng.htm].

UN Millennium Development Goals Website. www.developmentgoals.org.

UN Millennium Project. 2004a. *Millennium Development Goals Needs Assessments.* New York.

————. 2004b. "Interim Report of the Task Force on Poverty and Economic Development." New York [Retrieved on November 12, 2004, from www.unmillenniumproject.org/documents/tfoneinterim.pdf].

————. 2005. *Investing in Development: A Practical Plan to Achieve the Millennium Development Goals.* New York.

UN Millennium Project Website. www.unmillenniumproject.org.

UN Water (United Nations Interagency Coordination) Website. www.un.org/esa/sustdev/sdissues/water/Interagency_activities.htm.

UN WEHAB (United Nations Water and Sanitation, Energy, Health and Agriculture and Biodiversity) Working Group. 2002. "A Framework for Action on Water and Sanitation." [Retrieved on November 11, 2004, from www.johannesburgsummit.org/html/documents/summit_docs/wehab_papers/wehab_water_sanitation.pdf].

UN/WWAP (United Nations/World Water Assessment Programme). 2003. *UN World Water Development Report: Water for People, Water for Life.* Paris, New York and Oxford: United Nations Educational, Scientific and Cultural Organization and Berghahn Books.

van de Guchte, Cees, and V. Vandeweerd. 2004. "Targeting Sanitation." *Our Planet* 14 (4): 19–21.

Wandera, B. 1999. "The Post-Construction Management Challenge." Paper presented at the United Nations Development Programme–World Bank Regional Water and Sanitation Group for Eastern and Southern Africa Financing Community Water and Sanitation Workshop, November 29–December 2, Mpumalanga, South Africa.

WaterAid Website. www.wateraid.org.uk.

Water and Sanitation Program Website. www.wsp.org.

————. 2002. "Willingness to Charge and Willingness to Pay: The World Bank-Assisted China Rural Water Supply and Sanitation Program." Field Note. Washington, D.C. [www.wsp.org/publications/global_wtp_china.pdf].

Watson, G. 1999. "Good Sewers Cheap? Agency-Customer Interactions in Low-Cost Urban Sanitation in Brazil." World Bank, Washington, D.C.

Whittington D., J. Davis, and E. McClelland. 1999. "Implementing a Demand-Driven Approach to Community Water Supply Planning: A Case Study of Lugazi, Uganda," *Water International* 23 (3): 134–45.

WHO (World Health Organization). 2003. *World Health Report 2003.* Geneva.

————. 2004a. "Water, Sanitation and Hygiene Links to Health: Facts and Figures." Geneva. [http://www.who.int/water_sanitation_health/en/factsfigures04.pdf].

————. 2004b. "Statistics on Malaria." [Retrieved on November 12, 2004, from mosquito.who.int/malariacontrol].

WHO/UNICEF JMP (World Health Organization and United Nations Children's Fund Joint Monitoring Program) Website. www.wssinfo.org.

————. 2000. *Global Water Supply and Sanitation Assessment 2000.* Geneva and New York.

————. 2004. *Meeting the MDG Drinking Water and Sanitation Target: A Mid-Term Assessment of Progress.* Geneva and New York. [www.wssinfo.org/pdf/JMP_04_text.pdf].

World Bank. 2002. "African Experience in Water and Sanitation." Blue Gold Series. Water and Sanitation Department, Washington, D.C.

————. 2003. *World Development Report 2004: Making Services Work for Poor People.* New York: Oxford University Press.

————. 2004. *World Development Indicators 2004.* Washington, D.C.

World Commission on Dams. 2000. *Dams and Development: A New Framework for Decision-making.* The Report of the World Commission on Dams. London and Sterling, Va.: Earthscan.

World Commission on Environment and Development. 1987. *Our Common Future.* ["Bruntland Report"]. Oxford, U.K.: Oxford University Press.

World Panel on Financing Water Infrastructure. 2003. "Financing Water for All." World Water Council 3rd World Water Forum and Global Water Partnership. Kyoto, Japan.

World Summit for Children Website. www.unicef.org/wsc.

Worldwatch Institute. 2004. *State of the World 2004: The Consumer Society.* Washington, D.C.

Wright, Albert M. 1997. *Toward a Strategic Sanitation Approach: Improving the Sustainability of Urban Sanitation in Developing Countries.* Water and Sanitation Program, Washington, D.C.

WSSCC (Water Supply and Sanitation Collaborative Council) Website. www.wsscc.org.

————. 2000. "Vision 21: A Shared Vision for Hygiene, Sanitation and Water Supply and a Framework for Action." Proceedings of the Second World Water Forum, March 17–22, The Hague, Netherlands.

WSSCC (Water Supply and Sanitation Collaborative Council), USAID (United States Agency for International Development), and UNICEF (United Nations Children's Fund). Forthcoming. *Sanitation and Hygiene Promotion: Programming Guidance.* Geneva.

WSSD (World Summit on Sustainable Development) Website. www.johannesburgsummit.org.

WWAP (World Water Assessment Programme) Website. www.unesco.org/water/wwap.

WWC (World Water Council) Website. www.worldwatercouncil.org.

————. 2000. *World Water Vision: Making Water Everybody's Business.* London, U.K.: Earthscan Publications Ltd.

Zaidi, S.A. 2000. *Transforming Urban Settlements: The Orangi Pilot Project's Low-Cost Sanitation Model.* Karachi, Pakistan: City Press.